Religion and Hip Hop

Routledge Research in Religion, Media and Culture

EDITED BY JOLYON MITCHELL, DAVID MORGAN, AND STEWART HOOVER

Religion and Hip Hop

Monica R. Miller

Routledge
Taylor & Francis Group
NEW YORK   LONDON

First published 2013
by Routledge
711 Third Avenue, New York, NY 10017

Simultaneously published in the UK
by Routledge
2 Park Square, Milton Park, Abingdon, Oxon OX14 4RN

*Routledge is an imprint of the Taylor & Francis Group,
an informa business*

Library of Congress Cataloging-in-Publication Data

Miller, Monica R., 1981–
  Religion and hip hop / by Monica R. Miller.
    p. cm. — (Routledge research in religion, media, and culture ; 3)
  Includes bibliographical references (p. 195) and index.
  1. Religion. 2. Hip-hop. I. Title.
  BL65.C8M55 2012
  201'.7—dc23
  2012007936

First issued in paperback in 2013

ISBN: 978-0-415-74464-5 (pbk)
ISBN: 978-0-415-62857-0 (hbk)
ISBN: 978-0-203-10083-7 (ebk)

Typeset in Sabon
by IBT Global.

To Hip Hop,
"My Horkheimer" who helped me *crack the code*,
and imaginations daring enough to "*play*"

Contents

Acknowledgements

This project was made possible and enabled by the compassion, brilliance, love, and support of many people. I owe a debt of gratitude to the scholarship and mentorship of Anthony B. Pinn. This book stands upon his intellectual contribution to African American religious thought, his work on Hip Hop in particular. Beyond his scholarly contribution, his mentorship is unmatched in a profession where, all too often, the commitments of academic life often mean thin guidance for doctoral students and junior scholars. Over the years, he has come to serve as one of the most important influences on my academic formation. My gratitude cannot be contained in the words "thank you" for the encouragement and unmatched mentorship. Similarly, I owe an equal amount of gratitude to John L. Jackson, Jr. and Deborah Thomas. Their diligence in extending community, mentorship, and scholarly attention over the years has been immensely gracious. Jackson's suggestion, revisions, and multiple reads of this project were invaluable and contributed much to what it means to take up an "ethnographic imagination." His support of this book from the beginning has meant a lot to me and has continued to be an important conversation partner and sounding board—especially at the beginning stages of this project. Much appreciation to Ted Jennings at Chicago Theological Seminary for his friendship, mentorship and meticulous and careful teaching—his class on Jacques Derrida would come to be one of the most formative and important classes during my doctoral studies. Most importantly, Jennings taught me invaluable jewels regarding what it means to be *faithfully unfaithful* to the traditions by which we are accountable to (and how to "read the text closely"). I would like to thank Gordon Lynch for invaluable email exchanges related to the topic of youth and religion. These exchanges were immensely helpful for thinking through the subject matter. I owe a huge "shout out" to Russell T. McCutcheon whose approach to religion grounds this manuscript. His works *Manufacturing Religion* and *Critics Not Caretakers* were paradigm shifting for this project. These works altered my approach to religion in a rather profound way—they were the stimulus for my "Aha!" moment—albeit 150 pages into this book, thus, flipping my approach on its head and causing me to "begin again." These two texts are indeed transformational and offered me language to articulate my claims and a window into critical approaches to the academic study of religion. McCutcheon became a virtual mentor and conversation partner—his advice, suggestions, and critical queries over email greatly impacted and benefited this project. Mad props to him for his courageous and invaluable contributions to the academic study of religion and his passion for guiding students through that messy and complicated category we call religion. Many thanks, R! The wellness of the mind is contingent on the wellness of the body. Huge thanks to Monica A. Coleman for all her support, encouragement and for faithfully reminding me to take breaks and be well to myself. Doc C, you are a courageous beacon of light and I am so very grateful for your presence in my life! An immeasurable amount of gratitude to Bo Myung Seo, my doctoral advisor who always, so calmly, brings sharp and pointed thoughts to the table of intellectual exchange. Among many things, I am grateful for Seo's support of this project from its inception. Seo is a rarity in the academy and continually encourages a healthy balance of creativity and critical knowledge production. His commitment to interdisciplinary scholarship enabled the beginning formation of this project. A huge "shout out" to a host of warm and supportive friends and colleagues who have helped in many ways over the years: Kunitoshi Sakai, Cassie Trentaz, Adam Kotsko, Howard Wiley, Eddie Kornegay, Afri Alelani Atiba, Emily Bieber, Esq., Kasturi Sen, Esq., Nessette Falu, Tanji Gilliam of Oil House Productions, Wilfredo Gomez, Carol B. Duncan, Margarita Simon Guillory, Christopher Driscoll, Derek Hicks, Josef Sorett, Shayne Lee, Tamura Lomax, Thomas Beaudoin, Daniel White Hodge, and especially my dearest friend and colleague, Elonda Clay, to whom this book is dedicated to for her invaluable and constant gift of intellectual exchange about religion and hip hop over the past five years. This project would not have been possible without the many years of support and assistance of Ezekiel Dixon-Roman—one of the fiercest postmodern methodologists I know! To my beautiful Miller-Pace family in Long Island, New York, I couldn't have completed this project without such love and support especially my dear mother Charlotte A. Miller. I owe a debt of gratitude to Carol Ross, associate editor at Hyperlife Editing Services for her meticulous and dedicated editorial work and careful reading of this project from the beginning.

Much appreciation to the Routledge team for their fine job in seeing this project through and the editors of this series for their interest in and dedication to this work. To my colleagues at Lewis & Clark College and the department of Religious Studies in particular for their warm welcome, hospitality and support. To my Chicago "Good Brothers" (and sisters) for keeping me sane during doctoral studies—I love you all! Finally, to my Portland family (Elliot Young, Reiko Hillyer, Blair Woodard, Tia Vanich—of Saucebox, Jim Langlois, Deanne Patton, The Soul Mates Crew (Jarrod Lawson, Jay "bird" Koder, and Reinhardt Meltz), Kimberly Johnson, Ray Motameni, Suzy Watson, Reza Navidi, Alyssa Drennen) for the love, support, warmth and providing a home away from home—love to you all! Finally, to Jonah Kobayashi—your warmth, love, and continued support have been immeasurable—thank you!

Introduction
(Re)Finding Religion

The global and transnational ascendance of Hip Hop, with its multifarious cultural expressions and multiplicative practices—from break-dance, beat-boxing, rap, and graffiti to Hip-Hop's body-based aesthetics and distinctive clothing—has drawn wide-ranging attention. Nostalgic political hopes and expectations (of a politicized Hip-Hop nation), as well as social pathologization grounded in cultural depravity narratives, are among the sentiments expressed by a range of sources in recent years, including media outlets, faith-based institutions, and popular opinion. And as I shall explore in some depth in the pages that follow, my own field of religious studies has initiated explorations and explications of the manifestation of religiosity in the cultural form of Hip Hop.

Popular cultural topography is not flat or singular; rather, there are a wide range of cultural landscapes, some known and others always forming. Similar to what cultural theorist Raymond Williams suggests in and through his model of cultural types—there are always, at once, dominant, residual, and emerging cultural forms being destroyed, formed, and produced. While most cultural formations emerge organically from groups and communities, that is not to suggest that they are divorced from institutional elements or structures. But the formation of emergent cultures does pose numerous challenges to dominant institutions faced with how to engage and understand particular cultural developments, like Hip-Hop culture.

Religion and Hip Hop brings Hip-Hop cultural modalities, the demographic of youth, and the category of religion into sustained and critical engagement. The first chapter of this project, "Scapegoats, Boundaries, and Blame," spotlights the social backdrop against which Hip Hop is staged, and its uncomfortable social positioning as "deviant." My initial motivation to engage Hip-Hop culture was primarily to explore the "construction of meaning" in such "pathological" albeit popular cultural forms—thereby, proving the religious merit and not-so-nihilistic tendencies of those forms. The search—the quest for meaning—became, however, a frustrating and unobtainable fixation. The problem, it turned out, was an inevitable outcome of my positionality. In fact, the original title of this book, *Beyond the Black Church: The "Quest for Meaning" in Hip-Hop Culture*, is reflective of the *traces* of a tendency common to religious and theological studies: the privileging of the category of religion itself. My initial fascination with the coherence of meaning in popular cultural forms was inscribed with the traces of this history. Anxiety motivated by the public critiques and scape-goating of Hip-Hop culture shaped my motivation to find "evidence" that would prove the sentiments of *moral panics* and *nihilism* wrong. I would eventually come to find that searching for this "evidence" through the con-struction of and quest for meaning *as* religious was an impossible task. Frus-trated by my inability to prove the moral and religious merit of Hip-Hop culture, I did indeed need a new approach. How would I "prove" wrong the exaggerated claims of Hip-Hop pathology without showing the man-ner in which the subjects of Hip Hop were in fact making a conscious and intentional effort to search for meaning? This is a question that relies upon a logic of rendering Hip-Hop culture more respectable. And yet, no matter where I looked, or what products I explored, I would never fully apprehend a *presence* of meaning to classify, in an ad hoc way, as religious.

There has to be *something* religious in Hip Hop, right? After all, what would a "religious studies" project do otherwise? Not to mention that describing religion in the world is my bread and butter—I have got to find something *religious* about the cultural practices of Hip-Hop, or else I am going to be writing myself right out of my own discipline! And yet, after much excavation, endlessly searching for the construction of meaning, I realized that what we as scholars call religion—isn't so religious after all. We must begin again. We must begin by rethinking the religious.

And that is what I have attempted to do in these pages. The journey of rethinking is not unmarked by previous thought: it is in fact inevitably and densely scored and pre-scripted, it is a journey that takes place within the forest, if you will, rather than by some eagle-flight of un-historied con-sciousness. These scripts include, externally, the social positioning of Hip-Hop culture as deviant, in counterpoint to the ways in which Hip-Hop authors themselves are making use of religious stylings in presenting (and marketing) themselves. And then more internal to my field, my engage-ment is in and among the theorists who have worked to conceptualize the varied and problematic positionalities of religion, youth, and Hip-Hop cul-ture in discourse ranging across religious studies, social science literature, and public debate. I consider the ways in which the category of religion is theoretically configured and conceptually theorized among recent aca-demic trends, seeking to understand how religion is constructed (socially), understood (contextually), translated (historically), and negotiated in and about Hip-Hop culture.

Methodologically, then, this project *reads* and analyzes these categories across various discourses. From considering hegemonic and asymmetrical appropriations of rap music by black church-based discourse, to deconstruct-ing existing empirical studies on youth and religion that hold "religion" as a category of morality that buffers "delinquency," *Religion and Hip Hop* engages various positionalities through a discursive rendering. My intent is to explore *and* contend with how the categories of "youth," "Hip Hop," and "religion" are positioned and situated, and to further examine what purposes such configurations serve.

Taking up the thread of youth religiosity, I conduct an analysis of data on church attendance over time, adding to the knowledge even while finding that connections between belief and practice are complicated and not always best captured through empirical studies where survey instruments remain confined to traditional understanding of religiosity. Thus, although there is a consistent decline in youth church attendance over time, across race and gender, and especially in urban areas, this level of understanding is of necessity held separate from a more fundamental realization of the lived experiences of youth, as self-defined and self-manifested.

My gaze therefore moves to the manifestation of Hip-Hop culture in the urban dance form Krump, as documented in the film production RIZE and born by marginal youth of color in South Central, Los Angeles. Here, as in the recent burgeoning of Hip-Hop book productions, religious signifiers are indeed among the means used in marketing Hip-Hop cultural productions. Although cultural forms such as Hip Hop may refigure or replace institutional religiosity, beyond or before such marketing comes the bodily materiality of the subject, as evidenced in the authenticity of Krump.

But this is getting ahead of the game. In the remainder of this chapter of introduction, I will begin the process of orientation, first with some basic defining of two of my three referents, youth and Hip Hop. Then, and more densely, I will approach the situating of the religiosity of Hip Hop as a "proper object of study."

YOUTH, HIP HOP, AND RELIGION: SITUATING THE PROPER OBJECT OF STUDY

> "The institution of the 'proper object' takes place, as usual, through a mundane sort of violence."
>
> —Judith Butler[1]

Throughout this project, the demographic of youth is invoked in a variety of ways—sometimes directly, and other times in an indirect manner. At times, I refer to "discursive" constructions of youth bodies, and in other instances I explore practices popular among urban youth. In this sense, the rubric of "youth" or "urban youth culture" is deployed demographically (e.g., age) and culturally (vis-à-vis Hip-Hop material culture). The latter approach assumes that youth are influenced by, influencing, participating in, consuming, and producing Hip-Hop cultural modalities in a variety of ways. This project does not claim to be a face-to-face ethnography of youth in a strict sense. Rather, the ontology and demographic of youth is explored, discussed, and signified on from a multiplicity of dimensions. At times, their voices are extrapolated from virtual sources, film, to empirical data from social scientific studies.

Beyond a shadow of a doubt, the rise and evolution of Hip-Hop culture both globally and locally has altered and challenged the texture of American society in copious and unforeseen ways, and continues to do so. Hip-Hop culture historically is made up of four general elements: Mc'ing (the lyrical wing, such as beat-boxing and rapping), DJing, graffiti production, and dance (historically breakdance). Although these are the general elements that have historically defined the rubric "Hip-Hop culture," there is no one single definition for this term. As an emergent culture with strong historical roots in Latino/a and African-American communities, "Hip Hop" has become a contested term used by scholars in varying ways (e.g., to refer specifically to rap music or a specific style of dress). For the purposes of this work, I use Raquel Z. Rivera's working definition of Hip Hop as a conceptual framing. Rivera writes, "Hip Hop is a fluid cultural space, a zone whose boundaries are an internal and external matter of debate."[2] She further suggests that Hip Hop is "a profoundly diverse trans-local, multiethnic, and multicultural phenomenon." It is for these reasons that Rivera chooses to use the term *hip hop zone* to highlight (not explain away) "the dynamic tensions within Hip Hop and its constant drawing and crossing borders." When I refer to the "everyday practices of Hip Hop" I am talking about the localized expressions of youth embedded in and influenced by (and likewise influencing) the cultural terrain of Hip Hop, an everyday range of aesthetic style, and a plurality of mass-mediated cultural expressions.

Despite the popular and scholarly attention given to the manifestations of Hip-Hop culture, among these the strand of religiosity, less consideration has been given to exploring what *uses* religious rhetorics (and their effects) serve for various (and often competing) social and cultural communities of Hip Hop. While the lack of attention by religious and theological studies proper is best understood against the larger question of the *relevance* of popular culture for religious and theological analysis specifically and academic legitimacy more generally, those academics interested in the cultural repertoires of a life lived outside the confines of ivory tower discourse have considerable works to engage. Across a range of disciplines, the academy houses a wealth of intellectual productions that take up the cultural and social dimensions of popular cultural activity. Recent academic trends in religion by scholars such as Gordon Lynch, Anthony B. Pinn, Stewart M. Hoover, Nancy T. Ammerman, David Morgan, and Lynn Schofield Clark among others, have affirmed, and are representative of, intellectual inquiry into non-traditional everyday social and cultural practices from a multiplicity of perspectives. And what's more—these works share in common a push to affirm unrecognized cultural practices for their social and cultural significance.

Despite these engaging works, however, Hip-Hop culture occupies a precarious academic positionality as a marginal area of investigation throughout religious and theological studies. Theorists of color working from the corners of the humanities have,[3] through their scholarly commitment to theorizing marginal cultural productions (like Hip Hop), academically legitimated and socially de-stigmatized the study of (black) popular culture as a rightful academic endeavor. Public intellectuals such as these have concurrently, in many respects, given the cultural analysis of everyday life on the underside of America's belly an authoritative and rightful scholarly articulation. An equitable positionality in the marketplace of intellectual production does not, however, go without a price. While the bold work of black cultural critics and theoreticians has situated Hip Hop intellectually, this trend has threatened to commodify Hip Hop with an academic branding. Indeed, the take-it-to-the-streets passion among "thugged-out" intellectual warriors is, above all, politically courageous. Their tenacity is admirable, carving out a complicated space and terrain of intellectual pop-culture authenticity. In this space of cerebral hybridity, street corner "thugs" are not alone in their game to "keep it real"; public intellectuals similarly *compete* for social legitimacy in the commodified cultural marketplace of intellectual production. As a result of the "intellectualizing Hip Hop trend," the scholarly investigation of popular cultural phenomena has witnessed amazing moments of visibility, and in other instances has made Hip-Hop culture more vulnerable to moral stigmatization and academic questioning of its intellectual "properness." And yet, it seems as if the questioned status of Hip Hop as a "proper object" of study is wearing thin in a time when it's trendy to study popular culture in an intellectual fashion. The spectrum of mitigating polarities (of stigma and moments of possibility/recognition) is not specific to the academy, however. Similar spectrums of ideological positioning are likewise evidenced within public sentiments of Hip-Hop culture more generally. These competing polarities, moreover, do not exist within a vacuum. Rather, they reflect both the *causes* and *effects* of larger ideological public and popular opinion.

On both extremes, however, the study of Hip-Hop culture appears arrested between a *moral panics* paradigm (socially) and a *commodified* academic project (intellectually). Within these interstices, polar ideologies mitigate *and* police both stigma and popularity. Although writing with the British situation in mind, Stanley J. Cohen's theory of deviance is quite applicable to the episodic periods of pathologized Hip-Hop exaggeration within the North American context. Cohen argues that when a given society's reaction is "disproportionate to the actual seriousness" of the situation, the exaggerated risk often exceeds the actual conditions that are being signified on in a way that makes such claims both irrational and unjustified. In some cases, these *moral panics* sensibilities masquerade under the construct of "religion" as that which offers salvific and transformative possibilities to deviant cultural productions.

Worth quoting at length, Cohen describes *moral panics* as:

a condition, episode, person or group of persons emerges to become defined as a threat to societal values and interests; its nature is presented in a stylized and stereotypical fashion by the mass media; the moral barricades are manned by editors, bishops, politicians and other right-thinking people; socially accredited experts pronounce their diagnoses and solutions; ways of coping are evolved (more often) resorted to; the condition then disappears, submerges or deteriorates and becomes more visible. Sometimes the object of the panic is quite novel and at other times it is something which has been in existence long enough, but suddenly appears in the limelight. Sometimes the panic passes over and is forgotten, except in folklore and collective memory; at other times it has more serious and long-lasting repercussions and might produce such changes as those in legal and social policy or even in the ways the society conceives itself.[4]

Throughout this book, I explore the often misplaced and exaggerated ways in which youth practices and Hip-Hop culture are sometimes discursively constructed as "dirt," "risk," and societal "threat." Discourse that fashions Hip Hop and youth culture as an "exaggerated presence" to societal norms, is often grounded in and makes use of religious narratives. When religion is positioned socially and intellectually as the "sanitizer" of "deviant" cultural productions, this conflation produces (and maintains) dominant power. That is, religion becomes understood as a hegemonic, dominant, and hierarchical agent of moral maintenance and deviance management.[5] A more thorough investigation into the material culture of Hip Hop necessitates a *third* way, a more complicated theoretical posture situated and investigated with multi-dimensional interdisciplinary corrective lenses—not a unitary or teleological vision, but lenses that support and necessitate multiplicity and dialecticism concurrently. This ocular vision focuses on the functions, uses, dimensions, play, articulation, and fluidity of what uses of the religious accomplish. How do complex cultural and social configurations both manufacture *and* call into question the very category scholars refer to as the religious? A sustained analysis of the varied uses and functions of religious rhetorics, and a consideration of what type of social and cultural work(s) are accomplished by such deployments, is precisely the work (and perspective) not yet taken up by religious studies in its engagement with Hip-Hop culture.

Despite the perils of commodification, scholarship emanating from Hip Hop intellectual forerunners has affirmed the significance of taking up (black) cultural repertoires for academic and theoretical inquiry in the broader publics (and counter-publics) of everyday life. While cautioning against the dangers of engaging popular culture for intellectual inquiry, bell hooks invokes the possibilities thereof:

Voyeuristic Cannibalization of popular culture by cultural critics is definitely dangerous when the intent is purely opportunistic. However, when we desire to decolonize minds and imaginations, cultural studies' focus on popular culture can be and is a powerful site for intervention, challenge, and change.[6]

While the work of public intellectuals such as Cornel West and Michael Eric Dyson, among others, has yielded considerable and noteworthy contributions on the academic *and* public stage, cultural criticism that signifies on the representations of social life has done scant justice to theoretically interrogating intellectual categories such as religion. Thus, the existing methodologies of ideological, social, and cultural criticism of Hip Hop hold little promise for analyzing other material dimensions. The robust nature of Hip-Hop material practices calls for methodological variety. Certainly, cultural criticism has its place and has assisted in de-stigmatizing the intellectual object of inquiry. Employing a range of methodological assemblages holds much promise for moving intellectual discourse beyond ideological suppositions often unsupported by material data. Thus, a range of approaches can yield significant contributions for researching the cultural practices of everyday people, and methodological expansion becomes vital and necessary for a thorough interrogation of the worldview, stories, and life-worlds of everyday actors. But not only are new approaches warranted, we also should be looking towards an expansion of new sources—film, dance, virtual spaces. Otherwise, the voices (and life-worlds) of people being signified on remain in a subaltern position, voices that "cannot speak."[7] If the field of Hip-Hop studies is to continue in its growth and strength of intellectual contribution, critical trends must be applied to the object(s) of inquiry. Again, corrective lenses are necessary for a multiplicative and multidimensional vision and contribution to the field. In looking with the sort of redoubling vision enabled by a kaleidoscope or a prism, I hope to find that from among the interlayered luminosities of Hip Hop emerge previously unearthed dimensions of intellectual importance.

Why popular culture for the study of religion? Regarding the utility and possibilities of thinking together "popular culture" (as lived) and the category of "religion" (as imagined and theorized), sociologist of religion Gordon Lynch notes that these both "are concepts that help us to think about the world in particular ways,"[8] suggesting that both these concepts are not as neatly packaged as often thought and presented. My concern is not whether popular culture is "proper" enough for academic and scholarly endeavors, for I am with hooks when she states boldly that:

> to claim border crossing, the mixing of high and low, cultural hybridity, as the deepest expression of a desired cultural practice within multicultural democracy means that we must dare to envision ways such freedom of movement can be experienced by everyone.[9]

I am convinced that engaging popular culture is a type of "border crossing" where ivory tower meets the rugged streets. I embrace the affirmative possibilities of popular culture even with its inherent and complex complicities (such as homophobia, misogyny, classism)—pathologies that not only affect the social institution of Hip Hop but also mirror and pervade every aspect of American life. Thus, this project extends beyond such moral critique. I am more interested in *how* scholars of religion engage popular culture and *what* types of inherited intellectual genealogies (of religion) are traced into such projects. How does the inherited legacy of such thought constrain, limit, and enhance engagement? What perceived ideas of the religious are projected onto the objects of analysis? What do deployments of religious rhetoric accomplish and authorize within the Hip-Hop world?

THE STUDY OF RELIGION IN CULTURAL FORMS

> "Believing religion somehow to provide privileged access to some posited transcendent realm of meaning, they search for their hermeneutic philosopher's stones and fail to understand feelings such as fear or awe as 'taught' and therefore products of social life."
>
> —Russell T. McCutcheon[10]

The complex networks of social processes and human activity, which scholars have come to call "religion," form the central category of analysis in this work. This project critically takes up the category of religion as an object, a unit, a social function of analysis. I start from the assertion of McCutcheon, whose work this project is much informed by, that there is nothing in and of itself unique and irreducible—*"sui generis"*—about religion outside of its "disciplinary manufacturing." I borrow this rubric "disciplinary manufacturing" from the works of McCutcheon and Talal Asad,[11] who in different ways suggest that the category of religion takes place *within discourse itself*; in this sense, it becomes the manufacturing of scholars who have a variety of interests in maintaining the idea as a category of analysis. Also, it heuristically suggests that there is nothing uniquely religious; rather, certain practices and human activity *come* to be understood *as* religious. The emphasis on "manufacturing" suggests human activity in the construction of religion as a discourse, rather than a transcendent uncaused essence "out there" in the world.

This manufacturing of the category of religion may be better understood by considering it along with other such social constructions as gender and race, which carry such a heavy weight of "naturalness" as to appear innate, or *essential*—that is, to have their own pre-existing essence which is carried forward into societies. But broken down analytically and separately from meanings assigned by the dominant culture, little remains of essence to inform and support the retention of these socially convenient categories. Religion, like gender and race, is *assigned* and *performed* for social, political, and cultural reasons. Seen this way (religion as non-unique, socially constructed category), religion becomes available for examination in its effects and motivations within the culture. Equally, it becomes possible to push aside the category, to make it disappear, by reassigning its various manifestations to the bodies themselves that are performing the manifestation: giving ownership of 'religious' affect and effect to the individual within the culture.

This project comes at a critical moment in the study of religion, and of culture more generally, where scholars are involved in lively debate around how to approach such categories. For example, media and religion scholar Stewart M. Hoover pushes for less attention to the intellectual tradition of religion and more focus on analyzing practices, writing:

> I have argued elsewhere that the contemporary religious scene can be best understood when we step outside received categories of analysis (dictated to us largely by nineteenth-century and early twentieth-century social theory: secularization, functionalism, social movements, positivism, institutional studies, social structure, and the like) and instead follow the lead suggested by anthropological scholarship. We should see cultural practice as the central category, and understand the practices of contemporary lived lives as efforts to embody an evolved religious understanding. From this perspective, it is possible to look at important social categories such as structure, class, institutions, social movements, and so on, but in a way that grounds them in lived lives and lived experience, and which takes account of their cultural, symbolic, and discursive dimensions.[12]

McCutcheon, who advocates for a *redescription* of how scholars think of religion in general, argues, "Simply put, the discourse on sui generis religion deemphasizes difference, history, and sociopolitical context in favor of abstract essences and homogeneity."[13] Scholars such as Lynch argue for a critical reclaiming of the term "sacred" as a way into cultural analysis. The tensions around *how* to take up the academic study of religion force a more attenuated posture to not "what" religion is, but rather, to the very way in which religion is studied as a social formation. The academic study of religion inherits weighty baggage and imperialisms of many sorts, which combine to make the category appear self-evident as an object of study. So much so, that considerable rigor is required to see past and through the inherited construction. The caveat that taxanomical distinctions must be made within any project "searching" for the "phenomena of religiosity" or "meaning" "out there" (wherever "there" is) is vital.

This book investigates the uses of religion and manufactured zones of significance within the material culture of Hip Hop. What do such uses accomplish? What do manufactured zones of significance accomplish for certain cultural and social groups and localized interests? These questions necessitate an approach to religion that understands that this "folk

category," as McCutcheon argues, is a constructed taxonomy and ana-
lytic tool used to describe certain ways groups of people come to organize
certain human activity. Thus, there is no point searching for the religious
dimensions of Hip Hop, as if religion is a self-evident essence waiting to
be picked like an apple from the tree of popular culture. Anthropologist of
religion Malory Nye says it well when he challenges scholars in the field to
think about the category of religion in a less confessional way:

> We do not have to single out any particular definition of religion. It is
> not necessary to say that religion has any particular essence (or basis),
> nor that it plays any particular role in social, cultural, or psychological
> life. There is no activity, no way of thinking or talking, and no particu-
> lar type of place or text which is intrinsically religious. Instead religion
> is about a way of talking about the world, of perceiving differences and
> similarities with other types of activities.[14]

It is for this reason that Nye, among others, argues that there is nothing
unique about the idea of religion, or as Nye puts it, "it does not exist as a
'thing' in itself. . . . There is no essence of religion."[15] Persuaded by critical
trends of *how* to study religion, and in maturation of my initial aims, the
motivation for this project is *no longer* grounded in a metaphysical quest
for religious essence or presence in Hip-Hop culture. The religious analysis
of Hip Hop need not be conflated with a quest for meaning, if meaning is
understood as something decipherable of religious presence.

Instead, I consider how complex configurations of human actions/
activities/practices in Hip-Hop culture at times accomplish certain *effects*
through religious rhetorics. Through what material means do such configurations make their appearances? What do these uses accomplish? What are
their observable effects? Religion is a publically, socially, culturally, and
intellectually contested (yet taken for granted) term in our postmodern age.
Religion is often thought about in ways that privilege and privatize it as
an inward interiorized feeling grounded in the category of experience. It is
this strategy which maintains a *sui generis* phenomenologically grounded
positionality throughout the field today. This positionality, according to
McCutcheon, over-relies upon problematic, over-determined, and elusive
categories such as *experience*, *meaning*, and *psychical* necessities used to
justify the persistence of religion in the world. Religion is often thought to
uphold morality and order over and against fixity, constraint, and chaos.

Scholars of religion working within poststructuralist and postmodern
approaches make clear that theorizing religion as a social construction has
potential to free this category outside of claims to (interiorized) uniqueness and authenticity—a quandary that further relies upon metaphysical
abstractions such as "truth" and "personal experience." Social theorist
James A. Beckford warns against "the tendency to regard religion as a relatively well-defined object," suggesting that instead we "examin[e] critically

the social processes whereby certain things are counted as religious." And, not only is religion itself constructed and defined *by* humans, also the "public order, disorder, panics, and confidences" that surround this category "are constructed as emergent products of myriad human interactions."[16] This project does not seek to make apologetic claims for the religious, religious experience, or its inward subjective realities, a theme I engage more fully in Chapter 4. While I do not seek to deny these possibilities, in the spirit of Nye, McCutcheon, Beckford, and others I am persuaded that the academic study of religion should engage social *processes* and human activity, rather than (unique) religious essence and presence. While some may see this approach as overly reductionist, the logicality of such perspective becomes clear when the linguistic signifier "religion" is replaced by signifiers of identity, such as race and gender. To take any approach other than a social constructionist perspective to these terms is to say that there is something biologically "real" about these constructs. In other words, McCutcheon suggests that these are "folk terms" that house certain activity—not unique activity, just particular activity specific to particular social and cultural groups. A social construction/formation approach to the religious is a perspective that analyzes "the processes whereby the meaning of the category of religion is, in various situations, intuited, asserted, doubted, challenged, rejected, substituted, re-cast, and so on."[17] With a focus on human activity, Beckford reminds us that "we *are* human beings who live in the medium of meanings, contested as well as shared, we are on firmer ground if we limit our investigations to what we can know about the social construction of religion as process and product." Although it is appropriate and customary in theological studies to transcend the social constructionist perspective of religion to examine claims to truth and faith, this project does not engage such queries. Rather, the category of religion is figured as an interpretive category given meaning through the human privileging of certain human activities. As a social construction, it cannot and does not "do" anything outside of human activity, and because of this, its rendering, analysis, and signification is in a constant process of reproduction, negotiation, and contestation.

This approach informs how I assess the ways in which religion is utilized, constructed, and understood by engaging in theoretical and materialist interventions of cultural products. This work uses the theoretical to explore the empirical, while calling the theoretical into question by way of the material. This approach represents a departure from existing scholarship on Hip Hop and religion, which is dominated by confessional, theological, and hermeneutical approaches to cultural data. These approaches have constrained the wider possibilities of theoretical explication and conceptual expansion. Again, these approaches invariably say something about the manner in which the religious is understood. It is for this reason that McCutcheon, among others, advocates for developing theories of religion "as a social fact of historical, human existence" rather than "an uncaused

sui generis feeling or impulse."[18] Understanding religion as social formation also means that ideas such as coherence and consciousness become
interrogated. When we study culture and religion, like anything else,
we stay reminded that "we are not studying stable, self-evident things
so much as analyzing system-wide strategies whose result is to portray
the many as one and heterogeneity as homogeneity."[19] Terms such as
religion, the sacred, spirituality and so on, not only have complicated
inheritances, they are likewise discursive, manufactured, and disciplinary—words that have complex histories used to measure the validity of
certain (privileged) experiences. I am not concerned with whether there
is something religious "out there" in a metaphysical or ontological sense;
rather, I situate the category of religion within taxonomy and discourse.
Where it has analytical and taxonomical advantages, I place emphasis on
what manufactured zones of significance authorize in cultural practices
across diverse space and place.

The more common religious and theological approach to exploring
Hip-Hop culture is erroneously occupied with preserving truth claims
of what counts *as* religious among Hip-Hop source material. In other
words, the dominant methodological posture begins with an assumption
beyond social constructionism, often assuming the religiosities present
in cultural forms to be promulgated by belief and presence—rather than
considering religion as something constructed in and by practices for various interests. There is an apologetic assumption (grounded in the phenomenological tradition) within the larger field of religion and theology
regarding the construction of religion as something experienced in the
world, rather than manufactured in the interests of other social and cultural dimensions of life. This approach is problematic in its tendency to
analytically separate what "is" and "isn't" religious—representative of a
strategy maintaining religious uniqueness by asking what is decipherable
about the religious.

In seeking instead to hold up to a postmodern gaze the various manifestations of popular culture—in starting, that is, from the source material of culture itself rather than from pre-fabricated units of religious
meaning—my hope is to offer to the collective scholarly understanding
a fresh rendering of human processes, and a series of possibilities for re-
finding what we have categorized as religion. Exploring Hip-Hop culture provides an opportunity to theoretically interrogate, develop, and
rethink the category of religion as a series of processes that include construction, maintenance, and contestation. This process requires a theoretical shift of intellectual sources for the theorizing of religion, similar
to Lynch's challenge when he calls for more engagement with social and
cultural theory by religious studies: "Engaging with these wider theories
can generate further conceptual tools for thinking about how modes of
belief are contested and change through time, the relationship between
belief, social distinctions and social capital, and the relationship between

agency, practice and structure."[20] Representative of Lynch's attempt is the push for a more "intersubjective, mediated, and dynamic theory of religion," an approach that, he believes, "has the potential of helping us build much richer accounts of religious and secular subjectivity than accounts of religious meaning-making based on the personal creeds that research participants are able (or often unable) to narrate to us."[21]

In addition to interrogating the category of religion, this project initiates a filigree bridging over various gaps in research on youth and religion in the U.S. While this project doesn't engage the materiality of youth bodies in a face-to-face way, I do, where possible, make youth voices and practices central to this work. From a consideration of existing empirical studies on American youth and religion to exploring a dance subculture common among black youth, this project raises the question, explores, and reads the construction of youth in myriad ways.

Methodologically, this book applies what John L. Jackson, Jr. refers to as an "ethnographic imagination" to material cultural products as a way to explore mediums, practices, and texts that are representative of *both* the life-world contexts *and* products of American youth. In and through these mediums, youth re-appropriate, mediate, reproduce, construct, contest, recast, and create worldviews and social scripts through cultural practices. These mediums, products, and contexts occur in under-interrogated social spaces such as virtual reality, books, dance forms, film, and music production.

While this work is highly textual, it likewise expands current trends in the field beyond the more common religious and theological analysis of rap music by considering contested spaces where the materiality of cultural forms takes on a multiplicity of meanings. I am curious about the ways in which context mediates production, function, and use within the varied material representations and productions. With a "critic not caretaker" approach to religion in place, this project will explore a range of "textual assemblages" through various theoretical positionalities and paradigms, a perspective queer theorist Jasbir Puar refers to as "a queer methodological philosophy," arguing that "queerness irreverently challenges a linear mode of production and transmission: there is not exact recipe for a queer endeavor, no a priori system that taxanomizes the linkages, disruptions, and contradictions into a tidy vessel."[22] On the contrary, Puar contends that it is "more attuned to interwoven forces that merge and dissipate time, space, and body against linearity, coherency, and permanency."[23] In other words, this approach is a compilation and collection of material multiplicities that are highly discursive. This project represents, in part, an assemblage of Hip-Hop cultural materials at various moments of analysis, and in others, an assemblage of theoretical interrogations and (de)constructions. While the compilation of Hip-Hop material assemblages represents the worldviews and voices of those who produce and participate in them, its significance also becomes re-mediated through the scholar's theorizing

and apprehension. Throughout this project, such assemblages are manufactured—or rather, assembled—by the scholar (myself) in various (and often
biased) arrangements to manufacture a particular narrative. There is here,
even in the "material" apprehension and ethnographic imagination, no
access to the pure *thoughts* or *intentionality* of subjects themselves. Rather,
the reality of these practices becomes re-assembled through my own nar-
rativized constructions—bodies, voices, and "lived" realities are therefore
always discursively constructed.

As suggested earlier in this introduction, my current work offers fresh
insights into the ways in which religion is constructed (socially), understood
(contextually), translated (historically), and negotiated for those embedded
in and influenced by the life-world of Hip-Hop culture. Not only does this
book seek to contribute to the growing discourse in religion, youth, and
popular culture, but also, to theory and method in the study of African-
American religion beyond more traditional hermeneutical and confessional
approaches to religion.

RELIGION MEETS THE STREETS:
RECENT TRENDS AND LIMITATIONS

Scholarship produced by cultural critics in the early to mid 1990s, such as
Dyson's *Between God and Gangster Rap* (1997),[24] unapologetically put
Hip Hop on the academic "pop" scene in an explosive way. Various scholars of color working from corners of religion, culture, and theology likewise
began to take up this trend, such as Robert Beckford, Anthony B. Pinn, and
John Michael Spencer to name a few. Their works attempted, in a variety of
ways, to understand the socio-religious and theological significance of Hip-
Hop culture in general, and rap music in particular, with varying religious
and theological questions in mind.[25] The works culminating from these
efforts have affirmed the religious significance of (black) popular culture
specifically, answering a loud "yes!" to Pinn's important query posed in
Noise & Spirit: The Religious and Spiritual Dimensions of Rap Music
(2003): "Is there anything of religious significance in rap music?"[26] This
trend however is not representative of the field. Few scholars of religion and
theology in the U.S. have given sustained attention to the *complex* social
processes and formations of Hip-Hop culture from the academic discipline
of religious studies. Even harder has been the push to persist beyond the
dogmatic and institutional confines of Christian analysis and constricting
theological categories.

Scholars such as Pinn, Dyson, and West use the existential weight
expressed in black cultural production (such as rap music) to expand
existing notions of black religion, advance perspectives on racial identity
and political possibility, and construct liberative sensibilities of prophetic
Christianity. On the flip side, a more recent and troubling engagement has

emerged. This trend is representative of church-based attempts to engage with youth culture by "reaching" and "saving" the Hip-Hop generation through Christian evangelization. These church-based projects (attempting to keep the institutional church relevant in a changing cultural economy) cloak their religious messages with a thugged-out Hip-Hop twist. This troubling approach has culminated in a hegemonic project that relies upon appropriating the stylistic elements (e.g., appropriating rap music by replacing the original language with Christian terms and theology, making churches more "Hip Hop friendly" by dressing in clothing that is traditionally worn in Hip-Hop culture, and using Hip-Hop slang and vernacular intentionally in order to capture the attention of their target audience) of Hip-Hop culture as tools of evangelization.[27] These faith-based attempts are rather limited in their approach and thin in their analysis, and rely upon a limited and fundamentalist approach that assumes Hip-Hop culture as depraved—thus, limiting analysis from a top-down (opposed to a horizontal relational approach) master narrative.

Pinn's work on popular culture, more specifically rap music, offers attention to the polysemy of religious rhetoric in rap music including yet extending beyond Christianity. His work is appreciative of the religious *density* and social *complexity* of rap music as exemplified in his sustained attention to humanist orientations as one religious option found in the musical wing of Hip-Hop culture. Notwithstanding Pinn's contribution, the phenomenological sensibilities grounding his theory of religion remain lodged in a typing of religion as an innate and inward quest for meaning (and invariably presence) in ways that cannot live up to the postmodern stylings of Hip Hop—an argument that will be taken up more forcefully in Chapter 4. Methodologically speaking, scholars such as Pinn, among others, approach their religious and theological analysis by analyzing the lyrical wing of Hip Hop (rap music), carefully noting heightened attention to perceived religious contours of questions of "ultimacy" raised within the productions themselves. Understood in this manner, questions of "ultimacy" are assumed to hold ontological weight and express existential angst, and because of this, inherently invoke a *religious* orientation. This formulation (religion as ultimacy and orientation) seemingly relativizes and divinizes culture at large, unduly relying upon the phenomenological (and *sui generis*) intellectual traditions of Paul Tillich, William James, and Charles H. Long. This approach limits the category of religion to what McCutcheon calls a "private affair" tradition. In other words, instead of understanding religion as a folk category—a non-unique signifier and way of talking that houses particular human activity among certain cultural and social economies—the "private affair" tradition essentializes religion as a unique feeling and experience in the world.

Forging academic spaces of engagement, West, Dyson, and Pinn approach their analysis of and engagement with Hip Hop from a more relational perspective. While such scholars have certainly voiced criticism of the more damaging and symbolically violent elements of Hip-Hop culture, they refuse to fully determine Hip-Hop culture through ideological critiques of commodification, misogyny, and homophobia, among other social ills. They recognize that Hip Hop represents the best and worst of American society—that, in Hip-Hop culture, traditional ethical positionalities are altered. In other words, they are careful not to approach Hip Hop from a model of cultural depravity, deficit, or complete pathologization; rather, they deploy their social critiques rightfully, while also acknowledging Hip Hop's creativity and beauty. Their work offers ways to understand (without condoning) the more troubling elements of the broader culture. As in anthropological studies, morality becomes suspended to better understand complex logics of practice. For example, Pinn notes in *Noise* & *Spirit* (2003), "But we must also acknowledge that when not at its best, rap music provides a celebration of radical individualism and nihilism over and against community and hope."[28] While Pinn takes an intentional pause to reflect on the more troubled aspects of rap music, he doesn't allow rap's blind spots of oppression to diminish and overshadow a fruitful and critical engagement. He acknowledges that rap music is not alone in its promulgation of oppressive elements; similar trouble is likewise entrenched within texts such as the Bible and certainly spaces such as faith institutions. The latent and overt proclamations of social contradiction do not prevent a sustained analysis of the complexity and density of rap music.

Pinn's contribution to the study of religion and popular culture has yielded invaluable insights into the grittier and more complicated elements of religiosity as found in culture by offering an opportunity to value and critically engage alternate religiosities and life arrangements that force a categorical rethinking of what he refers to as the nature and meaning of black religion—those on the underside of the *underside* of black religion. Using non-traditional figures such as rappers Tupac Shakur and Snoop Dogg, for instance, castigated "thugged out" demagogues become figured as agents of transformation and conversion who point their listeners towards complicated life orientations.[29] It's often the case that the rugged terrain of rap music becomes the subaltern "Other" to more common sources of religious reflection such as the spirituals. On this point, Pinn pushes us to realize that the "thug" does not reject the world. Instead, "the mark of transformation entails an epistemological shift resulting in clearer vision concerning the possibilities embedded in the complexities of life."[30] This altered perspective forces a more complicated take on the form and shape of religious rhetorics packaged in wrapping often un-recognized by larger society.

Recent examinations of Hip-Hop tend towards a textual over-reliance on rap music, a methodology which while valuable in itself does leave other material dimensions of Hip-Hop culture (beyond rap lyrics) un-interrogated. The most common approach in religious studies has yet to extend beyond the singular methodology of sourcing rap music. An engagement with the fabric of Hip-Hop requires attention to the wide arrangement and assemblages of Hip-Hop material culture. While the method of "reading" popular culture for its religious significance yields important insights, attention to other dimensions makes room for a robust exploration of religious uses. It is my hope that future work will take advantage of a much broader range of empirical engagement. A plethora of ethnographic approaches have been applied to exploring religion among subcultures such as rave and alternative spiritualities more common to white communities[31]—but a thicker empirical and theoretical approach to the study of the religious uses within Hip-Hop cultural practices has yet to be undertaken.

My current exploration, of which this book is one result, engages empirical and material data through the textual in a variety of ways. It reads and constructs empirical data and explores seldom-engaged sites of Hip-Hop cultural activity, including youth voices when possible. Not explicitly concerned with intentionality, the project focuses on *effects* of religious uses by exploring the kind of work religious housing allows or authorizes among particular subjects across various cultural mediums. It is my hope that this work encourages a more expansive methodological and theoretical posture across African-American religious studies.

FILLING THE VOID: CRITICAL MAPPINGS

Religion and Hip Hop explores the category of religion within existing literature on Hip Hop and religion across various mediums and contexts specific to the reorganization of where practices are shaped and formed. While it is not the intention of this work to conflate Hip-Hop culture as a "youth" movement, I nevertheless hold the social cartography of Hip-Hop culture as an assumed sphere of influence given its local and global weight. I have chosen to consider products and contexts popular among many youth of color.[32] I am assuming that this demographic has been greatly impacted by the production of Hip-Hop culture (as consumers), while also taking the position that the more privileged and privatized aspects of Hip-Hop culture (studio time, record labels, knowing producers to get a deal) feed off of urban culture in general and the everyday creativity of youth culture specifically, in a dialectical manner. So, in this sense, urban youth are both consumers and producers of the broader culture of Hip-Hop production. The life-worlds of youth are seldom engaged in religious and theological studies. Likewise, it is this demographic that is often considered to represent an "at-risk," "criminal," or "vulnerable" population (heuristics that are contestable and ideological in nature; that is, these bracketed words signify value-laden ideations).

For example, social science literature and studies have shown that religious involvement among youth of color serves as a significant shield that buffers youth crime and criminal activity.[33] According to the Manhattan Institute for Policy Research among others, multivariate analysis suggests

that faith institutions act as a significant buffer against "crime" and "delinquency" for African-American youth. Similarly, the National Study of Youth
& Religion argues that youth involved in religion have a more "positive"
view on life in general opposed to youth who aren't involved in religion in
some way. Most data-supported surveys seem to suggest that (institutional)
religion provides a necessary structure that mitigates "deviant behavior."
Similarly, the National Black Youth Project survey found that black youth
are "significantly more likely" to express that religion is "very important"
compared to white and Hispanic youth, that they attend religious services
more than their white and Hispanic counterparts, and that they are more
likely to engage in religious activities outside of places of worship.[34] For
the purposes of these studies, religiosity is understood as religious activity
(such as reading scripture, praying, etc.) and involvement is understood
within institutional confines—so religion for the purposes of these surveys
is understood as activity *in* faith-based institutions. Again, the concept of
religion in these empirical studies centered on youth is left un-interrogated
and traditionally defined. Throughout this project, I explore how youth
bodies are *discursively* constructed in literature that often deploys religiosity as a sanitizing construct—a moral contraceptive, if you will, utilized
as a strategy to cleanse the sins of delinquent (cultural) transgressions. In
other words, I take the position that when religion is deployed as a moral
contraceptive to guard against threats of social contamination, religion thus
becomes a social strategy to manage what is conceived of as "deviance."

According to the National Black Youth Project, political scientist Cathy J.
Cohen argues that:

> more than any other subgroup of Americans, African American youth
> reflect the challenges of inclusion and empowerment in the post–civil
> rights period. When one looks at a wide array of some of the most
> controversial and important issues facing the country, African Ameri-
> can young people are often at the center of these debates and poli-
> cies. Whether the issue is mass incarceration, affirmative action, the
> increased use of high-stakes school testing, HIV and AIDS, sex educa-
> tion in schools, or welfare reform, most of these initiatives and con-
> troversies disproportionately impact young, often vulnerable African
> Americans. However, in contrast to the centrality of African American
> youth to the politics and policies of the country, their perspectives and
> voices generally have been absent from not only public policy debates,
> but also academic research. This research project will fill that void,
> placing African American young people at the center of our analysis
> and action.[35]

Discursive constructions grounded in youth pathology have often assumed
that (marginalized) youth bodies are fully determined by the structural
forces that create the conditions and contexts of their "pathologies." Within

this type of narrative the active agency of youth bodies becomes invisible. In the spirit of Michel de Certeau, I take the perspective that subjects are never fully determined, rather they are also active "users," and despite common assumptions, are not fully "passive and guided by established rules."[36] The process of agency/constraint and structural disadvantage necessitates a much more complicated posture. This work attempts to engage the alterity and misrecognition of "everyday practices" and "ways of operating," practices that embody contestation of domination, mediation of structure and agency, and creative ingenuity. I am with de Certeau when he calls for a different vision, or parallax view, of objects than what initially meets the eye, especially among socially dominated groups.

As briefly touched upon earlier—context matters. Spaces as virtual reality, film, and knowledge production are not only contexts of Hip-Hop cultural activity, they also represent products of such activity. I place particular emphasis on context and setting (outside of faith institutions) because little attention has been given to the uses of the religious among everyday practices *outside* of formal faith institutions. For instance, what the manufacturing of religion accomplishes for competing social interests within Hip-Hop culture is given recurring emphasis within this work.

By focusing on diverse spatiality of material culture, I attempt to mitigate against synthetic labels such as "churched" versus "dechurched" versus "unchurched" demographics, realizing that the whole issue of religious influence, mediation, and significance is messy and calls for a more complex approach, beyond what things "appear" to be.

AND SO . . .

It's time to begin the journey proper. Situating Hip Hop *socially*, Chapter 1, "Scapegoats, Boundaries, and Blame: The Civic Face of Hip-Hop Culture," locates the larger movement of Hip Hop against public popular cultural debate. Before initializing this book's intensive engagement with the theme of religion in relation to youth and Hip Hop, critical understanding of the social as well as theoretical positioning of Hip-Hop culture provides important contextual information, as well as offering the work's first opportunity to re-vise through re-visioning. It is crucial to give attention to the public context of Hip Hop, the civic face of its public portrayal. Intellectual analysis of how the public sphere in particular makes use of the landscape of Hip Hop is an attempt at such contextualization. Using the "Don Imus" controversy as a lens of analysis, this chapter is a theoretical and interdisciplinary exploration of the public positionality of Hip Hop using a recent event as a case study. Understanding the "public" role of how Hip-Hop culture is fashioned (and often scapegoated) in public debate offers a space in which to re-shape, re-theorize, and re-fashion existing problematics of Hip-Hop *public* opinion. This chapter calls for serious academic engagement with and rethinking of Hip Hop's cultural and social relevance. It relies on the theoretical work of Mary Douglas and queer theory to situate Hip Hop for nuanced analysis. Another formative influence is Cathy Cohen's most recent work on Hip Hop and black youth in *Democracy Remixed: Black Youth and the Future of American Politics* (2010).

Moving from the public face of Hip Hop to its self-publicizing face, Chapter 2, "Don't Judge a Book by Its Cover," engages the materiality of Hip Hop through what I have dubbed Hip-Hop knowledge productions. These knowledge productions are books written by Hip-Hop artists, often in conjunction with an established author. The latter end of 2009 saw an explosion of these cultural productions onto the literary markets. This chapter will consider recent books by rappers 50 Cent (*The 50th Law*), KRS One (*The Gospel of Hip Hop: The First Instrument*), and lastly, The RZA of Wu-Tang Clan (*Tao of the Wu*). By form, each book markets a particular religious aesthetic (e.g., the works of 50 Cent and KRS One are both fashioned after a Bible); by content, the use of the religious accomplishes particular social/cultural interests for each author/rapper. Moreover, each work produces particular *effects* through its use of religious rhetoric. This chapter will consider the ways in which each book uses the capital/weight of (the concept) religion for various human means and ends. This chapter doesn't set out to perform a hermeneutical or theological analysis—searching for the *meaning* of each text. Rather, by considering aesthetics, language, and textual assemblage, I explore what varying uses of religion in each text *authorize* for the artists themselves.

Chapter 3, "And the Word Became Flesh: Hip-Hop Culture and the (In)*coherence* of Religion," begins the book's more formal situation within the body of religious studies. It commences by charting the approaches to the religious investigation of Hip-Hop culture within the humanities. Although recent trends and considerations have given Hip-Hop culture academic visibility, thus securing this cultural production as a rightful source for religious reflection, current approaches in the field leave the category of religion un-interrogated and theoretically thin. More specifically, Chapter 3 engages three academic trends of Hip-Hop engagement in the humanities. I refer to these trends as: (1) The Black Church and Spirit of Market Maintenance, (2) The Critical in the Lyrical: Rapper as (Christian) Prophet, and lastly (3) Hip Hop as a "Quest for Meaning"? While all three trends retain important interests in *how* the religious in Hip-Hop culture is approached, left un-interrogated in all three approaches is, in fact, the category of religion itself.

With a discursive plotting of the intellectual terrain thus charted out, Chapter 4, "*Inside*-Out: *Complex Subjectivity* and Postmodern Thought," explicitly engages the last of the three trends explicated in Chapter 3—Pinn's theory of religion (*complex subjectivity*) as developed in his work *Terror & Triumph: The Nature of Black Religion* (2003), and more recent applications of his work in a 2009 special issue of *Culture & Religion* journal on "Hip Hop and Religion" co-edited by Pinn and Miller. This chapter argues that while Pinn offers an insightful way of thinking about religion useful for the analysis of Hip-Hop culture, there is what I call an *unintended consequence* lodged within his theory. This effect, I argue, is produced by his use of a common *trace* specific to the intellectual inheritance of the phenomenological problematics within the works of James, Long, and invariably Tillich (sources used to give shape to his theory of religion). In form, *complex subjectivity* remains faithful to the postmodern condition by understanding religion as human activity, yet by inheriting the modernist problematic of its intellectual sources its postmodern form becomes constrained by the *traces* of *sui generis* religion in its theoretical conceptualization. This limitation becomes more troubling when applied to cultural analysis. Its *traces* conceive of religion as an inward "self-evident" feeling lodged within observable human behavior. I contend that rethinking the problematic of *complex subjectivity* (inside/out) through postmodern sources gives attention to and makes space for a retheorizing of black religion. In Chapter 4, I rethink three problematics within *complex subjectivity* (problematics traced into Pinn and Miller's work) through Jacques Derrrida's concept of *play*, Pierre Bourdieu's concept of *habitus*, and lastly, McCutcheon and Beckford's work on religion as *social formation* and *social process*. Each work is paired with a particular problematic to rethink *complex subjectivity* by providing theoretical sources that assist in de-privileging religion as *sui generis*. My concern in this chapter is transgressing the conflation of the meaning-making dimensions of Hip Hop as *religious* quests.

While Chapter 3 offers a map of the intellectual terrain, and Chapter 4 engages one major approach to the religious when applied to culture, the fifth chapter, "Youth Religiosity in America: The Empirical Landscape" explores the mapping of American youth religiosity by reading closely the ways in which religion is empirically employed as a signifier of *difference* within existing studies on youth and religion. Religiosity, as measured in these studies, is seen as a sort of "buffer" for social delinquency. This process, which I refer to as "buffering transgression," keeps religion within the custody of an "arrested development"—a space of ultimate "moral" authority. This type of fashioning of religion contributes to the marked delineation and surveillance of subcultural practices. It, likewise, leaves the category of religion theoretically un-interrogated and in a position of moral sanitizer, at best. The heuristic "buffering transgression" is used to connote a process that employs religion as a moral contraceptive—buffering threats of cultural and social transgression. This chapter raises the question of the role of "religion" in empirical studies beyond moralizing claims and institutional referents, to expand the field of inquiry.

Concurrently with this deconstructive critque, the chapter sorts through and positions what is empirically known about the religiosity of American youth, and black American youth specifically, in a postmodern era of shifting approaches and experiences.

Most usefully, using longitudinal analysis I (with Ezekiel J. Dixon-Roman) conducted in the article, "Habits of the Heart: Youth Religious Participation as Progress, Peril, or Change?" (2011), it examines youth (black, white, and Hispanic) religious participation over time accounting for important social variables such as wealth, race, geographic region, and gender. Here, we explore the social distribution of the level and change in church attendance from 1992 to 2006. Empirical studies argue that despite impressionistic and non-data-supported claims, youth religious participation in America remains vibrant institutionally. While helpful in plotting the institutional terrain of American youth religious participation, these studies don't consider participation over extended periods of time. As such, these studies don't gain a view of the participative trajectory over time, accounting for social group differences. If religiosity (and religion understood as institutional) is figured as a "buffer" against crime and social delinquency, what implications would cartographical shifts in institutional participation have on "buffering transgression" models? Answering this query necessitates a shift of attention to non-institutional cultural practices, enquiring whether or not such activity produces similar "buffering" weight. Left under-explored among social science literature is the change, shift, and shape of institutional religiosity, both methodologically and substantively. If there is significant change, what are the demographics of the variation of such change over time? What does said change suggest for this demographic of the population? Given the shifting conceptions of religiosity in our postmodern context, does the context of the church still matter for youth (especially black youth)? If significant change is found, what youth social demographics predict such change in church attendance during this time? The chapter reports the answers I found to these questions in a recently published study using growth mixture modeling.

Moving from institutional religion to materialist interventions, Chapter 6, "Faith in the Flesh," explores one of many non-institutional cultural activities youth today are participating in. This chapter employs visual and virtual ethnography to explore the documentary film RIZE, by David LaChapelle, who chronicles a dancing sub-culture in the ghettos of South Central LA. In this chapter, instead of asking "What is 'religious' about this film?" I explore what is *accomplished* through the multidimensional social processes and manufactured zones of significance within various practices of Krump culture. I consider the themes and theoretical suppositions uncovered in this book, putting them in conversation with the data of RIZE. That is, this chapter uses the suppositions generated throughout the book as a lens of analysis while using the data of RIZE to challenge, engage, and enhance earlier theoretical arguments. Attention is given to themes such as "making do" (de Certeau), *habitus* (Bourdieu), *play* (Derrida), and *complex subjectivity* (Pinn) among others. Given that this chapter chronicles a dance sub-culture, specific attention is given to the body (to the extent that such ontology is discursively made available to the ocular gaze of the viewer) as site of significance within cultural formations and practices.

The conclusion "When the *Religious* Ain't So Religious, After All," which closes this investigation, leaves a door open to "begin again," by charting a new approach for future work in the intersections of religious studies and Hip-Hop cultural practices.

1   Scapegoats, Boundaries, and Blame[1]
The Civic Face of Hip-Hop Culture

"People putting their clothes on backwards—isn't that a sign of something going on wrong?"

—Bill Cosby, Speech for 50th Anniversary of
Brown v. Board of Education[2]

"Specifically, how has the public come to characterize and imagine young black people?"

—Cathy J. Cohen[3]

"I'm a nigger/he's a nigger/she's a nigger/we some niggers/wouldn't you like to be a nigger too?"

—Nas, "Be a Nigger Too"[4]

"That's some nappy-headed hos there"

—Don Imus[5]

Undeniably, the public face of Hip-Hop culture has witnessed moments of great pathologization in American culture. From Bill Cosby's famous May 14, 2004 tirade on poor black people/black youth and Hip-Hop culture, to Bill O'Reilly's continual blaming of Hip Hop and rap music for black violence and crime, to the Hip-Hop scapegoating witnessed during the 2007 Don Imus controversy, among a litany of other examples—social criticism of Hip Hop is no stranger to the public arena. Evolving intensity of Hip-Hop criticism has recently motivated Hip-Hop cultural workers to speak out more strongly in defense of their art form. In his new book *The Gospel of Hip Hop: The First Instrument* (2009), rapper KRS One makes a strong point against the logic of disassociating the lives and expressions of Hip Hop artists from their "heritage," as if there were some pre-determined way black culture "should" be expressed. "From the very beginnings of Hip Hop in the late 1970's," critques KRS, "we were always treated like aliens or 'outsiders' who had to fend for themselves while being criticized along the way. The sad thing, though, is that 'outsiders' are not studied or taken seriously at all—even if they are your children."[6]

   KRS's testimony is sharp and telling. Similarly, in a 2006 interview by The Source, when asked about Oprah Winfrey's public opinions about the content of his music, rapper Ludicrous replies by speaking to the powerful recasting potential of Hip-Hop culture:

> They need to understand that every time people in Hip Hop say 'bitch' we're not degrading women. They need to understand that in this language Hip Hop built, some words don't always mean something negative. What I'm saying is that in Hip Hop, there is a language. I feel like people should understand where we are coming from. We live it, and the people that criticize it so much have never lived it and are just hearing us talk.[7]

Here, both rappers express a growing sentiment among and within the Hip-Hop community. Despite the global growth and influence of Hip-Hop culture, culturally specific ideological debates regarding the "properness" of Hip-Hop culture furiously abound in the public arena. Not only is Hip Hop an understudied life-world within intellectual discourse, it also undergoes sharp stigmatization within the larger American society—a stigmatization evidenced in, and yet more conspicuously revealed through, the criminalization of poor black youth culture in general. Although this project acknowledges the reproduction of social inequality by Hip-Hop culture, I intentionally bypass the all too common (and easy) moral critique to focus on varied complex dimensions of Hip-Hop culture. This project recognizes Hip Hop to be similar to other aspects of culture—it internalizes (mirrors) and reproduces social domination, while also creating spaces of subversion. Notwithstanding the affirmative positionality of this project, the study of Hip-Hop culture cannot be divorced from its larger social reality and context. In other words, it cannot be understood in a theoretical vacuum producing myopic analysis. Thus, it becomes necessary to engage the public face of Hip-Hop culture by giving attention to the misplaced pathologization of public scrutiny within the larger publics. This chapter does not represent a "plea" for the properness of Hip Hop; rather, it's an attempt to use public events as a consideration of Hip Hop's civic face.

Understanding how Hip-Hop culture is fashioned in public debate offers a moment to re-shape, re-theorize, and re-fashion public opinion—in other words, a consideration of Hip Hop's cultural and social relevance among American society by considering a less considered analysis. Using the "Don Imus controversy" as a cultural case study, this chapter seeks to critically explore and deconstruct the case of the "nappy-headed ho" (as one example of "difference" in black popular culture) by bringing the work of Mary Douglas, Judith Butler, and black queer studies to bear on issues of censorship, performativity, and subversive resignification of identity. Overwhelmingly, black elites[8] argued that the primary transgression of Imus's "nappy-headed ho" tirade was American racism. Overt charges of racism by the black community failed to acknowledge the larger (and more latent) issues of gender (nonconformity) occurring beneath the seemingly racialized (and sexualized) tropes of degradation ("nappy-headed ho"). This narrowing was the result of displaced blame and pathologizing of Hip-Hop culture which became, as this chapter will reveal, the assumed bearer of responsibility for their repetitious and irresponsible use and deployment of "degrading" words.

DIRTY AND DEVIANT: MARY DOUGLAS AND BOUNDARY THEORY

Hip Hop is often understood as "out of bounds"—a cultural art form riding and challenging the moral peripheries of society. This typing of Hip Hop necessitates a consideration of how boundaries, often understood as self-evident and rigid, are in fact socially constructed within society. The weight of boundaries remains an important construct in the world. At the least, they give subjects the ability and capacity to maintain order from ever-immanent ideas and fears about chaos and destruction. As is the case with social constructions in general, ideas about "order" and "decency" are about boundary making— these things are real only insomuch as they are constructed. Boundary crossing poses threat and danger to the solidity of rules and norms within society. While boundaries prove to help maintain order, and give shape to what is eventually seen as normative, boundaries are always, at once, bound by ideology. They define what is "acceptable" and "un-acceptable," considering that which remains outside of such boundaries—the "outliers"—as danger.

The process of boundary making and breaking is poignantly captured in the anthropological work of Douglas's analyses of "dirt," the term she uses to theoretically talk about the construction of order/disorder and its relationship to the social body. She writes, "Dirt is essentially disorder. . . . It exists in the eye of the beholder. . . . In chasing dirt, in papering, decorating, tidying, we are not governed by anxiety to escape disease, but are positively re-ordering our environment."[9] Douglas argues that "dirt" becomes disorder when a prevailing notion of dis/order (read: *conformity*) is embedded in the process of re-ordering. To this idea, she adds that "reflection on dirt involves reflection on the relation of order to dis-order, form to formlessness, life to death."[10] Considering Douglas's assertion in light of Hip-Hop scrutiny, we are reminded that constructing Hip Hop as a "danger" or "risk" to the black community or society is less reflective of the actual dangers Hip Hop poses, and more representative of boundaries of properness, respectability, and morality. Douglas cogently reminds us that "Dirt is Dangerous," writing:

> The concept of dirt makes a bridge between our own contemporary culture and those other cultures where behavior that blurs the great classifications of the universe is tabooed. We denounce it by calling it dirty and dangerous; they taboo it. . . . How often is one threatened with danger for failing to conform to someone else's standards? Patently absurd threats and promises are used to induce conformity, especially in the nursery.[11]

Socially constructed and fabricated social systems remain stable by (in) conspicuously *including* and *excluding*—reordering dirt that seemingly gets "out of place," mitigating dis/order and chaos. Douglas's thesis of dirt as "matter out of place" anthropologically speaks to processes of cultural marginalization. Bodies that lie on the outside of constitutive borders and boundaries are labeled as threats, and must effectively be "policed" and put back into their proper place by those who occupy dominant positions within society. Douglas's thesis on dirt raises a plethora of critical questions about *deviance* more specifically—or in rapper KRS's language, those considered "outsiders" in society. I use the theoretical work of Douglas as a way to think about the altered ethics and epistemology of Hip-Hop culture. What's often cited as Hip-Hop cultural "pathology" is perhaps, as rapper Ludicrous stated above, an altered ethic that cannot be understood from the outside. He suggests one must live it in order to understand it. After Bill Cosby's 2004 speech and public condemnation of Hip-Hop culture, "Hip-Hop intellectual" Michael Eric Dyson responded in *Is Bill Cosby Right?* (Or Has the Black Middle Class Lost Its Mind?) (2005) by suggesting Cosby's critiques of Hip Hop are reflective of cultural differences between poor and middle-class black people. Dyson writes that Cosby's views:

> are widely held among a number of black constituencies—it is not unusual to hear some black poor and working-class members themselves joining Cosby's ranks in barbershops and beauty salons across America. But Cosby's beliefs are most notably espoused by the *Afristocracy*: upper-middle-class blacks and the black elite who rain down fire and brimstone upon poor blacks for their deviance and pathology, and for their lack of couth and culture.[12]

This quote invokes the long and telling history of cultural depravity narratives that have occupied the black middle-class imagination for years, including intellectual production. As such, the cultural deviance and pathology of Hip-Hop culture (or when white people do racists things and blame it on Hip Hop, thus causing self-blame anxiety in black communities) become related to class fissures. As a result, behaviors and practices of Hip-Hop culture are analyzed through a politics of respectability among middle-class and elite black enclaves. Douglas's thesis reminds us that what is often considered "deviant"—much like Howard Becker's thesis in *Outsiders: Studies in the Sociology of Deviance* (1963)—reflects a social construction of normative conceptions, not an "actual" reality. Further, constructions of what is deemed as dangerous are not made in the absence of intent. Douglas suggests that constructions of "danger" are politically, culturally, and socially motivated:

> Dangers are manifold and omnipresent. Action would be paralyzed if individuals attended to them all; anxiety has to be selective. We drew

on the ideas that risk is like taboo. Arguments about risk are highly charged, morally, and politically.[13]

This chapter will analyze how Hip-Hop culture is often utilized as the social and ideological scapegoat for social anxieties that extend beyond the control of art and entertainment. Hip Hop is not the progenitor of such complexities. Thought in reverse, it mirrors and internalizes the social pathologies of American culture at large, including society's inability to deal with "difference" in more general terms. As we will see, highlighting the pathologies of Hip Hop is often done to obfuscate and obscure more pressing social concerns of difference (e.g., gendered and sexual difference) within the black community. Hip Hop as *cause* of social ills, rather than *effect* of social ills, situates and frames it as crisis ridden and morally decadent.

"NAPPY-HEADED HOS"?

Who and what *is* the nappy-headed ho? Do "nappy-headed hos" exist ontologically, or are they just discursive realities, "deviant" signifiers that exist within the ideological matrix of language? These are queries related to tensions between the discursive and materiality to which I will return. This chapter is a performative of communal reflection that never took place. Here, I offer *critical* reflection by showing how the blaming of Hip Hop (for the Imus controversy) caused vital analysis on gender and sexuality to become obscured under the trope of race. That is to say, the ideological scapegoating of Hip Hop produced a denial of the "deviant" Other (the nappy-headed ho).

The discursive response by the black community to the Imus controversy was one that confirmed yet denied a cultural space for the "nappy-headed ho" in and through the hierarchization and "scaling" of assumed respectability. The process of scapegoating and scaling bodies emerges through the argument of the black community that a specific group of girls (on the basketball team) were *not* "nappy-headed hos"—invariably suggesting that "nappy-headed hos" were birthed in the misogynist lyrical imagination of black rappers. The black community fell into Imus's trap by scapegoating rap music as the counter-cultural space of blame, leaving a normative depiction of black womanhood in place and the materiality of the "nappy-headed ho" as a real but yet unintelligible "deviant" subject.

In Butlerian terms, the black community failed to subject a perceived linguistic injury to processes of subversion. That is to say, the bodily existence of the "nappy-headed ho" was left without a cultural home, as such. The hegemonic response by (some) elite cultural intermediaries affirmed the reality of the "nappy-headed ho" through its ideological non-embrace, privileging a particular brand of black femininity through purchase on respectable bodies, thereby constructing *difference* in and through processes of exclusion. By "ideological non-embrace" I am simply referring to both the affirmation and denial of the "nappy-headed ho." On one hand, the "nappy-headed ho" was acknowledged over and against a measure of more respectable black female bodies, via a "non-embrace" (i.e., "not these girls"). This move is both material and ideological, in the sense that this non-embrace can be understood at the site of cultural contestation and the struggle to give meaning to what is and is not "respectable." One could wonder, if a group of non-educated, poor, black female strippers were called "nappy-headed hos," would their "interpellation" have received such a widespread response by the black (elite) community?

From Kanye West's "George Bush don't care about black people"[14] to Imus's "nappy-headed ho"[15] and rapper Nas's controversial 2008 album originally entitled "Nigger," the familiar denominator of public discussion on polarizing issues in the black community has concurrently led to one frequent critique: the debased and decadent culture of Hip Hop is to blame; if it wasn't for Hip Hop then words such as "ho" and "nigga" would not be available for such careless use within society. This kind of rationale is what political scientist Cathy J. Cohen calls a "partial truth":

> . . . those familiar images and narratives of young black people engaged in seemingly deviant behavior that are accepted as truth—do not need irrefutable evidence to be effective. Such representations are used to justify the public's instinctive biases about certain groups, in this case that both hip-hop and its putative community of young adherents are pathological. Moreover, these narratives are especially effective in supporting distinctions between those seen as "respectable" black people—the eloquent black women on the Rutgers women's basketball team—and those characterized as deviant—the black rappers under attack.[16]

This chapter does not attempt to resolve the quandary of the Imus controversy; rather it intends to use the public "subjection" of the "nappy-headed ho" as an opportunity to theorize the discursive limits that took place in the public sphere. I seek to privilege the "disruptive" reality of the "nappy-headed ho" by creating intellectual space whereby the materiality of the "nappy-headed ho" can be reclaimed and recast in a way that embraces and celebrates the multiplicity difference.[17]

DON IMUS: "THAT'S SOME NAPPY-HEADED HOS THERE"

On the morning of April 4, 2007, radio host Don Imus prepared for another day of work, making jokes, and pissing people off on the air. However, what Imus proceeded to do on the morning of April 4 would shake the racial foundations of the black community, sparking months of conversation, debate, scapegoating, hypocrisy, misappropriation of blame, and lack of critical analysis. Public discussions culminated in a series of "town hall meetings" on the most watched daytime talk show, Oprah, which led to a highly publicized symbolic burial of the "N" word by the NAACP in July. In other words, the signifier "nigger" is an over-glorified word in Hip-Hop culture that allows folks like Imus to deploy similar words (like ho) in taken-for-granted-ways.

On the April 4 edition of Imus in the Morning,[18] Imus publicly referred to the Rutgers University all-female basketball team, which comprised eight African Americans and two Caucasians, as "nappy-headed hos." Imus's comment followed from one made by executive producer Bernard McGuirk, who referred to the team as "hard-core hos," and was further supported by sportscaster Sid Rosenberg's comment that "the more I look at Rutgers, they look exactly like the [National Basketball Association's] Toronto Raptors." The conversation went like this:

> *IMUS:* So, I watched the basketball game last night between—a little bit of Rutgers and Tennessee, the women's final.
> *ROSENBERG:* Yeah, Tennessee won last night—seventh championship for [Tennessee coach] Pat Summitt, I-Man. They beat Rutgers by 13 points.
> *IMUS:* That's some rough girls from Rutgers. Man, they got tattoos and—
> *McGUIRK:* Some hard-core hos.
> *IMUS:* That's some nappy-headed hos there. I'm gonna tell you that now, man, that's some—woo. And the girls from Tennessee, they all look cute, you know, so, like—kinda like—I don't know.
> *McGUIRK:* A Spike Lee thing.
> *IMUS:* Yeah.
> *McGUIRK:* The Jigaboos versus the Wannabes—that movie that he had.
> *IMUS:* Yeah, it was a tough—
> *McCORD:* Do the Right Thing.
> *McGUIRK:* Yeah, yeah, yeah.
> *IMUS:* I don't know if I'd have wanted to beat Rutgers or not, but they did, right?
> *ROSENBERG:* It was a tough watch. The more I look at Rutgers, they look exactly like the Toronto Raptors.
> *IMUS:* Well, I guess, yeah.
> *RUFFINO:* Only tougher.
> *McGUIRK:* The [Memphis] Grizzlies would be more appropriate.[19]

A flurry of outrage by the black community forced Imus to appear on daytime shows taking public accountability for his actions. On April 9, 2007, Imus appeared on Rev. Al Sharpton's radio show,[20] agreeing to speak publicly and honestly about what took place on that morning when the seemingly racist comments were made. When questioned by Sharpton, "What is any possible reason you could feel that this kind of statement could be just forgiven and overlooked?" Imus responded by saying:

> I don't think it should be. I don't think it can be. I think it can be for-given, but I don't think it can be overlooked. And I—when I originally apologized on Friday, I apologized. And I didn't say what everybody said, you know, if I offended somebody, I'm sorry, because I knew I offended somebody. So I apologize. But I didn't want to be portrayed, as often, an excuse saying, well, what we have is a comedy show, which it is. I'm not a journalist, I'm not Tim Russert, I'm not a politician. I don't have any—we don't have an agenda. Our agenda is to try to be funny. And sometimes we go too far and sometimes we go way too far. In this case, we went way too far.

He continued by saying that he did not deem nor intend for his comment to be "racial" in any way, adding:

> So I got on the air and I said, man, they are tough. I said, they got tat-toos, and then somebody else said something. And then I said that. And at the time I said it, because I'm talking about two African-American teams, and at the time I said it, I didn't think—I mean I don't know, I'm just telling you what I thought—I didn't think it was racial. I wasn't even thinking racial. I was thinking like a "West Side Story" deal, like one team's tough and one team's not so tough.

After the break, Sharpton brought his daughter (a college graduate from Tem-ple) on the show to face Imus, saying, "This young lady just graduated—went to Temple. She is not a nappy-headed ho, she's my daughter." Imus responds by saying, "I understand that." Sharpton continually tried to persuade Imus of the racial violence that took place and Imus rebutted by saying, "Why listen to the same kind of outrage, let me ask you, in the black community when rappers and other people in the black community, athletes in the black com-munity defame and demean black women, and call them worse names that I ever did?" Sharpton responds by adding, "I am one of them that is outraged." While acknowledging the tastelessness of his actions, Imus digresses into a lesson regarding the differentiation between *words* and *intent*, saying:

> I think what makes a difference in this context—and you can still call for me to be fired, that's fine—but I think what makes a difference, a crucial difference, is what was my intent? Am I some rabid, racist, vicious person who's on a rampage screaming and got on the radio and turned on the microphone and said, here's what I think these women are? That's not what I did.

Imus's rebuttal was followed by Sharpton's disavowal of these differentiations: "But the point is this: The question is not whether you're a rabid
racist with intent. If you commit a crime, intent may be an element, but the
crime is still there."

IMUS TO HIP HOP TO THE WORD NIGGER: BLACKS "RAP" BACK

The public dialogue between Imus and Sharpton started a whirlwind
within the black community. While racism was at the center of the
original conversations, what followed in the black community was
both expected and baffling. Although Sharpton's initial reaction was
to face and challenge Imus publicly, the nature of this debate quickly
turned from blaming Imus to placing responsibility on the Hip-Hop
community for propagating and supporting the racial and sexist tropes
of black women in general—understood and seen by *both* the black
and white communities as ammunition and a free pass to make similar judgments. Aside from numerous radio shows and public editori-
als, the first major response by the black community came from Oprah
Winfrey as she publicly called on members of the Hip-Hop community
to come face to face with the "precedents" set by their cultural productions that seemingly "allowed" folks like Imus to feel comfortable
enough to make such public comments with ease. Oprah's "town hall
meeting" was marketed as a highly public way to call attention to the
"real" issues by examining the misogyny within and among the Hip-
Hop community. Worth noting, Oprah was publicly criticized by the
Hip-Hop community because she seldom invited rappers to her show,
an oversight acknowledged the loudest by rap artists Ludicrous and
50 Cent.

The first town hall meeting, "Now What?" featured a former CBS executive, two journalists, two author/magazine editors, activist Al Sharpton,
and music artist India.Arie. The second show, "The Hip-Hop Community
Responds," featured Russell Simmons and Dr. Ben Chavis of the Hip-Hop
Action Network, record executive Kevin Liles, and the rapper Common.
According to sites such as Racialicious.com, one of the most visible observations made about this second airing was the absence of female rappers
whose careers are built on highly controversial sexualized themes. Also
present were female students telecast live from Spelman College in Atlanta,
GA. No mistake in school of choice: Spelman students made headlines a
few years ago when they disinvited rap artist Nelly from taking part in
a leukemia fundraiser after the unveiling of his (sexually explicit) music
video "Tip Drill" which featured him swiping a credit card between
the buttocks of a black woman. After refusing to take public accountability as requested by the students, his performance at the fundraiser
was cancelled.

Was Imus correct, right, or fair for pointing the finger at the Hip-Hop community? Did the black community support Imus on this point? From publicly debating Imus to blaming rap artists, the response by the black community was overshadowed by narratives of personal responsibility and a public minstrelsy of identity politics. Given Sharpton's face-to-face combat with Imus and Oprah's nationalized two-part town hall meeting, America certainly could not say that the black community had done nothing. Perhaps their doing something went beyond the call of duty. After all, they responded in a way that internalized and re-shifted focus (away from Imus) by holding rappers accountable for the content of their songs. Just shy of three months after Imus's public statement, the NAACP voted and agreed that the last (symbolic) step had to be taken—the burial of the word "nigger." They argued that if "ho" was an unacceptable and inflammatory word to be spoken and rapped about, then the word "nigger" (often used in rap music) must be taken head on.

On Monday July 9, 2007,[22] hundreds of "mourners" gathered together in downtown Detroit to bury the "N" word, the symbolic and longstanding expression of racism in American society. Two horses dragged a pine box with a bouquet of black roses, laying the coffin to rest at a historically black cemetery, headstone and all. Detroit Mayor Kwame Kilpatrick said, "Today we're not just burying the N word, we're taking it out of our spirit. . . . We gather burying all the things that go with the N word. We have to burry the 'pimps' and the 'hos' that go with that. . . . Die N word, and we don't want to see you 'round here no more.'" The Rev. Otis Moss III, Pastor of Trinity United Church of Christ, also added, "This was the greatest child that racism ever birthed." The NAACP Board Chairman Julian Bond added, "While we are happy to have sent a certain radio cowboy back to his ranch, we ought to hold ourselves to the same standard. . . . If he can't refer to our women as 'hos,' then we shouldn't either."

The funeral was the culmination of not only the Imus controversy, but also a response sparked by the racist comedic tirade of Michael Richards aka "Kramer," who was said to have gone "crazy" when he performed at a famous LA comedy club called the Laugh Factory. Becoming visibly disgruntled with someone in the crowd, Richards stated, "Fifty years ago we'd have you upside down with a f***ing fork up your ass. . . . You can talk, you can talk, you're brave now motherf**ker. Throw his ass out. He's a nigger! He's a nigger! He's a nigger! A nigger, look, there's a nigger!"[23]

MISSING THE MARK: BUTLER AND BLACK QUEER STUDIES IN CONVERSATION

The Imus controversy was not just racial, it occurred among the margins of sexed and gendered complexity. I find the limiting and conspicuous backlash by the black community to be a rather expected, predictable,

and yet curious retort. Although the phrase "nappy" undoubtedly elic-
its a pejorative racial history emerging from the racialization of white
supremacy (a linguistic trace of the commodity racism that pervades the
everyday lives of people of color), how exactly did the deployment of such
a term end with self-blame and call for personal responsibility of black
counter-cultural productions? While "race" overwhelmingly pervaded
the black reaction, the lack of critical attention and depth of analysis
beyond the idea of race left normative depictions of black womanhood
in-tact, and at best, denied the "nappy-headed ho." The response by the
black community not only *validated* Imus's comment but also gestured
towards the inability to embrace non-normative depictions of identity.
More egregious, it denied the possibility of cultural (re)signification (in
Hip Hop), bodily (re)presentation, and historical (re)contextualization of
perceived acts of injury.

   Through a theoretical engagement between queer theory and black queer
studies, the next section attempts rethink the case of the "nappy-headed
ho" through a more complicated and multifaceted starting point beyond
the primary lens of race. Using the work of Judith Butler, I argue that even
before the basketball team was raced, or what Cornel West might call "nig-
gerized," gender played a more prominent role in the Imus case than publically acknowledged by the black community. Not only were the gender
implications given little attention, but also, issues of sexuality were unacknowledged. I am persuaded it was the perceived gender non-conformity of
the basketball team that rendered them as "hos"—the insidious product of
"sexing" gender through race in more general terms.

   One is not hard pressed to see more occurring in Imus's deployment
of a "singular" racial slur (nappy). My point, more precisely, is that
"gender(ed) trouble" was overlooked and obscured under a more general
rubric of essentialized notions of race further concealed under a pathologizing of Hip-Hop culture as scapegoat and progenitor of out-of-bounds
words. Preceding the Imus slogan "nappy-headed ho," co-host McGuirk
notes, "The more I look at Rutgers, they look exactly like the [National
Basketball Association's] Toronto Raptors." Imus continues, "That's some
rough girls from Rutgers. Man, they got tattoos and . . . " with McGuirk
replying, "Some hard-core hos." Before Imus added "nappy-headed" to the
gendered and sexed list of pejorative attacks, there is here an opening to
read the gendered and sexed statements in a more "troubling" kind of way.
Unquestionably, these comments by McGuirk and Imus are specific to the
non-conforming *appearance* of the Rutgers basketball team. It was noted
throughout Imus's parody that these females were "rough" looking and
comparable to the men's Toronto Raptors. These radio jockeys were being
troubled by gender—or what they perceived as an illegible performance of
gendered norms. Nappy heads was at best a secondary thought in the linguistic injury directed at these groups of females performing or betraying
femininity vis-à-vis their sport and tough-girl looks.

In the beginning of *Gender Trouble* (1999), Butler notes that her work "sought to uncover the ways in which the very thinking of what is possible in gendered life is foreclosed by certain habitual and violent presumptions."[24] She continues by suggesting that the complexities surrounding ideas of gender and sexuality more often than not create a "crisis in ontology" whereby the limits of gendered possibilities and realities become policed and stabilized for the functioning of the heterosexual matrix. The open airwaves of the Imus show became the public domain whereby gendered non-conformity was regulated and policed from a white heterosexual perspective secured through racial tropes. The elicited (raced) phrase "nappy" should have come as no surprise; we are reminded that "racial presumptions invariably underwrite the discourse in gender in ways that need to be made explicit, but that race and gender ought not to be treated as simple analogies."[25] Likewise, white feminist theologian Laurel C. Schneider argues that identity categories are "co-constitutive," arising and emerging in and through other (socially constructed) categories such as gender and race. In writing about the ways in which white supremacy and ideologies of colonialism have fundamentally relied upon constructed categories as "biological," Schneider says, "Correlating race and sex or gender brings into question the natural status of all three categories, implying that they could be otherwise."[26] The policing of gender(ed) norms gives intelligibility and coherence to identities (like Imus) whose stability of self relies upon the permanence and fixing of the identity of others. Read with a more suspicious eye, the transcript between the radio hosts on that day evidences two white men who appear to be disturbed by a "rough" (looking) group of females. Butler herself notes that there exists a repetitive, recurring, and rhythmic drive to unearth the identity of people on the margins, referring to this as a quest for knowledge that relies upon policing the boundaries of identity performance. This policing is most evident in Imus's use of signifiers such as "rough" with overt references to the players' having tattoos, among other things. One could perhaps suggest that more troubling about this group of girls, beyond race, was their gender(ed) non-conformity, which created anxiety among a few white men uncertain of the sexual orientation of said basketball players.

Given the ideological matrix in which all subjects function, representation is unavoidable. In this case, representation was not "operative" in the sense that it extended legitimacy to this group of females; on the contrary, representation found at the site of language served as a normalizing arena which sought to regulate what these men saw as bodies "out of bounds." Butler notes that representation functions to both legitimate and normalize assumed identities. The interpellation of intersecting "multiple significations" cast at these females by the Other did not receive a recasting by the black community in a manner that disrupted this linguistic injury—in fact, it had quite opposite *effect*. Although Imus claimed his overall intent was not racial, nevertheless, black heterosexual men such as Sharpton rose to the occasion to speak for and on behalf of the female basketball team, citing racism as the primary offense (which is curious in and of itself, given that two of the players were white females), thus offering no attention to issues of gender. After the primary accusation of racism was publicly deployed, the remainder of attention was focused on the signifier "ho" as both a derogatory and demeaning word for educated black women. As such, the gendered constructions made by Imus were simply ignored, and likewise, the insignificance given to the gender(ed) implications of Imus's comments ultimately kept race as the functioning signifier of oppression, securing racism in a fixed, immutable, and eschatological manner. Ideas about the permanence of racism ignore the effects occurring within changing historical contexts. Similarly, maintaining the primary function of race as an ultimate signifier of marginality holds together the ways in which compulsory heterosexism and patriarchy function as primary signifiers of oppression.

Butler's work on gender is helpful in that it both distinguishes and disrupts the ways in which gender has traditionally been understood as "natural" biological process dictating and regulating sexuality. On the contrary, she argues that in the context of discourse, gender norms discursively constitute subjectivity in general. In this sense, gender is not innate; it is socially produced at the site of language, practices, culture, and activity. Equally important, Butler highlights the ways in which power functions as a structure that seeks to constrict and limit possibilities of transgressive practices that disrupt normative depictions. We know that a heterosexist economy of identity maintains coherence by relying upon gender binaries. As such, black queer studies reminds us that caution must be exercised when analyzing discourse on race, gender, and sexuality.

In the work *Black Queer Studies* (2005), E. Patrick Johnson and Mae G. Henderson note that "essentialist identity politics often reinforces hegemonic power structures rather than dismantling them,"[27] continuing on that "queer studies like black studies, disrupts dominant and hegemonic discourses by consistently destabilizing fixed notions of identity by deconstructing binaries." They further note the importance (and academic currency) of queer studies for understanding and exploring categories of marked "difference." Within the framework of a black queer analysis, we locate the tensions between weighing (and scaling) categories of difference, especially for communities where the marking of differences matters. In the case of the "nappy-headed ho" a black queer perspective welcomes and recognizes the complexity, importance, and intersectionality of identity, without feeling pressed to choose one over the other. It acknowledges that "monolithic identity formations" cannot "survive the crisis of (post)modernity."[28] For these scholars, extending queer studies to the realm of blackness means challenging notions of both heteronormativity and universalizing assimilation so that the "black" in queer functions politically, and endorses "the double crossing of affirming the inclusivity mobilized under the sign 'queer' while also claiming the racial, historical, and cultural specificity attached to the marker 'black.'"[29] The sub-field of black queer studies seeks to form a "dialogical" and "dialectical" kinship whereby each discourse does not *compete* for primacy or dominance, but rather complements and expands varied units of analysis.

The case of the "nappy-headed ho" offers an embodied site in which a black queer analysis is necessitated. As Butler herself notes, it's less about whether theories such as *performativity* have the flexibility to grapple with issues of race; rather, the question becomes, "What happens to the theory when it tries to come to grips with race."[30] The latter is perhaps a more meaningful endeavor. No singular or unitary lens of analysis will suffice when grappling with identity constructions in general; rather, due to their interdependent nature, one needs the layered strength of multiple lenses to accomplish such an exploration. The approach of black queer studies seeks to expand queer theory and consciousness beyond the more sinister constructions of identity while attempting to locate discourse in the realm of the political. In the article "Punks, Bulldaggers and Welfare Queens: The Radical Potential of Queer Politics" (2005), Cohen writes, "I envision a politics where one's relation to power, and not some homogenized identity, is privileged in determining one's political comrades. I am talking about a politics where the nonnormative and marginal positions of punks, bulldaggers, and welfare queens, for example, is the basis for progressive transformative coalition."[31] More importantly, Cohen challenges queer theory to expand beyond the binary of hetero/queer identity constructions centered on sexuality, while challenging black politics to consider the "possibility of change, movement, redefinition, and subversive performance—from year to year, from partner to partner, from day to day, and even from act to act."[32] Beyond arguments regarding identity as social construction, Cohen takes into account the role of power within and outside of queer communities. It is precisely the "broadened understanding of queerness" that can most effectively take into account and come to grips with an "intersectional analysis that recognizes how numerous systems of oppression interact to regulate and police the lives of most people."[33]

The racial backlash by the black community obscured and elided the gendered implications of the Imus case. While race figured primarily as an identity signifier for Imus strengthening his gendered and sexed commentary, reading these acts through an approach that takes black life *and* queer analysis seriously offers room to explore less obvious complexities beyond the primacy of race.

If the case of the "nappy-headed ho" was read through an intersectional queer analysis, what would we find? Perhaps the more important question is, why wasn't this case read through a posture of identity complexity? While I don't have the answers to these questions, I do maintain that scaling identity constructions at best fails to give intelligibility to the complicated lived reality. Referring to the scaling of race, gender, class, and nationality late political philosopher and theorist Iris Marion Young pointed out that in this pecking order of identity, "the privileged groups lose their particularity."[34] In this case, the primary trope of race functioned as a way to maintain dominant notions of gender, sexuality, and class in the black community. It's often feared that a queer approach to gender, class, and sexuality cheapens the *primacy* of racial analysis. In this case, race became the centralizing trope of communal unification whereby *all* within the "black" community could understand the injurious nature of Imus's linguistic tirade. I am persuaded that less focus on race would have created gendered and classed fissures necessitating deeper communal reflection and a more critical approach to what Cohen calls "advanced processes of marginalization"[35]—an approach to marginalization that doesn't flatten oppression, but highlights its insidious cleavages.

RECLAIMING THE "OTHER"

What's race got to do with it? If Hip Hop isn't to blame, then what is? While I have already argued that race figured as a co-constitutive signifier along with others, here I interrogate the response of the black community by asking two questions. First, why was the ontological reality, the classed body of the "nappy-headed ho," denied (although affirmed in a negative manner when compared over and against more "respectable bodies")? Secondly, why were the cultural edges of black popular culture scapegoated in a pathological manner? I argue that beyond the trope of race, the "nappy-headed ho" was not only discursively denied by the black community, she was ultimately deemed illegible, stigmatized, and indecipherable. This section explores the radical possibilities of (re)signifying assumed notions of difference and the meaningful role that popular culture in general can play in such reclamations.

Let us revisit some of the comments made by the black community. Al Sharpton, referring to his daughter whom he brought to confront Imus in person, said, "This young lady just graduated—went to Temple. She is not a nappy-headed ho, she's my daughter," to which Imus replied, "Why listen to the same kind of outrage, let me ask you, in the black community when rappers and other people in the black community, athletes in the black community, defame and demean black women, and all of them call worse names then I ever did," culminating with Sharpton stating that he is among those who are outraged by the demeaning dimensions of black popular culture. In Oprah's town hall meeting "Now What?" she reminds listeners, "These are educated girls, in college, do they look like nappy-headed hos." Coupled with the fervor to differentiate bodies according to class and the symbolic capital of education, the black community's outrage culminated in a moratorium-style charging of Hip Hop to stop using words such as "ho" and "bitch" and "nigger," resulting in a national burial for the "N" word.

Through this series of events, it is apparent that the "nappy-headed ho" was not denied; rather, she was excluded ideologically and dismissed discursively. It was repeatedly mentioned in a number of ways that while there may be a material reality referred to as "nappy-headed hos" somewhere in the world (perhaps she would figure as the black female "dyke," "welfare queen," or "jezebel"), of most importance to black communal response was a vigorous *differentiation* of bodies—that *these* girls were not nappy-headed hos given their educational and social status. Through this process of respectability the black community missed an opportunity to resignify injurious linguistic signifiers. Beyond the material, this is representative of the nature and function of ideologically assumed notions of respectability and class privilege. A rigid and inflexible appropriation of the phrase "nappy-headed ho" became a fixed object of thought caught in the stasis of a particular historical moment.

In *Bodies that Matter: On the Discursive Limits of "Sex"* (1993) Butler asks the question, "What bodies come to matter—and why?"[36] In giving thought to both the material and discursive realities of identity construction, Butler understands the important boundaries of the "repetitive inculcation" of naming itself. The ways in which a subject is both addressed and interpellated speaks to what bodies come to be understood as legible. Butler notes, "We see this most clearly in the examples of those abjected beings who do not appear properly gendered; it is their very humanness that comes into question."[37] The question of what bodies matter, and who has been rendered a life worth living, Butler argues, is not an "idle question." Rather, she states that this question becomes a reality raised and negotiated by all people—it is indeed a question located in the realm of the ethical. What "bodies matter" can ultimately find expression in the question of who is (and isn't) rendered legible—the "who" in society have the privilege to live a *livable* life.

On the question of the materiality of the body, there is perhaps an irreconcilable tension to be found within my own analysis of this event. In one sense, I locate the construction of the "nappy-headed ho" as a *discursive* reality—as a structure which exists within the linguistic parody of Imus's slander. And yet, she exists materially (in the world) as a being whose construction was affirmed by way of material denial (not *this* group of girls). Imus's comments were directed at actual bodies; his interpellation was denied, but only for a certain segment of black women—the educated. As such, this raises the question of whether my analysis risks presenting what Anthony B. Pinn calls "no-bodys" by way of attention to the discursive and textual in a way that seemingly denies the material. With the body as both starting and ending point, Pinn's new text *Embodiment and the New Shape of Black Theological Thought* (2010) addresses what can be known of the body, and moreover, the multiplicity of ways in which the body occupies time and space, paying close attention to particular complexities related to the body and social difference such as gender and sexuality. This text explores what can be known of the (black) body, in terms of discourse and substance. Bringing together Foucault and sociology of the body's attention to materiality, Pinn renders the body as both discursive *and* biochemical reality and suggests that the "*no-body*"-ness of black theology is a result of its purchase placed on the *sui generis* discourse of "liberative potential" of the "right religion," and seeking resolutions, all of which has seemingly ignored the multiplicity of "truth" more generally. But, why does "flesh" matter for the doing and thinking of theology? For Pinn, the answer is simple, yet poignant. He suggests that without the materiality of the body—the fleshy "stuff" of life—then what becomes of the object that theology claims to study?

In a recently published book review article of this text, "What about the "Body?" The *Absence* of its *Presence* in Black Theology (2012)," I suggest that Pinn leaves a tension unresolved—one that involves the quagmires of theory and method. How are fleshy bodies (as both discursive and biochemical) to be methodologically apprehended when the discursive is unavoidable? Are not things such as "race," "the category of experience," and gender always discursively constituted? Is this quandary perhaps the outcome of an excess of purchase and meaning placed on what is erroneously seen as "real"—while, what is *real* is already (and always) ideologically manufactured and discursively constituted. This brings us back to the quagmires of situating the body as both material and discursive.

Despite such tensions, Pinn raises an important point reflective of a longstanding debate within feminist analysis regarding how to locate the matter of bodies themselves—a tension felt in Susan Bordo's critique of Butler's construction of the textual body. On one hand, there is something physical and tangible about the body that Bordo wants to account for, an emphasis on the metaphysics of the body that can be understood as *real*. She argues forcefully in her 1987 text *The Flight to Objectivity* that poststructuralist and postmodern tendencies to treat the body as pure text run the risk of producing what she calls a "stylish nihilism,"[38] a characteristic of Butler's own deconstructive work. While Butler doesn't deny the body, she troubles it in a way that causes anxiety to those for whom the reality of the body is the starting point for critical reflection and analysis. Bordo argues that the body must be both located and situated in a way that doesn't deny experience itself; Butler reminds us that even the category of experience is constructed, ideological, and political. The tension between these thinkers represents a desire for and mourning of the material body (Bordo) and a theorizing of the body from a politics of deconstruction (Butler). Both agree that cultural constructions themselves are structuring structures of bodies in a way that can cause harm, danger, and illegibility. In other words, bodies themselves become victims of cultural constructions in the world. But what comes first for Bordo? The chicken or the egg? Cultural constructions or materiality—can the material matter of the body even be separated from the cultural? If so, *how*? What does materiality signify (if such is even possible) outside of the linguistic ideological realm that Butler so forcefully accounts for? Butler writes of *Bodies That Matter*, "I began writing this book by trying to consider the materiality of the body only to find that the thought of materiality invariably moved me into other domains. . . I could not fix bodies as simple objects of thought."[39] We are reminded that matter itself has a history—it is always, in this sense, discursively constructed and situated. Agreed that Butler's antibiological perspective in favor of linguistic foundations raises issues regarding "what of the body"—however, her turn to the discursive reminds us that bodies *are* the effects of cultural and social constructions, there is no pure body to be felt outside of such domains.

The "nappy-headed ho" was subjected in language and action—an *abject* body discursively pathologized and rendered deviant through social exclusion. Moreover, the discursive exclusion of the "nappy-headed ho" is figured most prominently in the construction of ideology, through the bordering of boundaries, the "set of foreclosures, radical erasures, that are, strictly speaking, refused the possibility of cultural articulation,"[40] according to Butler. While one cannot deny the pejorative historicity of this term over and against the fixity of white supremacy, the question still remains, what is so abject about this "nappy-headed ho" that instantiated such a tenacious and dogged rejection in the realm of the black counter-publics?

The ontological reality of the "nappy-headed ho" as legible construction within the black community was denied because she was less than "decent" to a community still trying to defend itself against white cultural depictions of blackness through strategies of respectability. By norms of "respectability" I am referring to the process Young identifies as:

> conforming to norms that repress sexuality, bodily functions, and emotional expression. It is linked to an idea of order: the respectable person is chaste, modest, does not express lustful desires, passion, spontaneity, or exuberance, is frugal, clean, gently spoken, and well mannered. The orderliness of respectability means things are under control, everything in its place, not crossing the borders.[41]

Similarly, Cohen's challenge for a black queer politics that extends beyond identity calls for a redefinition of those bodies that are out-of-place and stand on the outside of dominant orders. Redefining the political edges of what it means to be queer while expanding misrepresented notions of power, Cohen sees possibility of a leftist framework that doesn't deny that which is characterized as *abject*, but rather, embraces that which has been described as invisible. Such an expansion begins at the site of *non-privileged* members of a group—where the most "vulnerable" bodies in one's community have the chance to live, speak, and be realized. This reclamation of being black *and* queer creates "allow-able spaces for queer 'deviant' culture and the rest of the 'naturalized world.'"[42] To carve out such a space invariably means to reclaim and give new meaning to how we understand difference in general. Poignantly stated, Cohen asks, "How do we use the relative degrees of ostracism that all sexual/cultural 'deviants' experience to build a basis of unity for broader coalition and movement work?" In embracing difference, Cohen sees radical political potential in the identities of those who have been written off as "risky." If there's ever to be a radical democratic project whereby dismissed bodies who stand on the edges of "respectability" can live, constructions like "nappy-headed hos" must be reclaimed, embraced, and celebrated. Such reclamation has potential to debunk assumed notions of reason, authenticity, and universality. Dogged attempts at moments of freedom can only be had by acknowledging and privileging the most vulnerable in our communities. It is then and only then that "freedom comes to signify what it never signified before; jus-tice comes to embrace precisely what could not be contained under its prior description."[43]

RETHINKING *DIFFERENCE* IN BLACK POPULAR CULTURE

> "Only changing the cultural habits themselves will change the oppres-sion they produce and reinforce, but change in cultural habits can occur only if individuals become aware of and change their individual habits. This is a cultural revolution."
>
> —Iris Marion Young[44]

Rethinking difference means thinking differently about the political and transformational power of culture itself. Most cultural theorists from within the Marxist tradition agree that the struggle for hegemony and domination functions at the site of the cultural superstructure. In this place, one feels the pulse of the fight for dominance wrought between codes, representation, and style. Butler asks, "Does resignification constitute a political practice, or does it constitute one part of political transformation?"[45] In the case of the Imus controversy, black popular culture was considered a *cause* of social ills, rather than both *cause* and *effect* albeit with subversive potentiality. In this sense, white blame turned into black guilt and personal responsibility. While the term "nappy-headed ho" was understood as racially injurious, precisely what kinds of claims does this make regarding culture itself? In Butler's words: "When we claim to have been injured by language, what kind of claim do we make?"[46] Attempting to complicate more general and constricting notions of censorship, Butler challenges the complex nature of meaning itself at the site of the linguistic domain. Undoubtedly, words carry significant historical baggage and always remain contested signifiers.

Rather than getting stuck in the mud of particular historical moments, signification finds its most prominent role in reinterpretation beyond fixed hermeneutics. Butler asks, "Are we fixed by language?"[47] Undeniably, language can be deployed with intentionally to harm and injure, yet similar notions of violence are also reproduced when we fail to take seriously the fluid and contested nature of language itself. The only threat to what is understood as harmful in language is the *unwillingness* to think of the *play* of language for political possibility.

Examples of this type of resignification and play abound in Hip-Hop culture. Subversive recasting is evidenced in everyday uses of words such as nigger, black, and queer. This "redoubling" of language finds an interesting life, most often at the site of the counter-cultural edges of life, but too often society condemns that which holds potential for transformational politics. For example, the early 1990s in American life saw an increased push to ban rap music on both state and federal levels, citing it as nothing more than sheer violence. Questioning this rather conservative move to ban rap music, Butler asserts that such "collapse of speech and conduct thus works to localize the 'cause' of urban violence, to silence a discussion of the broader institutional conditions that produce right-wing violence," further suggesting that "in the United States, the turn against the lyrics of gangsta rap may also operate as a deflection from more fundamental analysis on race, poverty, rage, and how those conditions are graphically registered in Urban African-American popular musical genres."[48]

Rather than rejecting the radical potential already present in black popular culture, increased engagement is needed, a type of engagement that embraces the myriad of ways in which "difference" itself is lived. The idea of difference is not the problem; more problematic is the lack of appreciation for assumed and perceived notions of difference that become ideological stumbling blocks in the project of radical envisioning. Can there be emancipation through claiming the "nappy-headed ho?" Rather than allowing essentialized notions to reduce and explain away the messiness of difference, ideological differences that become complicated by class, race, and gender can effectively be undone and redone through practices of resistance in the cultural marketplace. Could this term have been re-appropriated and used as a tool of what Cornel West calls "tragic comic hope?" The activity of turning things on their heads is not new to black cultural life, yet certain bodies are representative of certain differences that have been given little attention.

While the NAACP sought to bury the "N" word its attempts were aborted and brought back to life by rapper Nas's 2008 CD originally entitled "Nigger." On this brilliant, creative, and politically subversive LP, Nas calls for a deregulation of the word "nigger" by challenging other minorities to "be a nigger too," suggesting that reclaiming this

word has potential to create a cultural revolution with political promise
by holding the historicity of the word "nigger" in tension with its everyday
meanings. In one video that was banned from BET (Black Entertainment
Television), Nas, talking to a group of Italian, Asian, Latino/a, and black
people, raps:

> I'm a nigger/he's a nigger/she's a nigger/we some niggers/wouldn't you
> like to be a/nigger too?

When coming to grips with the case of the "nappy-headed ho," what would
it have meant or looked like for the black community to take on Nas's
challenge? The cultural imperialism among black elites failed to embrace
its least of these. While black popular culture in general continues to "live
by unwritten codes in society" by abandoning and altering rules of conformity and cultural constriction, little attention is given to powerful acts of
reclamation like that put forward by Nas. Such a process can only begin by
coming face to face with the Other by critically engaging and problematiz-
ing the civic face of Hip-Hop culture.

This chapter has examined the dirtying and washing of the public face of
Hip Hop, seeking to look more deeply at the pathologization of Hip-Hop
as stand-in for more troubling societal un-wellnesses. As with Nas's disin-
genuous reclamation of "niggerhood," there is a back-and-forthness at play
in signification and re-signification, claiming and reclaiming, as the 'deviant' black bodies move around in the tension of repositioning themselves.
This doubling effect continues in Chapter 2, which moves one step closer in
towards the materiality of Hip Hop, while paradoxically being baffled by
the redoubling of meanings as religion is used, at times blatantly, as a tool
for self-marketing as well as a space of lived redemption.

2 Don't Judge a Book by Its Cover

"Hip hop just saved my life"

—Lupe Fiasco[1]

"Hip Hop Is dead"

—Nasir Jones[2]

"What is the gospel? The good news. What is the good news? The good news is that you can actually be Hip Hop and feed your family. You can actually be a DJ and wind up in Hong Kong, China getting $10,000 for twenty minutes. You can actually be a graffiti writer and end up in France somewhere selling your pieces for $20,000 a pop. This is what Hip Hop is experiencing today. But the mass media is just letting you know two things: Hip Hop is about bitches, hoes, and niggas. And: the whole music industry has collapsed. Damn. Not much left for the kids, is there? So the gospel of Hip Hop comes out as a self-help technique . . . I'm not just doing Hip Hop—I am Hip Hop."

—KRS One[3]

"I am suggesting that in 100 years, this book will be a new religion on earth."

—KRS One[4]

In December of 2006 rapper Nasir "Nas" Jones, self-described as the "Street's Disciple," proclaimed through his new LP "Hip Hop Is Dead" that the very cultural production American culture had come to love so much, was no longer alive. Rapping in one lyric, Nas states, "Hip Hop just died this morning and she's dead/she's dead." Clarifying whether he is referring to a metaphorical or ontological death of Hip Hop, in an October 2006 interview with Shaheem Reid, Nas described his lyrically based Nietzchian-like requiem on Hip Hop's passing in this way:

When I say 'hip-hop is dead,' basically America is dead. There is no political voice. Music is dead. B2K is not New Edition. Chris Brown is great, I love Chris Brown, we need that, but Bobby Brown sticks in my heart. Our way of thinking is dead, our commerce is dead. Everything in this society has been done. It's like a slingshot, where you throw the mutha—a back and it starts losing speed and is about to fall down.

That's where we are as a country. I don't wanna lose nobody with this, but what I mean by 'hip-hop is dead' is we're at a vulnerable state. If we don't change, we gonna disappear like Rome. Let's break it down to a smaller situation. Hip-hop is Rome for the hood. I think hip-hop could help rebuild America, once hip-hoppers own hip-hop. . . . We are our own politicians, our own government, we have something to say. We're warriors. Soldiers.[5]

In a "death-of-god"-like twist (God is dead *yet* not "really" dead), Nas has something different in mind than prophesying the *ontological* death of Hip Hop; in fact, the very production of his apocalyptic-like album is testimony to the fact that Hip Hop is in fact, very much alive and well. There is another kind of reclamation at work here: a process of casting out and re-integrating of identity, to renew and invigorate.

The paranoid arrangements of quotes that open up this chapter are lyrical vignettes speaking to the life/death/life potential of Hip-Hop culture. From Lupe Fiasco's proclamation that "Hip Hop saved me"—to Nas's death-of-Hip Hop blow—and KRS One's attempt to establish Hip-Hop culture as a new religious movement on earth, what is for certain is that artists of Hip-Hop culture explicitly make known through rap their perspectives on the longevity, power, and mortality of Hip-Hop culture.

Recently the literary market has been flooded by a flurry of artist-produced (and co-authored in some instances) Hip-Hop knowledge productions (books) that use religious signifiers or existential themes such as "fear/fearlessness" as an entry into authorizing particular ideological positionalities of Hip-Hop culture—albeit in very different ways. This chapter considers three of these 2009 productions: *The 50th Law* by 50 Cent and established writer Robert Greene (author of self-help books that engage themes such as power, seduction, and strategy); *The Tao of Wu* by RZA of Wu-Tang Clan (with Chris Norris); and lastly an 831-page book entitled *The Gospel of Hip Hop: First Instrument*, written by KRS One.

Beyond their troping of mysticism, religion, philosophy, and celebration and power of the "thug" experience, these books market an exterior aesthetic and style bringing attention to their mark on the world. Signifying power and authority, 50 Cent's book is fashioned after a black King James Version of the Bible. A soft black leather-like cover encases this book, a sword grounds the title, and the edges of the pages are lined with gold. RZA's book markets a Zen-like quality, with a black and silver cover emphasizing the "W" for his group Wu-Tang Clan; and lastly, KRS's book is fashioned after a Holy Bible boasting fancy embossed gold lettering and a silk bookmark inside, similar to ones found nestled away in Christian Bibles. Beyond the fascinating *styling* of these productions, attention to public reception of these works and what the works themselves more generally signify is paramount for a thorough analysis.

This chapter will flow in three sections, each section taking on one particular knowledge production by a certain rap artist/author. In stepping from the more general positioning of Hip Hop in the broader culture to a consideration of the uses of religion within Hip-Hop cultural productions, this chapter will not perform a religious or theological analysis; rather, it is my intention to consider how the language and construction of *authority* in these epistemological productions (sometimes accomplished through the use of "religious" language) authorizes and accomplishes some type of cultural work within the Hip-Hop culture world and throughout larger society. That is to say, this chapter, paying close attention to varied uses of religion, will ask, "What do these works seek to authorize, what are their effects, and how are such effects produced?"

Due to the length and density of some of the works under analysis, limitations of space preclude me from doing an in-depth analysis of each. That said, my examination will focus on various dimensions of each book that highlight constructions of authority while taking into account public reception of these works from virtual spaces (e.g., YouTube remarks, blogs, and more formal interviews) to highlight how spaces such as the world wide web have been morphed into spiritual pulpits and platforms, places of great debates, battles, and perspectives. As will become apparent, critical suspicion of each work is necessary; what will become most observable in some cases is that the content of a book cannot be assumed at first glance based on aesthetic stylings—for even the manufacturing of the appearance of book is meant to "do something," to construct a certain kind of significance and power. That is to say, Hip-Hop knowledge production bears witness to the old adage that says a book can never be judged by its cover.

50 CENT AND THE LAW OF "FEARLESSNESS": THE THUG'S GUIDE TO SELF-HELP

"That book looks like a Bible!"

—Ramo (a blogger)[6]

The 50th Law, the co-creation of rapper Curtis "50 Cent" Jackson with the book-making know-how of prolific writer/guru Robert Greene, does indeed "look like a Bible." As such, it might reasonably be assumed to have something "spiritual" or "religious" in mind; but on the contrary, the main theme of this text is *Fear Nothing* and maintain trust in, not a higher power, but the self. This belief in the self is, as 50 Cent proclaims, what enabled his "nine lives" survival of the violence of the ghetto, and his subsequent success in the gritty world of rap—and is an equally good fit for the booming publishing world of self-help. With the assistance of Greene, a professional in this field whose earlier work (see, for instance, *The 48 Laws of Power* (1998), *The Art of Seduction* (2001), and *The 33 Strategies of War* (2007)) had impressed 50 Cent, the gangster ethics that kept 50 on top are explicated in each of the tome's fifty sections.

In a promotional video for *The 50ᵗʰ Law* (a title that may be seen to follow the styling of the self-help master's earlier publications) Greene describes his life work as taking:

> the most powerful people in their field and kind of break[ing] them down, what is the essence, what's the core of their success . . . I call it their power sense of gravity.[7]

Deciding to take this same approach with 50 Cent, he shadows 50 to analyze the secret to his success. The key, he finds,

> is your fearlessness . . . you're the one that has less fear than they do, and that gives you a constant strategic advantage . . . adapt, take risks . . . this is to me the source of your power . . . this is the subject of our book *The 50ᵗʰ Law.* . . . Were you sort of just born this way? Or did you have to develop this attitude on the streets as a kid?[8]

To this question 50 Cent responds,

> It's absolutely something I had to develop . . . I think I have the same emotions as everyone else does . . . I can kind of adjust.[9]

50 Cent describes his vision for the book in this way:

> I think it's important for you to develop a plan. In this actual book, you know, I put down some of the concepts and ideas that I created, I expressed, all of my intimate thoughts with Robert so he could assess what I was doing without having technical terms to create a description of what my planning process was. Overall I'm really proud of this actual project. [Fans] will get a chance to pick it up September 8th, *The 50th Law.* 50 Cent. Robert Greene. It's gonna be great, you'll get a chance to read it and create your own five-year plan for success.[10]

Greene has in fact performed quite a feat with the material provided by 50 Cent, particularly when it comes to translating his street credibility into an intellectual credibility, which he achieves primarily by the packaging of 50's persona and story alongside the likes of such odd bedfellows as Malcolm X and Machiavelli.

Indeed, the 50 Cent and Greene collaboration extends credibility and capital to each of their respective "games." While such may be the case, the public has yet to be convinced. Comments from an online blog both praise and mock this endeavor—what could a ex-felon, drug dealer, and "thug" teach society about navigating the ropes of capitalism and the corporatized rap industry? One blogger "Cybervillian" remarks that:

50 is really educating the misguided hip hop community to success.
Now it's up to the kids not to try to be dumb like Cam'ron or Rick
Ross and actually be studious and intelligent while keepin it gangsta.
Knowledge is deadly that's why Ricky isn't a threat, nor camron, nor
ja rule, nor fat joe, nor anyone in rap. 50 is the smartest out. And now
is giving knowledge to those who wish to read into it. I'm definately
coppin this.[11]

Differing from blogger "Cybervillian," blogger "Wack Diesel" expresses a
rather mocking hesitation:

First Year: Find Somebody To Shoot U Nine 9 times
Second Year: Diss The Hottest Rapper Out
Third Year: Copy The Style Of The Same Rapper You Dissed
Fourth Year: Get Co Signed By The Two Biggest Names In Rap
Fifth Year: Diss Another Artists Everytime You Album is About
    To Come Out
There You Go, SO You Don't Have To Buy This Book[12]

In this marriage of opposites, 50 Cent and Greene pool their diverse
expertise to manufacture a particular cultural product that achieves certain aims. In the journal article published in 2011 that shares the title of
this chapter, I defined these achievements in these words: (1) it re-signifies
difference and ideas of "properness" by authorizing 50's experience of
"ghetto" life as the platform where his successful character of fearlessness
contributes towards his ability to navigate social mobility; (2) it uses *aesthetic* and *philosophical* weight towards establishing an intellectual origin
to the ideological marketing of "fearlessness"; and lastly (3) it sets out to
accomplish a "thugged-out" new-age human-centered approach to life in
more general terms.[13]

These are substantial acts of alchemy, and as such merit a closer
examination.

SELLING FEARLESSNESS: AUTHORIZING THE THUG'S EXPERIENCE

With so many "respectable" self-help books already produced, what could
a former drug-dealing thug from Queens who's been shot nine times possibly teach business students about climbing the walls of capitalism and
rising to the top of their corporate hustle? Throughout *The 50ᵗʰ Law*, as the
back of the book declares, the main message of this text is *nihil timendum
est*, fear nothing.

The marketing of 50's life experience (selling drugs, fighting, confronting
drug lords, going to jail) was in fact a useful strategy in cultivating "fearlessness" (thus making him one of the most successful rappers to navigate

the capitalistic conglomerates of the rap industry), which by *effect* re-signifies *difference* and alters dominant codes of morality by authorizing the
thug's experience of violence—as *productive*. This re-signification alters
boundaries of respectability and deviance by highlighting the affirmative
dimensions and blurring normative conceptions of deviance.

From the beginning, there is an authorizing of the thug's experience
via Greene:

> What struck me the most was that we had a remarkably similar way
> of looking at the world, one that transcended the great differences in
> our backgrounds. . . . He [50 Cent] developed this way of thinking on
> the dangerous streets of Southside Queens where it was a necessary life
> skill; I came to it by reading a lot of history and observing the crafty
> maneuvers of various people in Hollywood, where I worked for many
> years. The perspective, however, is the same.[14]

In the text *Authority*, Bruce Lincoln argues that "discursive authority is
not so much an entity as it is (1) an effect; (2) the capacity for producing
that effect; and (3) the commonly shared opinion that a given actor has the
capacity for producing the effect."[15] Thus, authority is not something that
is self-evident, rather, it is constructed in certain situations thereby producing effects such as "trust, respect, docility, acceptance, even reverence."[16]
Throughout *The 50th Law*, 50's experiences (which would under normal
circumstances be criticized) are highlighted and embraced for their capitalistic cultivation of progress and social mobility.

Through Greene, an established business man and accomplished author,
drawing parallels between his own life and 50's experience, authority is
both constructed and accomplished. By way of Greene's social capital,
moral categories and codes are now leveled. This is 50's story, as told to
Greene, by Greene. After listening to 50's life stories, Greene writes that
the most basic feature of 50's success is that "he is a master player at power,
a kind of hip-hop Napoleon Bonaparte. . . . I decided that the source of
his power is his utter fearlessness."[17] After all, 50 Cent never imagined he
would be alive after the age of 25, so as Greene writes, what more could
50 possibly lose?

Greene points out that in growing up on the dangerous streets of Queens,
NY the expression of fear equates to losing respect from others. No matter
what went down, you had to set aside the emotion and act with power; in
fact, acting with power created the feeling of power, until facing someone
with a gun was no big deal. Looking for something "positive" to market
in the gangster's experience of "criminology," Greene further establishes a
telling re-signification and affirmation of *difference* in drawing a parallel
between 50's learned-on-the-street business sense and the "freewheeling
types of the nineteenth century" Wild West. Speaking of such twenty-first
century rough-and-ready entrepreneurs, Greene posits that "Their spirit

fits the disorder of the twenty-first century. They are fascinating to watch and in some ways have much to teach us." [18]

In a Derridian-like redoubling of signification, *difference* is recast. Jacques Derrida reminds us that "in short, 'difference' would be 'improvisational anarchy.' It would be a bearer of negativity but also of an alterity that would ceaselessly escape from the same and the identical." [19] On one hand, 50's experience is lifted up in utter alterity—a strangeness that fuels something different than most successful people, yet on the other is representative of that which is not so different from what American society has seen. Put in this way, 50's (social and cultural) *difference* is not something completely "different" from the standard—it is a rather "a reaffirmation of the same, an economy of the same in its relation to the other, which does not require that the same, in order to exist, be frozen or fixed in a distinction or in a system of dual oppositions." [20] Greene reminds us that what he sees in 50 is no different than what he likewise witnesses among the "Hollywood" typologies of success.

The fearlessness that 50 lives out is extrapolated from the streets. In this book, the streets (as configured through 50's success and authorized by Greene) are no different than the business world: "The competitive dynamic (the streets, the business world) is in fact the same, but your apparently comfortable environments makes it harder for you to see it" [21]—in other words it's time for a new perspective, without fear. The re-casting of chaotic experiences (like 50's), where the popular imagination only pathologizes those acts it finds "criminal" and "deviant," becomes formative for an ideological shift of perspectives on "deviance" and "difference." In the ethnographic work *Off the Books: The Underground Economy of the Urban Poor* (2006), urban sociologist Sudhir Venkatesh highlights the logic of practice among poor urban residents of Maquis Park in Chicago, Illinois. While "conventional morality" is altered in the urban underground of the underclass, Venkatesh reminds us that "its boundaries are not so clear." [22] Venkatesh, like Greene, sees something more than just crime in the everyday practices of il/legal underground economic activity: "The hustle also involved a diverse set of strategies to make sure that the shady world did not completely ruin the social fabric," [23] and as such, "In the ghetto, advertising and marketing, credit and capital acquisition, enforcement and regulation, and other aspects of commerce seem as easily conducted via informal channels and outside the government's eye as through legitimate venues where the state is the arbiter and lawmaker." [24] Like Greene, Venkatesh sees something in the ghetto's im/moral economy worth noting: "Underground entrepreneurs possess skill, business acumen, and tremendous potential for innovative skills and strategies" [25]—here the hustlers' world becomes humanized.

The effects of authorizing 50's experience (as being "legitimate") invariably flip traditional morality on its head while also challenging reception of the public face of 50—and the Hustler writ large. Sociologist Howard Becker reminds us that the placement of the "outsider" is real and yet, similar to Mary Douglas's thesis on "dirt" as "matter out of place," is always socially fabricated. The construction of the outsider as deviant doesn't reflect the "true" essence of the deviant's behavior; rather "the term 'outsiders' . . . refers to those people who are judged by others to be deviant and thus to stand outside the circle of 'normal' group members."[26] With the authorizing effects of social capital in place, who can say that 50's criminal and violent experiences garnered from street life aren't effective? It's not that 50's ethics aren't "moral" or "valid" enough, rather that conventional codes and rules set in place don't authorize these types of experiences as beneficial or valuable in society. Becker reminds us that "rules are the product of someone's initiative and we can think of the people who exhibit such enterprise as *moral entrepreneurs*."[27] Set up in this way, 50 Cent is not required to offer an apology for his past life, nor does he have to repent for it; rather, this work authorizes his experiences and presents diamonds in the rough of ghetto underclass life.

The 50ᵗʰ Law serves to reverse Pierre Bourdieu's thesis on the importance of acquiring dominant *cultural capital* to survive—we are reminded that "the most powerful principle of the symbolic efficacy of cultural capital no doubt lies in the logic of its transmission."[28] While acquiring dominant capital may be necessary to navigate the interstices of social mobility, we are still left to wonder how the *habitus* of the underclass reflects, at times, a resilient social base for successful capitalist social mobility. Perhaps the answer remains in the emergence of *indigenous* forms of *cultural capital*.

AESTHETIC AND PHILOSOPHICAL WEIGHT

Similar to the argument I have been making for the non-unique status of religion as a concept, Lincoln would have us remember that authority, rather than having some capital in and of itself as an abstraction, is actualized as it is constructed and played out socially. So it is the details of enactment that constitute what we term authority. And thus it is to the details that we, as scholars, can look to reconstruct "what just happened." How did the thug off the streets gain capital as a philosopher? How is it that his work is now subject to aesthetic appreciation? Through what dynamic has the street hustler become validated as business entrepreneur? The preceding section answered similar questions in terms of re-signifying *difference* and "deviance," but there is more to the achievement than that. Validity and reliability are standard measures of scholarly instruments, and where these do not already exist they can, as will be seen, be borrowed.

The foremost instance of this borrowing of authority occurs in the styling of the volume after a Bible, most certainly a "proper" object of study. Authorities are compounded here: religious troping layers with the weight of the judge, also black-clad and serious. Concurrently, there is the title itself, embossed in (faux) gold in a Gothic font. Note the transliteration of the signifier "50" from the humble fifty cents to a modifier of the majestic and ultimate authority of the Law. Fifty is a weighty number (that is, one to which cultures have assigned weight), and in affixing his identity to it 50 Cent benefits from the weight of both the number itself and, in this work, its proximity to the temporal authority of the law. Thus, the otherwise 'deviant' who exists outside the law claims ownership of it, ascending in 'respectability' as if stepping on an escalator, and by symbolic adjacency the Hip-Hop practitioner is afforded both validity and reliability.

Bourdieu points out that the authority carried by language is constructed, rather than granted, to any user. He writes, "The naïve question of the power of words is logically implicated in the initial suppression of the question of the uses of language, and therefore of the social conditions in which words are employed."[29] For words to become powerful the speaker must also be seen as authorized: the symbolic weight is shared by speech and speaker. Bourdieu goes on to explicate that "the symbolic efficacy of words is exercised only in so far as the person subjected to it recognizes the person who exercises it as authorized to do so."[30] So a logical initial move on the part of Greene is the authorization of 50 Cent as one who should be listened to; the effect is similar to that of turning on the switch to allow the electricity of the power of words to flow.

What do Ralph Waldo Emerson, James Baldwin, Montesquieu, Dostoyevsky, Pascal, Nietzsche, Sun Tzu, and Machiavelli have in common with Curtis Jackson aka 50 Cent? Before Greene began his refashioning of 50, perhaps not much. But the collective intellectual and cultural weight of these past masters packs quite a punch, and in *The 50th Law* they are all fighting on the side of 50. Quotations from these and others such as Malcolm X adorn each section of the volume, and their strategies and philosophies are presented as aligning with those of 50 Cent. Thus, 50's authority is textually and visually grounded in the combined historical validity of cultural "greats."

The next section will engage the "human-centered" approach that I believe 50 and Greene's collaboration constructs, whereby the use of established philosophy and intellectual sources validates 50's experience through the *effect* of historical authenticity. Greene writes, "I then expanded on these discussions with my own research, combining the example of Fifty with stories of other people throughout history who have displayed the same fearless quality."[31] There is a market standard that must be met in order to effectively and persuasively sell the life-world of 50—it has to be couched and delivered in a particular kind of way. Not only do the poached intellectual quotes give "conventional" breadth and depth to 50's experiences, they also provide symbolic capital and weight by way of established epistemologies. The quotes and life-worlds of already established philosophical persons like Nietzsche, for example, function almost ritualistically throughout the book. It is not strange that 50 and said intellectuals may embody or espouse similar philosophies of life, but the *poaching* of these quotes functions as an intellectual ritual of authority that provides symbolic capital and power to sell 50's life. In a real sense, the troping of famous and "complex" quotes allows the reader to be more "accepting" of the authorizing of 50's world—it allows the literary marketing of the "thug's" life to "pass"—without being pathologized. In *Language & Symbolic Power* (1991), Bourdieu reminds us of "the *social* function of ritual and the social significance of the boundaries or limits which the ritual allows one to pass over or transgress in a lawful way"[32]—in other words, as Michel Foucault points out in *The Archeology of Knowledge* (1972), what often gives shape, will, and power to the modes of existence of discourse is in and through the very construction of ideas themselves. The patchwork of 50's life, the authority of Greene, and the established intellectuals used to support 50's life-world work together to shape the experience of authority and unity in this work, and further, to operationalize and provide persuasive power to the selling of *The 50th Law*. Here, 50's experiences of life are not "self-evident" in and of themselves; rather, they are mediated through, used in tension with, and grounded in intellectual authority, among other things. These "technologies of power," if you will, help give shape to the authenticity of 50's authorship and help quell the deviance of his social world and practices. Foucault says it best when he writes, "Who is speaking? Who, among the totality of speaking individuals, is accorded the right to use this sort of language (*language*)? Who is qualified to do so? . . . What is the status of the individuals who—alone—have the right, sanctioned by law or tradition, juridically defined or spontaneously accepted, to proffer such a discourse?"[33]

THUG METAPHYSICS AND EXPERIENCE:
MENTAL ALCHEMY AND REALISM

Experience—and the illusion of authority given to the category of "experience" (and what counts as experience) by any and all means—sells. This is why the troping of the category of experience has not only proved useful (as a category of reflection) among subjugated groups to validate themselves in uncontestable ways, but the illusion of power and authority that comes along with selling "experience" is above all a good marketing strategy. After his being affirmatively compared to great historical and philosophical giants of history—how could one *not* believe the power of 50's testimony? The constructions of authority used in this work market a tried and true way of being in the world—the power of *The 50th Law*.

Together, 50 and Greene set out to sell one thing: a particular metaphysics of self-help built on the foundation of mental alchemy and realism—the power of the self to succeed—no matter what, despite whatever austere conditions a person may face. Here, the *sui generis* approach of a particular philosophy (*The 50th Law*) functions through the category of experience which in turn is supposed to, in "theory," provide a non-contestable authority. This is a point forcefully made by the scholars whose work I will refer to repeatedly throughout this project. Russell T. McCutcheon in *Manufacturing Religion* (1997) and *Critics Not Caretakers* (2001) argues that *sui generis* approaches are supported in and through the rhetoric of "experience":

> The very reliance on the category of religious experience is evidenced of the widespread presumption that actors have sole authority for conveying what they take to be the meanings of stories and behaviors and the interpretations of events. Otherwise, speculations on just what is distinctive about religious experience would be met with the same critical gaze as currently meets nineteenth-century speculations on the origins of religion per se.[34]

Ultimately, *The 50th Law* (as a proven philosophy based on experience exemplified through the personification of 50) provides a philosophy that articulates *fearlessness*. Greene and 50 write, "Your fears are a kind of prison that confines you within a limited range of action. The less you fear, the more power you will have and the more fully you will live. It is our hope that *The 50Th Law* will inspire you to discover this power for yourself."[35]

They market that *fear* hinders success in social mobility and may be likened to an ir/rational emotion that has been the cause of irrational things, such as religion. They suggest, "Out of fear, we also developed religion and various belief systems to comfort us. Fear is the oldest and strongest emotion known to man, something deeply inscribed in our nervous system and subconscious."[36] This is a widely held perspective throughout American society.

You can be just like 50 Cent through this philosophy! Among competing truths, *The 50th Law* is selling 50 as the embodiment of this ideology: "The new fearless types, as represented by Fifty, move in the opposite direction"—it is these types who are not afraid, as they point out, to "hustle" and "let go of the past and create their own business model."[37] The construct of power is thus correlated with the "fearless" type—one must harness fearlessness in order to become, as this book suggests, a "free spirit."

Not only the spirit is freed through the life philosophy explicated by 50 via Greene. The mind also is harnessed in the realization of freedom. In a new-age-like maneuver, the mind itself becomes a powerful tool of and for freedom. Although the authors acknowledge the tangible structural and social inequities that challenge and often defeat in one's journey across the landscape of life, they emphasize the role of the mind in transcending external structure. No matter what environment one is born into and navigates, the responses and reactions of the mind are presented as being a powerful personal resource for reshaping reality: "With so many physical limitations, hustlers have learned to develop mental freedom. . . . Their thoughts have to keep moving—creating new ventures, new hustles, new directions in music and clothes."[38] And while this a personal tool within the reach and control of each individual, it has universal qualities that cut across differences (and obliterating differences is a repeating theme in this parsing of the grammar of the creation of authority). *The 50th Law* is universalized: "And the people that practice the *The 50th Law* in their lives all share certain qualities—*supreme boldness, unconventional fluidity,* and *a sense of urgency*—that give them this unique ability to shape their circumstance."[39] Not only does 50 Cent gain through adjacency to others, the flow works in reverse as well. Successful personages, and each reader of the *Law* is free to include him or herself in this assemblage, are ascribed characteristics "legalized" by 50 Cent, in a cross-transfusion of qualities through time and space.

In another back-and-forth motion, the tried and true method of the carrot and the stick, long familiar to those subject to constructed beliefs of all sorts, is brought to bear on potential adherents to the Law as scripted by 50 Cent: "It is all rather simple: when you transgress this fundamental law by bringing your usual fears into any encounter, you narrow your options and your capacity to shape events."[40] The Law, in this styling, becomes the enabler and the delimiter, but the authors also describe a dynamic by which a further force, a manifestation of the "invisible hand," steps in to scatter manna on the hillsides for those who "observe" the Law: "—it opens possibilities, brings freedom of action, and helps create a forward momentum in life."[41]

The language of religion is used here to instigate a metaphysics of belief and results. Through *observing* a particular practice, one becomes entitled to certain benefits, and through *transgressing* a codified power structure, one becomes subject to negative consequences. A certain acclaimed truth or ideology necessitates action on the part of the adherent, Foucault's "truth obligation" to "bear witness." Thus, there is a "next move" required by the consumer of the *Law*, because although "Fifty *had* to confront his fears; you must *choose* to."[42] We are provided with the example of what happened when 50 confronted his fears, and thus the ideology is validified through lived experience—lived by 50 Cent, and available to us in the grand capitalist meritocracy. In the locus of the mind, we, like 50, can choose to advance rather than retreat, even to the point of facing death without fear. "If we are afraid of death," proclaim 50 and Greene, "then we are afraid of life.[43]

KRS ONE: SELLING HIP HOP THROUGH RELIGION

While rapper 50 Cent pushes to humanize the "thug's experience" into a self-help philosophy through the authorization of *fearlessness* as a new mythos, longtime rapper, teacher, and Hip-Hop philosopher KRS One has attempted to bring Hip Hop back to its more *spiritual* roots in his new book *The Gospel of Hip Hop: The First Instrument* (2009). The virtual spaces of Myspace,

YouTube, and online blogs have become contested sites of religious, social, and cultural dialogue, a *virtual* battling over whether Hip Hop could in fact be a new religion on earth in the next 100 years. On the flip side, many are debating if KRS One perhaps represents a dried-up nostalgic Hip Hopper stuck in the mud of a specific historical moment when Hip Hop was mythically *conscious*. One blogger who goes under the name "Drew Guevara" retorts, "KRS is no longer hip hop. Hasn't been since Nelly went at him. How's that for gospel?" Meanwhile others like blogger "JasonCTown" remain convinced that "dude always lays the truth down, and always has a different take than most any other rapper out there."[44] Self-proclaimed as the "teacha," KRS mentions in one interview that his new book "explores the spirituality of Hip-Hop, the divinity of Hip-Hop."[45] A cursory look at the over-800-page book confirms his attempt. And what's more, although his book is aesthetically fashioned after the Bible, KRS One makes clear that separate from more established organized religions, he feels something new on the Hip-Hop cultural horizons, stating, "I respect the Christianity, the Islam, the Judaism but their time is up,"[46] alluding to a new Hip-Hop religion on earth by telling online source AllHipHop, "I don't have to go through any religion [or] train of thought. I can approach God directly myself."[47] Bloggers in their virtual makeshift-like pulpits have debated whether KRS is attempting to establish a new world religion, not qualified by race or ethnicity, but rather, Hip Hop (which apparently transcends these signifiers). On the flip side, others are convinced that religion has nothing to do with it—rather, KRS One's latest strategy is about getting Hip Hop back to a more conscious or pure element. In an online YouTube discussion over KRS One's new gospel, blogger "Ebonysweet601" says:

> It's not about "religion" first and foremost, there is enough religion running ramped around the globe. It's not about bashing KRS One either, he is a human being just like everyone of us. Some folks don't want to admit that HIP HOP is not the same. The REAL hip hop was back in the days, period. Disagree if you want too, but the truth is the truth. The old school is in a different class, bottom line. Know this, God is not religion and neither is Jesus, they are both very much ALIVE.[48]

According to this perspective, KRS One's use of religious rhetoric has a more pragmatic strategy in mind—to re-establish the *realness* of Hip Hop at a time in which the game has completely changed—a time in which the "conscious" element of Hip Hop is missing. So one wonders why the over-abundance of religious rhetoric to make his point? In fact, one blogger wondered the same. "4Skeptik4" states that KRS One's latest efforts can be chalked up to:

> Self-glorification. That is this Hip Hop movement. Pride. "I am God" is essentially this movement . . . but truth says "I deserve and am nothing w/o God." Is there anything you have that wasn't given to you?

NO—how does a book about re-establishing Hip Hop in the lions den of commodification turn into a theological critique of the divinity of the self?[49]

The book is chock-full of data and is expansive in scope. This section will limit itself to considering one very small yet important aspect of KRS One's approach, an aspect that is creating very different and complicated perspectives on his book among the Hip-Hop community: his use of religion. In this way, Hip Hop becomes conflated with religion—Hip Hop *as* religion—a Tillichian/Geertzian-like collapsing that confuses the categories and constructions of both religion and culture. To make his point, KRS One epistemologically relies upon and buys into a phenomenological framing of spirituality and religion to raise Hip-Hop culture to the throne of power—*as* religion. While KRS One may have a "new religion" on his mind, here I focus on what the language and logic of religion/spirituality accomplishes in this text and how it assists in the production of cultural authenticity in a more general sense, by engaging the very first parts of KRS's book: "A New Covenant," "The Love," and "The Promise Land." It is the authority established in these beginning parts that establishes the ethos of "The First Overstanding: Real Hip Hop."

From Islam to Christianity and beyond, most religious movements rely upon an enlightened leader. In *The Gospel of Hip Hop*, KRS establishes himself as the prophet of Hip-Hop culture; and while Jesus called himself the "The Way, Truth and the Light," KRS self-referentially does the same, writing for the present and the future in an eschatological manner. KRS writes, "In my time (your past) I am called the *teacha*, I was present at the *first time*. I am the *first born*. I am from the *Age of Leo*, and I have come to call our Hip Hop nation into existence."[50] He continues, "I am known as *Knowledge Reigning Supreme*; I build and destroy, heal and inspire with the right combination of words."[51] In this prophet-like establishing, KRS begins to build the divinity of Hip Hop—but this divinity is not specific to the self; rather, it is specific to the cultural identity of Hip Hop. He writes, "I AM HIP HOP! I am not just doing hip-hop, I am Hip Hop."[52]

KRS One's theology doesn't remain consistent throughout—we are taken through complicated iterations of many theological dimensions, and a theological analysis of the text would produce nothing. Rather, by making use of those already engrained religious ideologies (such as the "God" being referred to as the "I am that I am"), KRS makes use of the already established power of traditional theology, specifically Christian thought, to make a case for the grandiosity and significance of Hip-Hop culture. His use of traditional religious phrases such as "good news" is a *play* on the good news of the Christian Bible. He works from the premise that "God"—however conceived in the mind of the reader—is above all things "real." And if "God" is real, and KRS is self-described as "the teacha"—a witness to the activity of God within and around Hip Hop—therefore he can proclaim, "GOD IS REAL! And Hip Hop is evidence of God's real existence and Love."[53] The use of already established "religious language" allows KRS to advocate for a strong politics of Hip-Hop cultural authenticity. Above all, by means of the rhetoric of faith, philosophy, religion, and self-help language, KRS establishes a spiritual base by which he can tell the "true" and "real" story of Hip-Hop culture—its evolution, historical phases, ritualistic elements, and what it means to be a global citizen of Hip-Hop culture.

Strategically, KRS One divinizes the culture of Hip Hop. His approach mirrors religious studies approaches to the subject matter. He constructs the anthropology of Hip Hop *as* religion, similarly to how both Pinn and Miller (as will be discussed in Chapter 4 of this project) employ a Tillichian view of culture more generally. In his critique of the universalizing dimensions of Clifford Geertz's construction of religion, Talal Asad argues that "there cannot be a universal definition of religion, not only because its constituent elements and relationships are historically specific, but because the definition is itself the historical product of discursive processes."[54] According to Asad, there is no transhistorical essence carried within concept of religion as such. Geertz's perspective on religion, in a similar way to other suppositions of the category of religion, remains captive to the formulation of religion as *moods* and *motivations* endowed with meaning. He, like many others, remains invested in what's decipherable about religion—the *sui generis* trapping. Critical trends in the study of religion suggest that *sui generis* framings of religion create illusory distinctions of religious/non-religious in an effort to both create and maintain a disciplinary and phenomenological distinction of something that can be called "religious" by nature. We are reminded that there is nothing unique about what comes to be understood *as* religious. A more interesting exploration is why certain practices, experiences, and ideas *come* to be regarded as religious among certain cultures and communities. Like McCutcheon, whom my approach to religion in this project heavily relies upon, Asad reminds us that:

> the argument that a particular disposition is religious partly occupies a conceptual place within a cosmic framework appears plausible, but only because it presupposes a question that must be made explicit: how do authorizing processes represent practices, utterances, or dispositions so that they can discursively related to general (cosmic) ideas of order? In short, the question pertains to the authorizing process by which "religion" is created.[55]

Throughout his book, KRS constructs an essence of meaning and cosmic order of Hip Hop by using the social power of established Christian theology. Through the use of Christian theological capital, KRS One focuses on the meaning of Hip Hop as self-evident. An overemphasis on meaning is above all what Asad calls problematic. Again, a change in thought structure is needed; Asad writes, "This happens when he [Geertz] insists on the primacy of meaning without regard to the processes by which meanings are constructed"[56]—or stated otherwise, who and what practices, through the use of *power*, are understood and/or generally accepted as meaningful? Having taken issue with the ways in which scholarship on religion in Hip Hop collapses the religious investigation of Hip Hop as a "quest for meaning," or "ultimacy," Asad sums the problematic of this approach nicely when he asks, "What kinds of affirmation, of meaning, must be identified with practice in order for it to qualify as religion?"[57]

KRS strategically capitalizes off of the phenomenologically based vocabulary already inherent in private, public, and scholarly understandings of religion grounded in the "incontestability" of "experience." Having established himself as the "I" of Hip-Hop culture (which plays off the way in which the "God" in the Christian iteration establishes power: "I am that I am"), KRS uses the capital associated with "God" talk to establish the "realness" of Hip-Hop culture. For him, Hip-Hop culture is divinely inspired and was therefore sent to the people. Similar to the God authentication that occurs in Liberation Theologies (the activity of liberation being proof of God's activity in the world), KRS tropes the liberation theological motif (God on the side of the oppressed) to create the illusion that Hip Hop's value in the world is a divine one. Now that a God is on the side of Hip Hop, KRS One can evangelize the people of Hip Hop to become citizens of the "real" Hip Hop—by buying, reading, and believing *his* Gospel. Either way one reads KRS, by establishing a link between culture and religion through cosmic appeal, rediscovery and reclamation of cultural forms is indeed an embrace of religion. KRS One boldly proclaims "our original culture which is our true religion."[58]

KRS struggles against the capitalistic take-over of Hip Hop. He argues that Hip Hop no longer reflects the pureness of its beginnings, an epoch when "conscious" rappers were legendary. Given such "backsliding," KRS makes a Christian-like plea:

> It is time to repent and grow up! Rapping about crime and murder may sound good amongst those who have never committed such acts, but for those of us who are REAL IN THE FIELD, we send this message to our young people—YOU DON'T REALLY WANT IT.[59]

Making a witty comparison, KRS One argues that people today are treating Hip Hop like they are treating God, by only seeking "the hand and not the face. . . . They would rather use GOD/Hip Hop than live GOD/Hip Hop. . . . Hip Hop saved us and made us not only rich, but important and well respected worldwide. How can we forget GOD . . . How can we forget about Hip Hop—the craft that feeds us and gives us identity?"[60]

Here, KRS uses "God" language to create equitable authority for Hip Hop. The "God" concept brings along prepackaged social power and cultural purchase; through the visual and textual interchange between the signifiers Hip Hop and God, KRS produces a persuasive illusion and effect. By using theological language, he is attempting to establish that like "God," Hip Hop has a "saving" ability that (divinely) inspired the development of the other ritualized elements of Hip-Hop culture such as graffiti, breakin, and fashion. Therefore, Hip Hop (as a saving force) is constructed as an invisible hand that inspires the aspirations and motivations of people to produce its cultural elements, at times divorcing Hip Hop from the people as an all-embracing divine entity. KRS even goes so far as to call the gospel in which he writes a "disinfectant"[61]—an analogy that creates the illusion of the transformational ability of Hip Hop, and with strange echoes of Mary Douglas's work.

We know that language has authorizing ability. Bourdieu reminds us that the authorization and legitimation of words are likewise dependent upon the social conditions by which they are deployed. Through the building up of symbolic capital, KRS creates a Hip-Hop mythology. Bruce Lincoln's work reminds us that the concept of authority is not abstract—rather, it is dynamic, formed, and occurs in concrete events. With a belief in the godlike persona of KRS already established, he can now begin his ministry of the Gospel of Hip Hop—a ministry that is based on the performativity of religion itself.

It is no accident that the subtitle of KRS's book is "The First Instrument." The rhetoric of instrument provides a sense in which this book represents more than words—it's a vessel of communication, not something to be *read*, but rather, *lived*. Furthermore, in order to live it one must purchase the book to receive the cosmic instructions on what a life lived after, and marked by, the Gospel of Hip Hop in fact looks like. This book in and of itself becomes a symbolic structure, a structuring structure which has the ability to "exercise a structuring power"[62]—one that constructs above all an illusion of "reality" itself.

It is apparent throughout this text that the troping of religious rhetoric functions as a strategy to advocate something more for Hip Hop. The uses of religion do not signify something of belief; rather, they function to mediate a message of power. KRS notes that Hip-Hop culture is without a "home base, no financial backing, no religious affiliation, no political organization, not even a race or ethnicity that it can call its own."[63] Grounding this message with transcendental power, KRS adds, "Such a culture is indeed beyond this World and its power structure. Such a culture reveals the activity of GOD—the Love that rescued us."[64] It is a liberation-theology-like construction: if Hip Hop *is* the activity of God in the world, who then can contest its power and might in a culture where religion *is* power in a spiritualized market economy? And yet ritualistically, KRS continually reiterates that the gospel of Hip Hop is not really that religious, although it respects all religions and sees itself within them "—ALL OF THEM."[65] If such is in fact the case then why does KRS see the need to make any correlation between Hip Hop and religion at all? Again, I argue that it is the "genealogy of religion"—the imperialism and power that come along with religion—that gives KRS's cultural evangelization a metaphysical origin and spiritual mythos. Hence, it becomes believable by appearing to be cosmically ordained.

In the Covenant section of this text, KRS declares that time is running out. In an apocalyptic-like twist, he writes that the end of the "grace period" is quickly approaching. If one doesn't heed *this* gospel then God's judgment will be upon one. Again, KRS uses Christian theological themes by grounding his *Gospel of Hip Hop* within the future. Furthermore, the culmination of this Gospel is situated within messianic time, what Derrida would term the "*to come.*"

KRS characterizes Hip Hop as a culture *not* constructed *by* humans. Rather it is the transcendental illusion of consciousness that resides within the interior comportment of subjectivity. He writes, "It [Hip Hop] is the term given to the inner force that inspires us to self-create"[66]—he even refers to Hip Hop as an *inner urging*. Mentioned elsewhere, KRS argues that his gospel is not about religion in the strict sense (Islam, Christianity, etc.) but rather that the culture of Hip Hop *is* religion. This conflation is accomplished by employing a strategy of divinizing culture, similar to what I find problematic in academic literature that engages Hip Hop and religion respectively (e.g., culture is religion and religion is culture). In what seems to be a departure from his original proclamation, KRS uses the medium of culture as mode to access the divine: "OUR culture is OUR direct connection to GOD." And even bolder: "OUR CULTURE IS OUR RELIGION AND OUR RELIGION IS OUR CULTURE"[67]—in other words, participation in this new iteration of the gospel as proclaimed by the "teacha" (KRS) culminates in a form of religiosity. Again, KRS relies upon the grounding of "experience," "feeling," and "motivation" to argue that *this* Gospel is a "confirmation" not a re-education to those who *intuitively* acknowledge what is already present within them. In "The Promise Land" section, KRS proclaims that Hip Hop is proof of God's existence—interaction with Hip Hop is likewise interaction with God. This is the brilliant effect of collapsing religion as culture and culture as religion.

Lastly, a turn to the "The First Overstanding: Real Hip Hop" section reveals what his use of religion accomplishes in this book—the promotion of what he calls "Real Hip Hop." And where does one find such knowledge in order to learn the practice of "Real Hip Hop?" KRS writes, "This instrument [*The Gospel of Hip Hop*] begins the creation of 'HipHop's' faith."[68] The central concern of *The Gospel of Hip Hop* is established in this section: "I AM HIP HOP! And upon this faith (our belief in ourselves as Hiphoppas) we can achieve TRUTH."[69] In order to make this pronouncement effective, KRS finds it necessary to build his gospel upon the *already* established, lived, and authenticated power of religion in the world—as well as theological codes and grammar that ground such talk. Before he could sell his "I AM HIP HOP" brand to the world in this eight-hundred-page opus, he had to prove and provide metaphysical foundations to his rather humanist proclamation. His troping of religion is textually strategic and existentially persuasive—and in a marketing sense, it makes KRS's gospel of Hip Hop much more symbolic—hence, much more situated in crisis.

His manufacturing of the Gospel of Hip Hop (as reflective of his material interests) is done through the form, shape, rhetoric, and tradition of religion—more specifically, Christian theological themes. The troping of these categories gives the appearance of a logical, unified, self-evident, and plausible argument. A closer look into the processes by which KRS builds his case both reveals and provides a conceptual apparatus for the metaphysically reductive and spiritual minded. It is through the construction of a religious base that KRS effectively sells and markets his Gospel to the world. Keeping in mind however, that (whether consciously or unconsciously) strategically using (already established) religious "truths" as the mythological and cosmological foundation (as construction of authority) doesn't mean that KRS is in fact selling religion. On the contrary, through religious themes, he is selling "real" Hip Hop and his prophetic (and divinely inspired) role as the "teacha" of this new movement. Perhaps *The Gospel of Hip Hop* will indeed be a new religion in the next "100" years. KRS has already established it, rhetorically and metaphysically, as such. According to the virtual pulpits of the world wide web, however, many Hip Hop "citizens" have yet to be persuaded.

THE ONE IN THE MANY: RZA AND THE WAR OF LIFE

From the projects of Staten Island, New York to fame, rapper RZA of the Wu-Tang Clan (named after Shaolin martial arts) is no stranger to religion and philosophy. The book sells the idea of "Tao"—the one and many ways of RZA, whose life has been influenced by many veiled philosophies. RZA charts throughout this work the impact of numerous religions upon his life journey (Hinduism, Buddhism, Christianity, and Islam). This is further accompanied by less religiously obvious impacts: the streets, comic strips, chess, kung fu movies, and Bruce Lee. One online blogger, "L Ruano," compares RZA's new book to a Hip-Hop "Siddhartha" masterpiece, writing, "The Tao of Wu is a nonfiction Siddhartha for the hip-hop generation—an engaging, seeking book that will enlighten, entertain, and inspire."[70] Being filled as it is with everything from esoteric numerology to the street philosophical mathematics of the Five Percent Concepts of Islam, it comes as no surprise that this book presents seven lessons/pillars of wisdom from the wisdom of Wu—seven being a number of significance to numerous religions signifying *completion*. By the end of the book there is a sense in which RZA, the person, is finally complete.

One cannot help but feel enlightened by reading RZA's work. Unlike 50 Cent and KRS One, RZA isn't marketing a particular ideology or way of life—rather, this book functions as his spiritual autobiography through the heuristics of wisdom seeking. In a personal interview on G4TV.com, RZA explains, "The word Tao means way and theres many ways you know that we try to find wisdom, and in this particular book, I took stories from my life, things I learned from my life and I put it into a book."[71] While RZA's wisdom is imparted through his music, there is something different about *reading* rather than *listening* to RZA's life stories: "A song is entertaining . . .but to sit there and have to read something and learn from it means you have to . . . make it a task."[72]

Here I would like to engage one among many dimensions of RZA's book: the creation of a philosophy of life. Notwithstanding the many veiled philosophies used throughout, RZA doesn't use his spiritual path as a legitimating tool of Hip-Hop culture, or religion. Rather, he creates a philosophy of life *as* war, a military technique where at various moments in life he employs hybrid-like tactics and strategies, changing them up when they no longer seem to work. One way after another, RZA is always beginning again. Above all, RZA uses his experiences to call into question various streams of thought even while applying various streams of thought to enhance his life experiences. He is representative of a patchwork of poached *taos* of life, fully persuaded by none but master player at all ways of seeing in the world.

THE WISDOM OF WU: TACTICS AND STRATEGIES

RZA's unique combo of Eastern philosophy, chess, and kung fu movies have all, in some way, contributed towards constructing "war" (tactics, positionalities, strategies, etc.) as a heuristic by which to navigate the hills and valleys of his tumultuous life. The many "taos" that become a part of RZA's life represent, among other things, a strategic pragmatic application and mapping of various ideologies from which to make use of or rethink various positionalities in his life. He makes use of *hybrid* steams of thought at various moments; however, these thought structures don't become totalizing, in a determined sense, in RZA's life. RZA represents and embodies a quintessential postmodernist subject—*poaching* what he can and when he can as a life strategy, never being fully *faithful* nor *unfaithful* to one or the other, yet making use of the category of "experience" as a contestable way to call into question the very foundation of the thought structures themselves. His philosophies are fluid and openended, always morphing, changing, according to the "training" of life and struggle. And yet, while he represents a postmodern way of being and doing in the world, there are hints of universalizing tendencies in his philosophy. The "tao" becomes one for the many—the textual representative of all ways of life represented in and through one path of life. If RZA is selling anything here, it is nothing more and nothing less than the ideation of "wisdom" itself. RZA upholds no politics of respectability as to where such wisdom may be found.

Sometimes referred to as "Hip Hop's Shaolin warrior," RZA embodies, according to founder of the USA Shaolin Temple, Sifu Shi Yan Ming, the very philosophies by which he studies. No need for a soapbox by which to evangelize; Ming writes that in the presence of RZA, "You feel his wisdom in what he says, how he stands, how he moves"[73]—an embodiment of Buddhist and Taoist philosophies.

There are many different ways of operating in the world, but when you're from where RZA is from—the Van Dyke projects of New York City—your options, like many ghettos, are limited. And yet, the people constrained to limited life choices and options find a way to "make do," often utilizing the arts and culture. These modalities become in many cases not only outlets for creativity and expression, but also opportunities.

Before RZA was able to physically move from the Van Dyke projects of New York City, he constructed myriad ways of operating in the world that would carry him throughout life. It was on these mean streets where RZA learned the art of making do and strategic life skills that one would otherwise encounter in more formal educational settings. He writes, "That's the projects—math and economic class on every block. . . . You learn civics, government, law, and science every day—especially science. Because being in the projects, like being in jail, is a science project. One that no one expects you to leave."[74] In 1992 he found his break, and was able to leave. The "lessons of life" in one of New York's most dangerous places became, for RZA, the very foundation he would continually refer back to. De Certeau reminds us that "strategies are able to produce, tabulate, and impose these spaces, when those operations take place, whereas tactics can only use, manipulate, and divert these spaces."[75] These differences according to de Certeau depend on various modes of "style" and "operating" in the world. While de Certeau makes the practices of strategies and tactics almost a plastic-like distinction, his theoretical basis for both is rather persuasive and compelling. He sees the extra-ordinary aspects of what most folk would call mundane consumption and production: "Without leaving the place where he has no choice but to live and which lays down its law for him, he establishes within it a degree of *plurality* and creativity. By an art of being in between, he draws unexpected results from his situation."[76]

In *The Tao of Wu*, RZA tells the story of how veiled philosophies from kung fu movies, street mathematics, and even chess provided tactical and strategic calculations for the maneuvering of success. De Certeau reminds us that strategies and tactics have different functions: "I call a strategy the calculation (or manipulation) of power relationships that becomes possible as soon as a subject with will and power can be managed. . . . It is also the typical attitude of modern science, politics, and military strategy."[77] He adds:

> By contrast with strategy, a *tactic* is a calculated action determined by the absence of a proper locus. No delimitation of an exteriority, then, provides it with the condition necessary for autonomy. The space of a tactic is the space of the other. . . . It takes advantage of "opportunities"

and depends on then, being without any base where it could stockpile its winnings, build upon its own positions, and plan raids. . . . It must vigilantly make use of the cracks that particular conjunctions open in the surveillance of the proprietary powers. It poaches them. It creates surprises in them. It can be where it least expected. It is a guileful ruse.[78]

Compelling about de Certeau's thesis read through the life of RZA is that the art of war as employed by those who have no choice but to do so is seemingly accomplished by *making do*. RZA embodies a multiplicity of "ways of seeing" that serve as enlightenment in one moment and a strategy and tactic in the next.

At the tender age of thirteen, in watching the kung-fu film *The Thirty-sixth Chamber of Shaolin* RZA glimpsed his future. Only nine years later he formed the Eastern-inspired, kung-fu-like style of Hip Hop, and eight years after that he got to see with his own eyes the real Shaolin mountain nine thousand miles from where he grew up. He argues that the Shaolin mountain reflected how "we really were what we'd always claim to be: men of Wu-Tang."[79]

At the age of twelve, RZA was introduced to divine "mathematics" by his cousin Daddy-O—what Daddy-O called the "Twelve Jewels" (Five Percent Concepts of Islam). It was the pragmatic aspects of "doing the math" (drawn from the lessons of the 120 called "The Lost and Found Lessons") that taught RZA something about the wisdom of making a way. Although he couldn't change the "math" of his environment and life (e.g., constant addition of family members moving in because of abject poverty), he began forming mental strategies to "think" differently about his situation. He writes, "I had faith that my mind could transform my surroundings. Mathematics would form my first governing principles."[80] He recalls how his material body may have been living in the poverty of "hell" but his mind was free to strategize a different way of being in the world. It was Daddy-O who introduced RZA to the Lessons, but cousin GZA revealed to him the knowledge of God (the black man) that would lead RZA to "knowledge of self." At the young age of twelve, RZA had mastered the lessons of the Lost and Found Nation of the Gods and Earths.

According to RZA, his knowledge of the Lessons effectively helped him to understand the Bible. With the knowledge of self in place, he was able to read the Bible with new insight. RZA finds truth in many modes of thinking: whether it be Eastern thought, Christianity, comic books, or chess, he utilizes these philosophies for certain seasons of his life. For RZA, the wisdom of these philosophies must be applied in the "right" season—that is what makes them truths. The lessons provided an ounce of freedom for RZA—but as a good strategist, he knew they wouldn't provide "freedom from yourself? That's a whole different story."[81] Armed with knowledge of self (the Lessons), the art of war (kung-fu movies), and an Islamized re-read of the Christian Bible, RZA turns to the martial arts of chess, what he dubbed "metaphysics as a board game."[82] He doesn't just see chess *as* a board game; rather, chess for him is "reflective of life."[83] But don't think RZA didn't apply his supreme mathematics to the metaphysical board; he certainly did. Playing the position of "God" on the chess board helped him to check-mate. He writes, "In the end, the best strategy, the best tactic you can have in chess is the same one you should use in life: Never give up. Never let them count you out."[84]

And RZA's philosophical *poaching* didn't stop at chess—he writes of the influences of film as well:

> From *Thirty-Sixth Chamber* you get discipline and struggle. From *Shaolin and Wu-Tang* you get the warrior technique—plus the idea that bad guys are sometimes the illest. Then, from *Eight Diagram Pole Fighter*, you get the brotherhood, the soul. You get the idea that, This guy right here? He's stronger than me. Maybe he can take it a little further than I can. Let me throw my power behind him so we all rise up.[85]

The name of RZA's clan (Wu-Tang) would be influenced by warrior strategies: "The name says that we're Wu-Tang warriors, we're from Shaolin, and we're a Clan, which means family."[86] RZA didn't stop there. He was in search of something more physical that would lay down the law of the art of war in more concrete terms. Soon after, he began training in Shaolin techniques of martial arts and inner Taoism with Sifu Shi Yan Ming. For RZA, the different stages in learning kung fu not only reflected the stages of life, he was also able to combine the mathematics of the lessons with the numerology of the chambers. Studying with Sifu allowed RZA to combine all the elements of his past philosophies—into the one body of Hip Hop.

The Wu-Tang Clan's approach to the rap "game" of Hip Hop embodied an Eastern orientation. RZA writes, "Wu-Tang Clan did take a martial arts approach to hip-hop—to the sound of music, the style of the lyrics, the competitive wordplay of the rhyming, the mental preparations involved."[87] Soon after, RZA transformed his basement into an all-out studio. He compares the spatiality of his make-shift studio to a:

> . . . dojo—Japanese for "Place of Tao"—a space for gathering, training, spiritual growth. It might not have looked it. All we did in that basement was make music, smoke weed, and cook turkey burgers. You'd hear burgers frying, chess games going, and the video game Samurai Showdown being played. But everything else was music.[88]

The makeshift dojo-inspired studio in no way reflected the peace of Zen, however. RZA described it as being a space of "organized confusion" but given the master *poacher* he is, RZA finds something greater among the chaos. By embracing uncertainty, chaos, and confusion, he remained open to possibilities and failures, without fear. Now a successful rap group, the

Wu-Tang Clan may have embodied the great spiritual truths of Shaolin, according to RZA, but that didn't mean their philosophies were bullet-proof to the problems of life: "The world had some wisdom to throw right back at us."[89] The many veiled philosophies of RZA's "taos" transformed his perspective and approach to the rap game while other spiritual truths (such as "turn the other cheek") assisted him to "the Path of the Warrior." RZA writes, "A lot of us need to think like a warrior in our lives, even when we're at peace."[90] While many interpret "turn the other cheek" as an adage of peace, RZA turns this idea into a strategy of survival: "A war-rior would take Jesus's advice in a martial arts kind way. In a street way, it means, if a nigga gonna punch you in the face, you pull back, then come in and fuck him up for real. . . . That's when turning the other cheek becomes a strategy, not just righteous living."[91] This application best summarizes RZA's use of the many and great poached philosophies representative of his life. And in the final culmination of his art of war, the personification of a street warrior, RZA writes:

> On 9/7/97, I became humble. And ever since then, the person people meet named RZA is all right. Ever since that day, I've been able to talk to people about my life, to tell them I'm not a Muslim, a Buddhist, a Christian, a gangsta, a thug, or a prophet. I'm not any one of these things, although in one way I'm all of them. On that day I became me: a humble warrior, a student again. I became free. I found peace. And I've had it to this day.[92]

As RZA reflects on the idea that a good teacher is always a student, despite all he has learned and acquired, he goes back to basics; he finds comfort in going back to learning it all over again. In beginner piano and chess books made for kids RZA is learning new *tactics* and *strategies* for the "season" in which he finds himself. RZA is a master of using religious and philo-sophical "truths," testing them according to his life, deconstructing them when they don't work—and not being afraid to *confess* he must recognize their shortcomings and *begin again*.

DO THE MATH: CONSTRUCTING CONNECTIONS

The phraseology "do the math" is well known street slang in many urban ghettos. Derived from the "Divine Mathematics" of the Five Percent Concepts of Islam, "do the math" also means "you betta recognize"—cause something don't add up (e.g., make sense). Doing the "math" reflects a personal aware-ness among those living in the austere conditions of the hoods' busy complex transactions—dominated by everyday sleight of hand and slick hustles. It means to connect the dots and reveal what's "really" going on—doing the math embodies a hermeneutic of suspicion necessary for survival.

Thinking the knowledge productions of 50 Cent, KRS One, and RZA together, I have to acknowledge that the "math don't add up"—something is off. Taking these books on face value—perhaps we were hustled? Although we were aesthetically made to believe that at least two of these works (50 Cent and KRS One) were divinely inspired, further investigation concludes that the math don't always add up, and a book can never be judged by its cover. Throughout this chapter, I have attempted to, in each knowledge production, consider how uses of religious and/or philosophical language are deployed for producing various *effects*—whether it be power, authenticity, or a polysemy of life strategies. Moreover, this chapter has attempted to explore religious uses in cultural forms by paying attention to how particular thought structures are grouped together, constructed, and troped for ulterior *means* and *effects*. It is often the case that the use of religion, spirituality, philosophy, or street metaphysics in popular culture doesn't represent belief in a confessional sense, rather, it shows the manner in which the use of these *structures* (by the power already vested in them socially, intellectually, culturally, and so on) constructs authenticity, authorization, and consent for something more practical and pragmatic, in life.

In 50 Cent, the use of already established philosophers and aesthetic appropriations of the Christian Bible allows him to sell a self-help philosophy based on fearlessness. In KRS One, we witnessed the *aesthetic* construction of power (in the form of the Bible) and textual use of already established (Christian) parables and theological suppositions to gain metaphysical and transcendental support for the selling of authentic Hip-Hop culture. Furthermore, he uses the power of established religion to ground his own self as the Hip-Hop "teacha." Lastly, RZA uses religion, philosophy, spirituality, and popular culture as a means by which to construct a more pragmatic philosophy of life based on *tactics* and *strategies*. Beyond engaging the books themselves, I have tried when possible to incorporate public voices of Hip-Hop participants by engaging the internet, which houses much of the conversation and debate on Hip Hop. The use of virtual and visual ethnography allows the use of public voices alongside of academic discourse.

The current work undertakes a *redescription* of the religious by focusing on what *uses* of religion—figured as human activity and manufacturing—accomplish, authenticate, and authorize in the cultural activity of Hip-Hop. Accordingly, this chapter performs a new religious studies approach to Hip-Hop scholarship. Approaching each one of these texts in a phenomenological manner, searching for essence of "meaning," yields little insight—in fact, the religious scholar may encounter more confusion than clarity. In many cases, the use of religion in these works doesn't *mean* anything in the strict sense. Rather religion *functions* as a means by which to *authorize* particular social interests. It is tempting to "look" for the religion in these works; in fact, as religious studies scholars that is what we are trained to do. But we must also keep in mind that the very thing we are looking for is not there; there is no genie in the bottle. The complexity of the three works engaged in this chapter forces a different perspective and approach by beginning with what the content of these books has already shown: don't judge a book by its cover—it may not be what you think it is. The uses of religion within Hip Hop material productions remind the scholar of religion that we must get beyond our modernist lenses of religion *as* feeling, and get up to speed with religion *as* effect, strategy, and manufacturing of social, cultural, and political interests. Chasing meaning is like chasing waterfalls—it is an impossible and endless task.

3 And the Word Became Flesh
Hip-Hop Culture and the (In)coherence of Religion

"All too often theorists have taken religion as a relatively unproblematic unitary and homogenous phenomenon that can be analysed and compared across time and space without proper consideration of its multi-faceted and socially constructed character."

—James A. Beckford[1]

"Fully comprehending hip-hop demands decoding its intricate use of language to the point where one is able to recognize relatively obscure and cloked references to veiled philosophies."

—John L. Jackson, Jr.[2]

"I'm the religion that to me is the realist religion there is. I try to pray to God every night unless I pass out. I learned this in jail, I talked to every God [member of the Five Percent Nation] there was in jail. I think that if you take one of the 'O's' out of 'Good' it's 'God,' if you add a 'D' to 'Evil,' it's the 'Devil.' I think some cool motherf**ker sat down a long time ago and said let's figure out a way to control motherf**kers."

—Tupac Shakur[3]

From rap lyrics, music videos, signifying tattoos, lyrical shout-outs to god, and trendy stylistic configurations declaring "jesus is my homeboy"—that concepts, symbols, and ideations of religion occupy a precarious space in Hip-Hop material culture is undeniable; that this reality has been taken up fervently and interrogated consistently by U.S. scholars of religion and theology is debatable. While "the word" increasingly becomes flesh in material cultural practices, religious discourse in American academies has yet to get up to speed with the changing cartographies of Hip-Hop cultural productions. Although U.S. scholarship in fields such as sociology of religion, for example, has forged sustained engagement with the intersection of religion with popular culture (such as cyber-culture, alternative spiritualities, rave culture, and so on), boasting methodological diversity, and U.K. scholarship continues in producing a plethora of work on youth religiosity and cultural practices, U.S. discourse on religion and Hip Hop is significantly lacking theoretically, descriptively, and empirically—with the exception of a few notable treatments.[4] As such, this chapter initiates a conversation regarding *how* religious studies scholars may begin thinking about engagement with the "im/possibility"[5] of religious rhetorics in Hip-Hop cultural productions by complicating current trends in the field. Within each trend, I pay close attention to how religion is figured and what purposes such figuring serves.

How does popular culture manufacture religion? Through what means? To what ends? How does popular culture "do" or perform religion—or thought another way, how does popular culture, such as Hip Hop, turn out, disrupt, or call into question the very category the scholar seeks to investigate? How is religion figured theoretically (on behalf of the scholar) and how might it move, transgress, or disrupt in material culture? These queries conjure many discursive possibilities and at the same time, these rhetorical questions concerning the category of religion cannot be divorced from (and are certainly complicit in) the disciplinary imperialism and power hierarchy carried with concepts such as religion. Anthropologist of religion Talal Asad asks a simple yet poignant question in his complication of Geertz's universal assumption and deployment of religion, writing: "How does power create religion? What kinds of affirmation, of meaning, must be identified with practice in order for it to qualify as religion?"[6] Putting it another way, Jonathan Z. Smith asserts that:

> while there is a staggering amount of data, phenomena, of human experiences and expressions that might be characterized in one culture or another, by one criterion or another, as religion—there is no data for religion. Religion is solely the creation of the scholar's study. It is created for the scholar's analytic purposes by his imaginative acts of comparison and generalization. Religion has no existence apart from the academy.[7]

With that in mind, in this chapter I turn more specifically to the small yet seminal literature that frames and grounds academic discourse on religion and Hip Hop specifically. Surveying the different approaches to the study of religion (and the social significance) in Hip-Hop culture is accomplished through a close reading of general trends, conclusions, assumptions, and methods that have dominated this area of study within the U.S. Moreover, I complicate the more common approaches to the category and analysis of religion when applied to popular culture, by paying close attention to the ways in which religion is defined, assumed, and understood against the texts of popular culture. As suggested in the introduction, the most common approach by U.S. scholars studying the religious significance of popular culture has been limited to a textual analysis and reading of rap lyrics for various purposes. Thus, this approach is methodologically limited. Textually based methods of analyzing the religious significance of Hip-Hop culture are useful, but a primary focus on rap lyrics has left other dimensions of material culture unexamined. While this project is not exempt from a "reading" of popular culture, Lynch reminds us that this approach is often taken at the expense of understanding the function of such texts in the context of people's everyday realities. We must remain open to the problematic tendencies of mapping the category of religion (as theorized) onto practices (as lived). The tensions between the imagined and the lived are made evident in Talal Asad's pushback against Clifford Geertz's connection between religious theory and practice on the level of cognition. Asad argues that:

the connection between religious theory and practice is fundamentally a matter of intervention-of constructing religion in the world (not in the mind) through definitional discourse, interpreting true meanings, excluding some utterances and practices and others. Hence my repeated question: how does theoretical discourse actually define religion? What are the historical conditions in which it can act effectively as a demand for the imitation, or the prohibition, or the authentication of truthful utterances and practices? How does power create religion?[8]

With similar questions in mind, this chapter *reads* recent academic trends and intends to unpack, complicate, and challenge traditional approaches throughout the field. These perspectives produce effects such as configuring religion as a dominant tool of surveillance (utilized to sanitize Hip-Hop culture as "deviant" Other by over-determining its cultural signification as religious), or using the gritty edges of Hip Hop as a means by which to enable democratic possibilities vis-à-vis prophetic Christian rhetoric situated within a context of black struggle. Other effects include maintenance of *sui generis* framings of religion in Hip-Hop culture to enable the persistence of religion (vis-à-vis the trope of "meaning").

Each approach retains its own respective problematic(s), possibilities, and interests. Some remain the product of hierarchical and power-laden strategies that seek, albeit not always consciously, to divinize Hip-Hop culture for the purposes of religious market maintenance. Moreover, problematic and asymmetrical approaches (power-laden) are more often than not complicit with inadequate modernist theories of the religion that cannot contend nor come to grips with the changing religious cartography of our postmodern condition.

With the exception of the work of Anthony B. Pinn to which I turn more specifically in Chapter 4, the category of religion in the literature on Hip Hop and religion has traditionally been understood from the perspective of institutionally (dominant) recognized forms of religiosity, namely those of Christian or Islamic expressions. That is to say, the more common approaches to engaging the religious in Hip-Hop culture deploy the category of religion in a way that leaves (dominant) notions of power un-interrogated at best, and institutionally confined at worst. Such conflations often misrecognize what the uses of religion accomplish for competing social and cultural interests. In other words, a top-down approach that begins with traditional categorical religious assumptions offers at best a thin analysis of the changing cartography of what we identify *as* the religious in culture, whereas a more relational approach would take into account the cross-pollination and mediation between social influence of dominant forms of religiosity and cultural practices—constructions that often take on and make use of religious value and capital for less obvious social interests. While the former approach offers little regarding the spectrum of how religiosity may be understood, created, and practiced, the latter approach contributes significantly to understanding how religion is manufactured, called into question, and produced among various cultural and social economies. In other words, it is necessary to take a cautionary pause in regarding the category of religion in these trends. While most literature employs religion in an *a priori* (self-evident) way, I argue that this category is not without its limitations when being thought theoretically and employed empirically. A similar caution is made by Nye when he calls for a re-evaluation of the category of religion in relationship to theory and method, suggesting that this category:

> be reconstructed in terms of practice theory as religious practice or religioning. . . . That is, I would suggest that religion scholars not only learn to reconsider how they think of culture, but at the same time they should make a similar conceptual shift with their use of the term religion. That is, the practice of religious studies should not be the 'study of religion', but the study of religious practices—of religioning. . . . If we try to talk of religioning rather than religion the result is a completely different set of expectations. Religioning is not a thing, with an essence, to be defined and explained. Religioning is a form of practice, like other cultural practices, that is done and performed by actors with their own agency (rather than being subsumed by their religions), who have their own particular ways and experiences of making their religiosities manifest. A discourse of religioning also moves away from looking at 'religion' in terms of 'religions' (Christianity, Islam, Hinduism, etc.), but instead looks at religious influences and religious creativities, and the political dynamics through which certain conceptualization of religious authenticity are produced and maintained.[9]

The push towards religious *influences* draws attention towards practices as well as offering a window by which to understand human interests in uses of religion, more generally. Here, I begin by surveying three general trends in order to chart the current terrain of this small area of discourse. I closely *read* how religion is figured in each trend, and what end such figuring serves. Thus, it is the third trend (engagement of Pinn's theory of religion *complex subjectivity*) that becomes the primary focus of Chapter 4.

THE RELIGIOUS STYLINGS OF HIP-HOP CULTURE: RECENT ACADEMIC TRENDS

> "However little may be known of religion *in the singular*, we do know that it is always a response and responsibility that is prescribed, not chosen freely in an act of pure and abstractly autonomous will. There is no doubt that it implies freedom, will and responsibility, but let us

try to think this: will and freedom *without autonomy*. Whether it is a question of sacredness, sacrificiality or of faith, the other makes the law, the law is other: to give ourselves back, and up, to the other. To every other and to the utterly other."

—Jacques Derrida[10]

The above quotation from Derrida captures the tensions, paradoxes, ambiguity, and im/possibility of the category of religion. In Derridian language, the quest for religion, the search for its kind and knowledge, is in and of itself an *aporia:* among the "blind spots" of metaphysical argument.[11] Taking the positionality that religion is manufactured and constructed, religion is always and at once aporetic: that which can be thought, yet never fully thought nor never fully experienced. While Chapter 4 will engage Derrida's poststructuralist turn to *play* with meaning and presence, the above quote situates the very complexity that this project attempts to struggle both *for* and *against*—that is to say, as Derrida reminds us, signification and meaning are unstable, thus leaving us with nothing more than a glimpse and presence of undecidability. Above all, a crisis of meaning.[12] There remain many operationalizable possibilities by which to define the category of religion—and yet, we are reminded that this concept has a history of its own as a contested term. Contingent on the disciplinary intent of its deployment, its definition has served and continues to serve the interests of various political, social, and cultural projects. Whether religion is configured as the "opiate of the people" (Karl Marx), "ideological state apparatus" (Louis Althusser), or the "unconscious" (Sigmund Freud), the category of religion continues to be disputed categorically, contested ideologically, and mediated socially and culturally. My concern in this chapter is not with apprehending or isolating a "proper" definition of religion, I am more interested in reading what attention to the religious in Hip-Hop culture has accomplished for various trends. My focus throughout this project remains fixed on (reading) what this category purports to do (in discourse and in the data of material culture), how it is figured, and what such uses accomplish. Dominant religious language holds much purchase in our world at large and is often, by proxy, used by communities in many contexts for various functions. With that said, the scholar mustn't assume that traditional arrangements of meaning (grounded in "belief") are being held in place on the basis of rhetorical and linguistic signifiers. In other words, our theoretical suppositions of this category (religion) often retain a variety of e/affects when methodologically employed as data. This project, at its core, explores the concept of religion from a particular positionality—remaining aware that apprehending signification and meaning is an impossible task. Its renderings never do full justice to lived reality. Meaning, as such, always seems to escape the grasp of the lurker, leaving traces of signification in what purports to be *presence* itself. Understood in this way, the isolation of meaning remains deferred, because it is, in and of itself, unobtainable. Close attention to recent trends in the field is vital for rethinking and redescribing what intellectual examinations of the religious in cultural data attempt to expose—what does such "religious" attention achieve? The uses of religion in Hip-Hop culture cannot be fully trusted (e.g., in a confessional sense, as a matter of belief)—its religiosity (if one is searching for religion as meaning and presence) cannot be assumed, trusted, and apprehended in ways that scholars of religion and theology are traditionally used to (that is, if religion is being understood as *sui generis* belief). Put another way, there is a "paranoid" fixture to Hip Hop's religious play. Anthropologist John L. Jackson Jr. puts it in this way: "'Believing' means using a very different heuristic entirely. And this privileging of belief is caught up in hip-hop's entrenched faith-based leanings more generally, in hip-hop's spiritual fundamentalism,"[13] going on to mention that what we find in Hip Hop is a "useful incomprehensibility" that is anything *but* "easy listening."[14]

Religious discourse (as imagined) is a precarious stranger to popular culture (as lived and performed). The few, albeit formative, U.S. academic trends in the field demonstrate a sustained commitment to thinking these areas together. While the range of Hip-Hop material culture (beyond rap music) remains marginal in these attempts, even more fugitive among them is focused attention to the idea of religion. That is to say, it becomes a simple task to cite "the religion" *in* popular culture through attention to more explicit proclamations and claims to (recognized) forms and beliefs. However, seldom considered is the complexity and multiplicity of popular culture's religious stylings—stylings, or manufacturings, that often don't fit neatly into prepackaged phenomenological typings. The survey text, *Religion and Popular Culture in America* (2000) by Bruce David Forbes and Jeffrey H. Mahan is helpful in its classifications of four typologies and patterns of engagement throughout the field (religion in popular culture, popular culture in religion, popular culture as religion, and religion and popular culture in dialogue).[15] However, "religion" and "popular culture" tend to be seen in this and similar texts as two separate domains, thus retaining a false uniqueness of two terms that are, in reality, not so distinct. We are left to believe that the concept of religion is self-evidently decipherable in popular culture—left wondering *how* popular culture activity makes *use* of religion in ways beyond simple proclamations to belief. The reality is that the terms "religion" and "popular culture" do not describe two distinct and competing realms, for such distinction only remains in the eye of the classifier.

This chapter descriptively analyzes three academic trends of engagement, while understanding these trends to be fluid in their positionality. For taxonomical purposes I categorize dominant trends in the field under three rubrics: (1) The Black Church and Spirit of Market Maintenance, (2) The Critical in the Lyrical: Rapper as (Christian) Prophet, and lastly, (3) Hip Hop *as* a "Quest for Meaning"?, as ways to read more closely the gaps, assumptions, and perspectives that inhabit this small area of study. This chapter not only contextualizes such attempts, but offers insight into the manner in which the concept of religion is fashioned and deployed in such uses—and for what purposes. I argue that in two out of the three representative attempts, the category "religion" remains uninterrogated, uninformed by the formations and uses of religion already present in Hip-Hop culture. This chapter ends by suggesting that the third trend is most useful in its posture yet its intellectual inheritances (by way of sources, taken up in Chapter 4) constrain its form and contribution to theory and method in the study of religion. This problematic necessitates an engagement with postmodern and poststructuralist sources in ways that are perhaps more faithful to the structure of the theory itself than its (current) sources and uses allow.

THE BLACK CHURCH AND SPIRIT OF MARKET MAINTENANCE

Dominant institutions in society maintain power and privilege through internal and extemporaneous processes of *othering* often exerted on an (un)conscious level. Institutions such as faith-based spaces are often maintained through the perpetual "othering" of "foreign antibodies" further evidenced within the social inventions of "creation myths," "moral panics," acts of "symbolic violence," and exaggerated moments of "crisis." Within this process, the "other" becomes constructed as *deviant*, that is, someone in need of "salvation"—a subject in need of civilizing rescue by the "decent" mission of dominant institutions, norms, and values. The market of the church is maintained, in part, through socially constructing alternative worldviews as "dangerous" and "deviant" and as such in "need" of baptism through institutional import and cleansing. This, among other things, is what I mean by "market maintenance."

Recent academic trends that begin their engagement of Hip Hop from a "black church" paradigm seemingly fashion faith-based institutions hierarchically, over and against "marked" social spaces such as "corners" and "streets." This illusion of dominance is often accomplished through manufacturing plastic social distinctions separated by artificial divides that appear real—distinctions that include classifications of religion. In other words, the larger question for church-based projects is whether Hip Hop can, on its own, display a form (and use) of religiosity outside of the institutional confines. Or, must such cultural productions undergo a process of institutional importation into more socially recognizable spaces to be counted as "authentically" religious? Certainly, institutional importation affirmatively serves "market maintenance" of faith-based institutions in a so-called era of secularity and "religious crisis." The more important question to push here is *whether* such engagements offer a moment of authentic relationality, given the manner in which such cultural phenomena are engaged. The ideological positionalities of black church perspectives towards "deviant" social spaces have been captured in sociological surveys such as *Streets of Glory* (2003) by sociologist of religion Omar McRoberts and *Black Picket Fences* (1999) by sociologist Mary Patillo-McCoy. Certain aspects of their studies highlight the growing *ideological* tensions between issues of "decency" and "degeneracy" through the churches' perspectives on the "street."

In *Streets of Glory*, McRoberts ethnographically explores twenty-nine churches in a tough Boston neighborhood referred to as Four Corners. Among the rich and meaningful data collected and analyzed (suggesting that the infrastructure of the church is both meaningful and important in poor urban areas, among other things), his chapter on "The Street" provides telling empirical data about the ways in which many of the churches in his study *identified* and *understood* the "streets": (1) as evil other to be avoided at all costs, (2) as a recruitment ground to be trod and sacralized, and lastly, 3) as point of contact with "at-risk persons" who need to be served.[16] What can be inferred from such data is that while proselytization was not always a goal, most of these churches overwhelmingly agreed that the "street" is a deviant place, and in order to become safe, one must "come into" the space of the church to be religiously efficacious. It can be inferred in such suppositions that religious production, consumption, and uses occurring *within* and *among* the streets are not given serious consideration by these church perspectives.

Patillo-McCoy's ethnographic research of eleven churches in the Chicago neighborhood of Groveland suggests that while the institutional church at times serves as social buffer against violence, a majority of the demographic self-identify as being "defenders" of a "decent" lifestyle, over and against illicit street activity. On this point, she notes that the institutional church is often utilized by parents as a way to keep youth "off the streets," and in this sense the church becomes utilized as an "institutional" buffer mitigating "decent" and "street" populations.[17]

The perspectives captured in the rich ethnographic work of McRoberts and Patillo-McCoy are neither surprising nor new. Working within a model of market scarcity, such ideological critiques assume that "deviant" street practices need institutional import within the church to be constituted as acknowledgeable.

The qualitative data from the work of McRoberts and Patillo-McCoy are representative of not only faith-based perspectives, they likewise reflect similar dispositions evidenced within church-based academic trends engaging Hip-Hop culture and religion. Problematic positionalities of market maintenance show up in the pathological *rhetoric* deployed as a means to engage youth of color, embedded within Hip Hop. Such works display an erroneous assumption that "de-churched" and "un-churched" youth stand in need of institutional guidance—seen in this way, youth bodies become potential converts for the Christian market by leaching onto and sanitizing Hip-Hop culture as its bait.

Most recently, scholars who occupy dual social spaces between the academy and the street, and who work hard to encourage engagement between the institutional black church and youth who participate in Hip-Hop culture, have begun to produce scholarship under the auspices of this intent.

Sociologist, minister, and professional DJ Ralph C. Watkins, in *The Gospel Re-Mix: Reaching the Hip-Hop Generation* (2007), expresses a willingness to engage in meaningful cross-generational dialogue, asking questions such as, "How is the church to become hip hop in order to reach the hip-hop generation?" He continues his query by asking:

> How do I sit at the table with people from the hip-hop generation? They need help, and I need help. When I look at hip-hop culture and what it is producing, I see the illness as well as the health. I see the sickness that needs to be healed. We need to go and sit with them, touch them, love them, and heal them. They are in need of a doctor. These comments are not meant to degrade or put down the culture but are an honest assessment. There is much good in the hip-hop culture, but there are also parts of it that are unhealthy and not good for our youth or community. As much as we must celebrate hip hop, we mustn't look at it or any other cultural production uncritically. We must bring the values and principles of the Bible to bear on our interrogation of cultural phenomena. The question for me, as I looked at the good and bad of the culture, was, How do I gain access?[18]

One is not hard pressed to feel the pulse of cultural depravity and social pathology here—albeit complicated by a sincere spirit of willingness to engage a very under-engaged cultural sector of American society. Like much social and cultural criticism, Watkins's ideological perspectives and exaggerated claims of "deviance" and "cultural sickness" are rather thin and unsupported, although he remains upfront that his main objective is to "win souls for Christ." Throughout this text, Watkins uses signifiers such as "reach," "save," and "reclaim the lost" when referring to Hip Hop—the segment he refers to as "the culture outside the church." The use of Hip-Hop culture as "bait" for the purposes of church-maintenance strategy (to combat decline and irrelevance) is debatable and contestable. Throughout, Watkins remains consciously unapologetic regarding strategies of appropriation—seldom addressing whether such strategies are fruitful and relational. On the contrary, he expresses concerns about the "dangers" of bringing a deviant culture "inside the church." He writes, "The church has to continually struggle with the appropriation of culture and the integrity of God's word."[19] Although Watkins is certainly no stranger to Hip-Hop culture as evidenced in his own participation as a DJ, and to Hip-Hop cultural competence in his position as a professional sociologist, one of the more troubling dimensions of Watkins's text is how he directs and encourages (in a manual style way) the church to take on the views, taste, and worldview of the subaltern class in the interests of the dominant institution.[20] Instructions within the text are used to guide how the church can (and should) *become* Hip Hop and what stylistic elements the church should use for its masquerade. For example, Watkins argues that "Hip hop squared wants the church to be a little ghetto, but being ghetto is the one thing that most middle-class African Americans and our churches have run away from . . . what will a church that is a little ghetto look like?"[21] Here, the church, traditionally not self-described as "ghetto," must put on the worldview and ethos of the "ghetto" to attract relevance among youth. While the book throughout boasts a plethora of problematic suppositions, I agree with one of its contributors, Otis Moss III, when he writes in his chapter entitled "Real Big: The Hip Hop Pastor as Postmodern Prophet" that "hip-hop culture and the generation that created it is the first genera-tion of African American youth to develop and produce cultural products without explicit 'soul sensibilities' or outside the black church. As a result, Hip-Hop culture as an art form develops outside the faith-based ethics of the black church."[22] Here, Moss acknowledges the religious and ethical alterity of Hip-Hop culture, although the term he uses to refer to the com-plexities of this generation, "Post-Soul Crisis in the Black Church," remains lodged in a leitmotif of catastrophic dualistic exaggeration. Developing a framework for a "post-soul worship" whereby the church incorporates ven-eration elements of Hip-Hop culture, Moss himself cannot seem to tran-scend the linguistic pathologies that pervade such attempts. He writes, "I believe every church, if it is serious about ministry in a postmodern age, can transform its worship to reach the hip hop generation."

The trend of "black church and spirit of market-maintenance" continues in *The Hip-Hop Church: Connecting With the Movement Shaping Our Culture* (2005) by Efrem Smith and Phil Jackson, offering a peek into the inner workings of black church engagement with Hip-Hop culture. In the preface, Hip-Hop scholar Bakari Kitwana ostensibly falls into the same rhetorical pathologies as does Watkins, writing, "If hip-hop brings people to have faith, makes youth come to church who previously didn't want to go, and helps hip-hop kids nurture a relationship with God, then why not?" Throughout, Smith and Jackson employ a language of cultural depravity similar to the one that plagues Watkins's text. Rhetorical signifiers such as "reach" become erroneously deployed towards a demographic (youth) that is assumed to have little participation in the institutional black church by way of its Hip-Hop commitments, and again false "distinctions" grounded in dichotomous claims are deployed. In this work, the space of the church and the cultural phenomena of Hip Hop are set up in an oppositional manner, creating an illusion of disconnection (herein emerges the fantas-mic exaggeration of a manufactured "crisis"). The task becomes how to connect these two bifurcated opposites competing for the same subjects and existential weight. This disposition is evidenced more forcefully when Smith and Jackson (rightfully) argue against impressionistic sentiments that figure the church and Hip Hop on a "collision course" where "both battle for the hearts and minds of young unchurched people within hip-hop culture."[23] While this may be true, they fall prey to the same slippage they seek to deconstruct when they push for a model of coexistence using Hip

Hop as bait for evangelization: "As pastors, we lead churches that use elements of hip-hop not only in the worship experience but also as outreach tools."[24] Although Smith and Jackson rhetorically advocate for a more relational approach to Hip Hop that doesn't exaggerate its dangerous presence, by advocating for a model of co-existence they inevitably display an ideological positioning of depravity by developing a church-based strategy of outreach to de-churched and un-churched youth vis-à-vis secular cultural appropriation. Moreover, the manufactured opposition between the space of the church and Hip-Hop culture creates an illusory and plastic antagonism that ignores the reality of dual membership in multiple communities and gives little consideration to how young people negotiate multiple commitments over a variety of spaces.

The trend of "market maintenance" must be applauded in its attempt— yet deconstructed in its (perhaps unconscious) conflicted ends. Set up in this way, Hip-Hop culture becomes a strategy of outreach for the market maintenance of faith-based institutions. Such a tactic is based on the exaggerated (non-data-supported) fears of narratives of church decline. Not only do these works lack sufficient empirical evidence that youth participating in Hip-Hop culture are overwhelmingly "de-churched" and "un-churched," they also lack knowledge of the weight religion is given in Hip-Hop culture. Overall, this approach is reflective of an insufficient and inadequate engagement with Hip-Hop culture by positioning (and privileging) ecclesiological spaces as ultimate (and only) agent of change and transformation.

THE CHURCH APPARATUS AND EXTENSIVE HEGEMONY

The competition for spiritual and existential space masked under asymmetrical patterns of engagement contributes towards grave misunderstandings of and misgivings about Hip-Hop culture writ large—thus calling for deeper theoretical analysis of passionate yet myopic attempts by those who seek (whether consciously or unconsciously) to maintain the functioning center of faith institutions masked under synthetic tactical engagements. This problematic thus leads this work into a theoretical engagement with the constructs of *ideology* and *hegemony*.

Given his formative contribution to the area of ideology and instructive insight into how the organization and webs of signifying practices attempt to constitute subjects themselves, here I turn to the work of French Marxist political philosopher Louis Althusser. More specifically, I read the aforementioned trend of engagement with Hip-Hop culture through Althusser's formative theory on *ideology* as explicated in his widely read essay "Ideology and Ideological State Apparatuses."[25]

According to Althusser, the social function of *ideology* has little to do with consciousness; that is to say, it is a rather profoundly "unconscious phenomenon." For Althusser, ideologies are understood as "systems of representations," which include *images* and *concepts* but more importantly "structures" that impinge and impose themselves onto society. Here, he breaks with Marx's *scientific* concept of ideology by reworking such ideas within "non-scientific language." According to Althusser, there is no (mass) "critical reflection" upon ideology's existence and effects because the hailing of ideology becomes highly *consented* to by the mass public, often unknowingly. This consent is similar to what Pierre Bourdieu refers to as *doxa* and what Antonio Gramsci calls *commonsense*—that is, the taken-for-granted and unexamined assumptions subjects retain in society. We remain partially unaware of *ideology* because, according to Althusser, it acts upon its subjects as indivisible—with the appearance of having no history, in a totalizing manner. For example, *implicit* ideologies could be messages reflected from advertisements often reflecting normative assumptions and ideals. These codes, often explicit, reside within the stream of our common sense, and thus, ground our general assumptions that become part of our conditioned reality. More often than not, we do not reflect critically about these assumptions; they become internalized dispositions (what Bourdieu would call the *habitus*) that for the most part remain unconscious and unexamined. Thus, ideology becomes the "sub-conscious ideological framework" that "constitutes" one's ideological perspectives. Ideology, then, is part of what determines how subjects live their lives.

In his foundational essay "Ideology and Ideological State Apparatuses," Althusser theoretically situates his concern regarding the placement of the exploited subject by examining the processes by which subjects maintain and reproduce their own condition of oppression. Within the context of this query, Althusser conceptually develops the notions of "Ideological State Apparatuses" (ISAs) and "Repressive State Apparatuses" (RSAs). For the purposes of this chapter, I focus on the ISAs that ground the function of religious systems. ISAs, for Althusser, are specialized institutions that remain distinct from RSAs and that include the following sectors of society: the religious (the system of different churches), the educational, the family, the legal, the political, the trade union, modes of communication (press, radio, television, etc.), and the cultural (literature, arts, sports, etc.). On the function of the ISAs, Althusser writes:

> The (Repressive) State Apparatus functions massively and predominately by *repression* (including physical repression), while functioning secondarily by ideology. (There is no such thing as a purely repressive apparatus.) . . . For their part, the Ideological State Apparatus function massively and predominately by *ideology*, but they also function secondarily by repression, even if only ultimately, this is very attenuated and concealed, even symbolic. (There is no such thing as a purely ideological apparatus.)[26]

Understood in this way, the institutional church maintains its function through ideological domination and control, often occurring within the symbolic realm. The work of Watkins and of Smith and Jackson symbolically fashions the church as a "safe" and "clean" place, where social pathologies can thus be eradicated. In *rhetoric,* places like the "corner" and the "street" are constructed in competition with religious institutions; that is, they become a competitive market for the "market maintenance" of the church's function. In order to be effective in membership maintenance, that which remains on the outside of its confines must be differentiated by *otherness* and constructed as deviant. This construction persuades the masses that in order to be "religious" or "holy" one must undergo importation *into* the church (membership). Moreover, stigmatized social spaces and cultural life-worlds (like Hip Hop) become stigmatized so that the *function* of the church remains intact. Nowhere do any of these readings suggest that Hip Hop on its own can function as an autonomous manufacturing zone of religion. Reversing the thinking would suggest that faith institutions become imported into Hip-Hop culture to understand larger society—an ideological reversal that would challenge the authenticity, power, capital, and function of such spaces. The danger in separating Hip-Hop culture and the church is the creation of a false distinction, giving the illusion that there remain no mediating factors or shared culture between the two classificatory domains. A different posture of relationality is necessitated. If market maintenance is the ideological posture of such engagement, faith institutions will not be able to legitimate alternative religious sensibilities—they will always remain in constant opposition. Within religious institutions (among other dominant institutions) subjects are taught ruling *ideologies* that ground and give shape to what "is" and should be considered "appropriate," "acceptable," and "decent" in the larger world. Althusser argues that religious institutions function through repression and violence secondarily, and by ideology primarily. In the works of Watkins and of Smith and Jackson, one is not hard pressed to see how ideology hails and interpellates the subjects of Hip-Hop culture—how it "recruits" and "acts" upon them in precise and calculated ways under a complicated ideological discourse promising spiritual transformation and moral order. Understood in this way, the recognition of and engagement with Hip Hop by works such as these is necessarily partial—on one hand, acknowledging the existence of Hip Hop's cultural significance and yet on the other, advocating for institutional importation, which implicitly suggests that actors within Hip Hop are not yet fully subjects prior to such religious apprehension. Thus, like the signifier "God," the functioning center of the church in these works mirrors what Althusser calls the "Subject *par excellence.* . .who interpellates his subject to him by his very interpellation."[27] As such Hip-Hop culture, baptized and sanitized in the purity of the church, thus "mirrors the reflection" of the ultimate "Subject."

While Althusser's work provides immense theoretical insight into the *function* of *institutions,* I now turn to the work of neo-Marxist cultural theorist Antonio Gramsci, whose widely used theory of *hegemony* is helpful in explicating internal processes of domination and subversion. Moreover, his theories are especially relevant in understanding the social processes of contemporary (counter) culture.

Gramsci's adoption and advancement of the term *hegemony*, most notably expressed in *Prison Notebooks* (1971), represents a clear break with traditional Marxist interpretations of *ideology*. Opposed to the signifier "domination," Gramsci uses the term *hegemony* when attempting to understand how subordinate groups often become *active* participants in their own subjugation. He uses the inner workings of the cultural superstructure to draw out this claim, especially formation in the area of civil society (which includes the church). Although Gramsci dissects *hegemony* into the segments *coercion, consent, domination, leadership,* and *common sense/good sense*, this section focuses on Gramsci's analysis of *limited* and *expansive hegemony* to further understand the processes by which Hip Hop under the first explicated trend (market maintenance) becomes co-opted and used as a tool of domination.

In response to the un/conscious processes of co-opting Hip Hop for the purposes of evangelization, I ask a question back to such texts: "Why must the church become Hip-Hop?" In order for the hegemonic process to be effective, Gramsci argued that a truly hegemonic group (in this case the church) takes on part of the worldview of the subordinate group (in this case, Hip Hop). Understood in this way, the church functions within the *ideological* operation of *hegemony* as an organization and institution that contributes towards the symbolic dissemination of dominant meanings and values. Bourdieu likewise argued that *hegemony* (in his language, *domination*) relies heavily upon practices of "symbolic violence." In the case of Hip Hop and the black church, here the black church uses what Gramsci calls "taste judgments," where outsiders become shamed for their chosen "way of life." This, however, becomes obscured under processes by which the church—in its own self-interest—takes on the "tastes" and "values" of the subaltern (Hip-Hop) group in the name of membership expansion and institutional participation.

In this Neo-Marxian analysis, the goal of domination is to pass from *limited* to *expansive hegemony*, a space where a large majority of the people "spontaneously" and "actively" give their consent to the hegemonic bloc—without the use of repression or coercion. In a Gramscian sense, once the church dons the worldview of Hip Hop over a religious cloak, the church becomes a hegemonic bloc by taking on the interests, tastes, and values of the subaltern in the attempt to maintain control. Through *expansive hegemony* a false sense of security is created that secures the subaltern position of ultimately living out the worldview and values of the hegemonic class.[28]

Works instantiating the prominence and necessity of the institution, in the spirit of market maintenance, ideologically fail to consider unconventional religious production outside the normative purview of the church as noteworthy. In seldom acknowledging any such reality, the *rhetoric* implies a need to be sanitized, baptized, and re-appropriated to become acceptable. Moreover, the church maintains a normative set of *ethical* and *moral* codes that become pitted against the seemingly deviant practices of cultured street productions. The frontal attack and culture/spiritual struggle between the approach of church-based trends and Hip Hop reflects what Gramsci labeled *war of position*: the struggle that takes place at the site of the cultural superstructure for control over meanings, values, and signification

THE CRITICAL IN THE LYRICAL: RAPPER AS (CHRISTIAN) PROPHET

Scholarship situated between the black church and Hip-Hop culture, whether insider or outsider to the academy, represents a brand of engagement where dominant religion is left intact—and the religiosity of the larger culture is left un-interrogated. The manner in which such engagement occurs recognizes the potentiality of Hip-Hop culture, and yet manages to miss the opportunity to engage it spatially on its own terms.

There are, however, scholars whose work advocates for a different kind of approach—one situated within cultural and social criticism espoused by black "organic intellectuals" who straddle the roughness of street sensibilities and the ivory towers of intellectual production. At a time when Hip-Hop culture was not seen as worthy of serious academic reflection, considered less than a "proper object" of study, forerunners such as Cornel West and Michael Eric Dyson (among many others) risked their academic professionalism and intellectual integrity to take a closer listen to the gritty edges of cultured street sensibilities. Referring to Dyson himself, Mark Anthony Neal in the foreword to Dyson's text *Open Mike: Reflections on Philosophy, Race, Sex, Culture and Religion* (2002) writes, ". . .and that's what made him 'real' for us 'thug nigga intellectuals' who actually hold it down in the academy, and the fo' real 'thug niggas' surviving the triple Ps: penitentiaries, projects, and poverty."[29] This strand of engagement is grounded in intellectual tenacity and political courage in its brave call for attention to socially marked cultural phenomena.

From among the ranks of scholars who work from similar positionalities as Dyson and West, I examine these two specifically as representative of a particular kind of engagement with Hip-Hop culture—an engagement that deploys religious (Christian) rhetoric and rhetorical signifiers (and ideas) to unearth rugged and transgressive social and cultural practices. In this sense, the uses of religiosity that ground such cultural and social criticism differ from a "market maintenance" approach as explicated above by affirming dimensions of Hip Hop that embody a discourse of prophetic Christianity whether bodies participate in faith institutions or not. Although this approach contributes towards a more political vision of what West calls prophetic Christianity, one has to wonder if this approach constricts the polysemy of uses and functions of religiosity evidenced in Hip Hop by confining such analyses to a Christian matrix.

Now a seminal text for anyone exploring the connections between Hip-Hop culture and humanities writ large, audacious, and bold, Dyson's work *Between God and Gangsta Rap: Bearing Witness to Black Culture* (1996) put Hip Hop on the humanities map. A cursory glimpse of the book's cover begins the (intellectual) play with and construction of religious markers: the invocation to "God" in-scripted on the knuckles of a clenched black fist paralleling the inscription of "gangsta rap" etched into the materiality of the black body. And between these two worlds, Dyson, a public intellectual and ordained Baptist minister, begins this work. Before we arrive at the preface, we encounter the summons of a poem, "the Baptist beat" written by Thomas Sayers Ellis, a piece that binds polarities of difference: "sinners and worshippers," "hustlers, survivors. All that terrible energy."[30] Here we get a religious image of what this book signifies: religious redemption through cultural transgression—a binding of the sacred and profane. In the preface, Dyson begins to "speak in tongues" in the spirit of 1 Corinthians 14:13. We have yet to get to Dyson's main thrust about gangster rap, and yet we have already encountered a host of Christian religious play.

Throughout, Dyson performs an array of cultural surveys, bearing witness to the austere conditions and celebrations of black culture in American society by engaging a host of figures in Hip-Hop culture. He arrives at his intellectual rapture on gangsta rap in the twenty-fourth "verse" (chapter) and sustains this rapture to the book's end—the section he labels the "benediction." Surveying gangsta rap personalities from Ice Cube to Public Enemy, Dyson unearths how such lyrical icons challenged the very moral, social, and racial foundations of American society. While insightful, beyond the brilliant social commentary on gangster rap the religious exploration is thin. What remains religiously significant in this work however is the deployment of (black) religious (church-based) tropes that ground Dyson's cultural and social criticism. This is accomplished through strategies such as adorning the thug bodies of gangster rappers with divine-like capital and prowess vis-à-vis black Christian church-centered rhetoric.

This adornment of religious capital is even more pronounced in Dyson's fuller engagement with late gangster rapper Tupac Shakur (Pac) in *Holler If You Hear Me: Searching for Tupac Shakur* (2001), where he critically examines existential themes within Pac's lyrics, among them religion, posing weighty questions on the pressing issues of life, figured as religious. In the chapter "But Do the Lord Care," Dyson writes, "It might help to remember that Tupac was obsessed with God. His lyrics dripped with a sense of the divine."[31] Pac's early mentor Leila Steinberg expressed to Dyson that "his songs were calculated to take you back to the Bible. Take the song 'Blasphemy,' for example, where he talks about ten rules to the game. What were the ten rules? What did the Ten Commandments say?"[32] Dyson notes how the roughness and rebellious nature of Pac's music offended more traditional beliefs and organized religion, suggesting that "rap and religion do not color our interpretation of their often-opposing creeds"[33] but continues, juxtaposing unpopular and unacceptable views as prophetic, to point out "a central moral contention of Christianity that God may be distinguished in the clothing—and maybe even the rap—of society's most despised members."[34] Here, Dyson flips the script on traditional Christianity: between the materiality of the "thug" body (in his experiences of a thug life) and art (in his socially offensive and transgressive lyrics), Pac becomes figured as a suffering servant, a typology of a black Jesus on the quest for social (and black) liberation. It is in this intellectual typing and framing of rappers as urban griots[35], that religious rhetoric strategically points towards and is connected with a larger "hip-hop spirituality. . .to support the quest for authentic black selfhood."[36] In this sense Pac becomes the prophetic griot of all things subversive. Dyson writes:

> In Tupac's raps all parties to death, evil and suffering get a hearing—and lashing—including the crack addict, the welfare mother, the hustler, the thug, the pimp, the playa, the bitch, the ho, the politician, the rapper, the white supremacist, the innocent child, the defenseless female, the crooked cop, and the black sellout.[37]

Explicated in this way, Pac becomes the progenitor of all things critical, operating within and discerning a "thug theodicy" and "thug theology" from the underside.

In a precarious turn from concentrated social and cultural criticism of Pac's life story and existentially styled lyrics, Dyson jumps to an examination of the religious significance of Pac's tattooed black body. Pac's inked body is figured as expressing the many/ness of his social complications and existential angst. Dyson writes:

> Tupac's body has become metaphoric in the way that John Brown's body has, or even John Henry's. But his breathing and walking body, his living and loving body, his rapping and acting body, his angry and defiant body, is the body that matters the most, because without it, we would have no record of his spirit etched into our hearts and minds. It is that body that is hard to believe is no longer here.[38]

This beautifully written chapter is full of brilliant social and cultural criticism of Hip Hop and what Pac's body signified to a world that, by the "dangerous" nature of his presence and being, could not hear what his (socially) wounded black body was saying. Through a deployment of Christian rhetoric, Dyson reads the signification of Pac's body as "sacrificial lamb" whose quest is figured as and defined by the "Black Jesus." While Dyson's social and cultural criticism of Pac specifically and Hip-Hop culture more generally is finely executed, it must be noted that this brand of intellectual

engagement with Hip-Hop culture is void of a more nuanced investigation into the uses of religion (beyond Christian rhetorical deployments that
fashion outlawish and outlandish thug rappers as postmodern typologies of
liberation demagogues) within Hip Hop. In Dyson's apprehension of such
subject matter, dominant Christianity remains intact and his treatment and
advancement of religion, as an intellectual category, remains unexamined.
What does the use of religion in Pac's music, beyond a theological reversal
in the spirit of liberation theological suppositions (as suggested by Dyson),
purport to do? For example, when Dyson argues "that Tupac represented
something very suggestive and certainly very articulate within black culture: he embodied the conflict of the language of hope and the rhetoric
of hopelessness,"[39] Pac's existential wrestlings with life's hard questions
become stifled within a motif of crisis, pain, and despair. Pac's religious
lyrical play with traditional theological signifiers becomes fixed within a
framework of liberation and struggle, the despondent "thug," the "cosmic
ally" who is on a perpetual search for the "Black Jesus." Pac's religious
play as strategy to unearth social ills (and reflect on his own complicities)
becomes lodged within his inheritance of Christianity. I would not go as far
as Dyson to proclaim:

> In one sense Tupac was the secular articulation of a religious belief in
> the possibility of identifying with a God who became what we are. A
> crucial source of hopefulness in black Christian culture has precisely
> to do with believing that God identifies with our condition as the
> underdog.[40]

Analyzing strictly in this manner is to flatten what the use of religion accomplished for Pac: a religious complexity that both utilizes and breaks with
traditional Christian norms and ethics. Something more is required (and
necessitated) of religious and theological reflection regarding what seem to
be expressions of "existential" realities. Linguistic play (within Hip-Hop
culture) requires an alternative approach to the analysis of religious grammar and themes, an approach that requires a turn from traditional theological notions of *belief*. Pac's complex performativity of Christian capital
calls for an engagement that extends beyond suggestions that "what Tupac
was searching for [was]. . . . this Tillichian modality of existence, this
embrace by ultimate concern, and to stick with Tillich, this 'courage to be'
in the face of the death and destruction he witnessed in his neighborhood
and in his life."[41] Although statements such as these offer a wonderfully
articulated liberationist and theodical perspective, they risk flattening the
messier uses, functions, and negotiations of Pac's religious troping while
overdetermining the intentionality of Pac's quest as religiously and politically transgressive.

Picking up this idea of the political transgressivity of Hip-Hop culture,
the work of West concentrates in part on the transformative democratic

potential of such 'deviant' groups. West is a social commentator par excellence, with a passion for "telling it like it is" in the hopes of "making it like it should be." He is also a deeply thoughtful author and scholar. He makes the point that by being *faithfully unfaithful* (a term that will be explored in Chapter 4 in the context of my examination of Pinn's concept of complex subjectivity) to America's democratic traditions, democracy can be formed afresh. Thus, marginalized voices have the potential to open up and revitalize social and political structures that otherwise have a tendency to become static and stagnant (not to mention heavily weighted in the dominant direction), instigating a picking apart and reworking of the hegemonic fabric. Like Dyson, West is interested in how the voices of Hip Hop culture interpolate the moral, social, and political soundscape, through what amounts to a Socratic critique methodically and repeatedly questioning the make-up of our structures and beliefs, a questioning most notably vocalized in rap lyrics. Seeing rap as a creative musical expression of black angst updating the earlier spirituals and blues, West argues for acknowledgement of Hip Hop as both prophetic and political: "a paradoxical cry of desperation and celebration of the black underclass and poor working class, a cry that openly acknowledges and confronts the wave of personal cold-heartedness, criminal cruelty and existential hopelessness in the Black ghettos of Afro-America."[42] He argues also for a more politicized and public role for the scholarly observer of such phenomena, writing: "I do not believe that the life of an academic—or at least all academics—should be narrowly contained within the university walls or made to serve narrow technocratic goals."[43] This broader conceptualization of the role of the academian is certainly one he himself has embodied with great impact.

One problem with the politicization of academic positioning is that it leaves the object of study particularly open to rhetorical manipulation. Here, Hip Hop becomes contested ground used to underscore and exemplify a particular (outside) agenda, in this case the worthiness of the (poor, young, black) participants in democracy-in-the-making. Seen this way, what was a lived materiality becomes a meaty substance for the consumption of those seeking to read meaning (their meaning) into the words and acts of others. This is not to say that Hip Hop bears no traces of its genesis and continuing existence on the underside of America's urban centers, or that the enactment of Hip Hop culture does not perform a cathartic celebration, reclamation, and proclamation. Or even, indeed, that it not is through and by such acts that democracy is pushed and pulled into a truer representation of its component citizens. Rather, it is a caution that he who is reading determines what is read and how its meaning is decided and relayed.

West styles these street philosophers as both prophets of destruction and agents of redemption, within our degenerating (but still salvageable) society. While "the best of rap music and hip-hop culture still expresses stronger and more clearly than any cultural expression in the past generation a profound indictment of the moral decadence of our dominant society,"[44] and in the America of today black youth find themselves "up against forces of death, destruction, and disease unprecedented in the everyday life of black urban people,"[45] through the rigor of unrelenting self-questioning and questioning of "the system," these underdogs have the transformative potential to restore society to an optimum—or at least better—condition. And is it working? It may remain unclear whether democracy has yet benefited but, according to West, in "an unprecedented cultural breakthrough created by poor talented black youths in hoods of the empire's chocolate cities, hip-hop by now has transformed the entertainment industry and culture here and around the world."[46]

West draws a distinction between prophetic Christianity, which is a lively and robust transfer of divine power to the believer, and Constantinian Christianity, in which by contrast power is entrenched in the institution. For West, democracy is threatened by the destructive strands that are present in culture, as in religion, along with liberatory longings—a dualism that he sees to be repeated within Hip Hop. Thus, the productive and the counterproductive vie for ascendance in a morality play enacted on the stage of modern America. If this was indeed a play, the stage set would be a visual rendering of the decay of the nation, writ large as *nihilism*:

> a philosophic doctrine that there are no rational grounds for legitimate standards or authority; it is, far more, the lived experience of coping with a life of horrifying meaningless, hopelessness, and (most important) lovelessness.[47]

In an ongoing eclipse, the lights are going out on hope and meaning as "moral consistency" and "ethical integrity" exit stage left. But do not fear: the corrupt dominant institutions are about to be challenged by the hitherto marginalized voices of a Hip-Hop nation. Justice shall be renewed and the crisis alleviated.

Thus troped as prophetic and political, Hip-Hop becomes a subversive (Christian) engagement with the mainstream, and the superimposed rhetoric tends to take over the original text. From the meaning-deprived depths of nihilism, Hip Hop is seen to emerge clad in shining raiment and bearing aloft the almost-lost treasure, its gift to democracy. As the following section will explore, this grail of "meaning" is lifted up in the present historical moment with religious scribings intact.

HIP HOP AS A "QUEST FOR MEANING"?

It is in the work of the third trend of engagement that a robust exploration of religion and Hip-Hop culture begins to take shape. Pinn is among the first of religious studies scholars to take up the task of charting the religious work of Hip-Hop culture in a sustained manner. His efforts evidenced in works such as *Noise & Spirit: The Religious and Spiritual Dimensions of Rap Music* (2003) among numerous published articles, book chapters, and scholarly presentations assisted in putting rap music and Hip-Hop culture on the radar of the religious studies terrain. His work, in which I participated as co-editor, on a 2009 special issue of *Culture & Religion* journal dedicated to the topic of "Hip Hop & Religion," continued this trajectory. Together, these works are marked by an effort to highlight the religious diversity and theological complexity of Hip Hop's religious terrain, unearthing complicated dimensions of rap music's religious stylings. These works are foundational in their attempts to show how rap music is not only rich with religious play, it also has more complicated dimensions than immediately meet the eye. While works such as these have carved out multiple spaces within the field, methodologically common among them is an over-reliance on rap music as a lyrical stand-in for the larger material practices of Hip Hop (which is bigger than rap). Theoretically, the category of religion in these works remains, in part, un-interrogated (e.g., self-evident and assumed) and grounded in (and trapped by) the pursuit of phenomenological sensibilities. In other words, these works begin from the supposition that "quests for meaning" in Hip-Hop culture can be understood *as* religious. This perspective unduly relies upon the universalizing and interiorization of religion as inner feeling, assuming religion to be decipherable as presence evidenced in certain markers of human experience. Less attention has been given to rethinking religious uses in Hip-Hop culture beyond this perspective. In analyzing what the use of religion accomplishes, beyond perpetual quests for meaning figured as religious, we can achieve a more robust examination of religion in the interests of and for various human efforts, rather than stopping at explicating such efforts as existential pursuits and questioning.

In the introduction, I established as central to this project the question of whether or not there is anything of religious significance in Hip Hop. As a scholar of religion, Pinn has concerned himself with charting the nature and meaning of black religion while also working to expand frames of analysis beyond static (Christian) theological confines. His first book-length treatment of rap music, *Noise and Spirit*, highlights the religious diversity within rap music, boasting examples from Christian, Islamic, and humanist sensibilities, among others. The contributors to the volume explore the religious density and existential dimensions of this cultural art form.

Similar to West's construction, rap music in *Noise and Spirit* is understood and placed in historical relationship to the larger lineage of music (such as the spirituals) and cultural pursuits of freedom among people of African descent. Through this connection, it is suggested that the medium of music, in part, enabled hope of a better life under dehumanizing conditions. Pinn writes, "It was through this cultural expression—enslaved Africans' efforts to express a sense of self in a hostile world—that memories of a former home were maintained and were used to make sense of their new existential and ontological space,"[48] asserting that songs such as these helped provide meaning to what otherwise seemed a meaningless world. Situated in this way, rap music becomes connected to the spirit, voice, and space for struggle and resistance against structures of racial domination specifically, and varied oppressions in general. For Pinn, the evidence of religiosity, or lyrical wrestlings between the sacred and the profane, is exemplified through the existential articulations of "Ultimate Concern"— the hard questions of life. Pinn is careful to acknowledge the "paradox" and "existential" slippage in rap itself—and through a Tillichian lens of analysis, "existential" questions (configured as questions of "ultimacy") expressed in the music become figured and understood as religious. The ontological angst and weight of the deep questioning that takes place both merits and warrants a religious recognition, according to Pinn. Distinct from others, Pinn executes carefulness in his understanding of rap's religiosity; for example, he argues, "The line between religious belief and practice is often blurred," explaining that he:

> uses religious studies (including theological exploration) as a means of providing additional depth to our understanding of rap music by surfacing its more implicit religious dimensions, making clear that what we hear in rap music is a deep wrestling with meaning itself [figured in the hard questions of life].[49]

Differing from Dyson's approach regarding Tupac in particular, Pinn doesn't take (and isn't beholden to) traditional religious signifiers at face value. He understands that there is more density and play in rap music—a play that often deconstructs the very religious signifiers we are searching for. For example, Pinn argues:

> While Tupac continues to make what is a rhetorical use of the God concept, the final answer to the absurdity of life is not found in a God silent, if present. It is found in human activity. At best, God is suspect because, in a thugged out, Marxist twist, there is a link between deception and the presence of traditional Christian religion.[50]

Pinn's acute attention to the suspicion of, inversion in, and play (couched within a humanist and human accountability framework) with religiosity begins to get at how the religious imagination of rap music is not only analytically deceptive (or what John Jackson, Jr. refers to as *paranoid*)— but also, tricky and semantically distrustful. A deeper look is necessitated by rap's religious thickness, one that requires a shift in the grammar used when theorizing the religious—a shift from belief (in religious presence configured as meaning) towards redescribing what a religious exploration of Hip Hop seeks to uncover. This suggested shift is taken up more forcefully in Chapter 4.

While Pinn's *Noise* & *Spirit* put rap music on the religious studies topography, he has continued in his sustained reflection on rap music. Born out of two American Academy of Religion panels in which Pinn served as respondent, came the 2009 special issue on 'Hip-Hop and Religion." Pinn and Miller (and here I switch momentarily to co-authorship read from the outside, as it were, in the interests of discursive clarity) describe the reaction to rap music among confounded scholars of African-American studies, wherein "the theologian is confronted with alternate categories of meaning; the biblical studies scholar is challenged by new sacred texts; the ethicist is confronted by altered moral and ethical postures and so on." They point out that "we are slow to interrogate rap for what it is and what it might help us understand about the geography of culture and the nature/meaning of African-American religion."[51] The authors express a desire to use the engagement of rap music as a way to theoretically develop African-American religion. This special issue was asked to think about the intersections between culture and religion. With this in mind, the authors argue that "religion is the substance of culture, and culture is the form of religion"[52]—an eerie echo of rapper KRS's proclamation: "OUR CULTURE IS OUR RELIGION AND OUR RELIGION IS OUR CULTURE." The cultural processes of rap are erroneously framed within a Tillichian formulation, one that reduces (and confuses) the complexity of culture (as lived) with religion (as imagined and theorized). Again, further work on the category of religion is required. Using Tillich and Charles H. Long on the ideas of "ultimate concern" and "orientation," the theoretical positioning of religion framing this special issue argues that "religion so conceived cannot be understood as confined to rigid structures, but rather, the religion of any people is more than a structure of thought; it is experience, expression, motivations, intentions, behaviors, styles, and rhythms."[53] Although Tillich's loose positioning of religion (as questions and concerns of "ultimacy") makes room for interpretation beyond strict Christian assumptions, this positioning situates religiosity within the problematic realm of private experience, presence, and meaning grounded in existentialist concerns. While this formulation enables exploration beyond religiously explicit rhetorical pronouncements in rap, the housing of "ultimate concern" (Tillich) and "orientation" (Long) remains phenomenologically situated within a (Christian) inheritance and intellectual genealogy that's preoccupied with apprehending meaning itself. Moreover, rubrics such as "ultimate concern" as borrowed from Tillich and traced into the work of Pinn are theologically grounded in a particular positionality of faith. Tillich writes, "Man, like every living being, is concerned about many things, above all about those which condition his very existence. . . . If [a concern] claims ultimacy it demands the total surrender of him who accepts this claim . . . it demands that all other concerns . . . be sacrificed."[54] As we can see, the inheritance of such language carries unexamined theological baggage in the re-appropriation of Tillich's work for the examination of rap music's religiosity. I would argue that couching the religious within such theological inheritance makes claims on behalf of faith (in a confessional sense) not evidenced in the empirical reality of such cultural productions. Continuing in the intellectual inheritance of Long and Tillich, the guiding theory of religion for this special issue takes up:

> religion as the *quest for complex subjectivity*, a quest that gives expression to the search for and struggle over meaning making—the making of life meaning. This *complex subjectivity* charts the nature and meaning of the religious, embracing movement, change and porosity, a quest for meaning that makes use of the raw data of life and culture to inform its theoretical and ontological movements.[55]

While Chapter 4 takes up *complex subjectivity* in a more sustained manner, for now it is clear that such an affective quest is, once again, concerned with the struggle for meaning as a religious quest. Understanding the inimitable occupation of the religious that occupies much of the rap world requires a rethinking of the grammar used to describe the religious as well as attention to the ways in which, at times, intellectual inheritances of particular traditions often constrain the very work such theory attempts to perform. Frames such as Tillich's "ultimate concern" and Long's "orientation" come loaded with particular disciplinary histories; therefore, we must give consideration to the larger discourse from which such thought arises. The phenomenological impulses of these intellectual inheritances maintain dominance on (interiorized) meaning and presence—stretching the realm of religion far beyond its reach as human activity and formation. Robin Sylvan, who also inherits the religious genealogy of Long, is critiqued by sociologist of religion Gordon Lynch for his overextension of religious functions of popular music (Sylvan relies upon the religious thought of folks within the *sui generis* tradition such as Eliade and Otto to analyze the "religious" dimension of popular music), a caution which is applicable for work on Hip Hop and religion. In *Traces of the Spirit: The Religious Dimensions of Popular Culture* (2002), Lynch argues that Sylvan:

> tends to neglect the much wider range of social and cultural uses that playing and listening to music have. If popular music is religious—in Sylvans' sense—then can the term 'religion' be appropriately applied to a wide range of different leisure activities. . . .the danger with Sylvan's approach is an over-stretching of the category of 'religion' to the point of its dissipation and a disciplinary imperialism which imposes the category of 'religion' on cultural practices in ways that distort or obfuscate their lived meaning for those involved in them.[56]

The scholar of religion searching "for" religion in popular cultural forms walks a fine line. The next chapter engages the category of religion in a more theoretical manner through a continuation of this third trend of Hip Hop engagement. More specifically, I closely read Pinn's theory of religion (*Complex Subjectivity*) by way of postmodern theory to rethink its intellectual inheritance of the phenomenological tradition and preoccupation with collapsing the quest for meaning *as* religious. I am persuaded that grand transcendental illusions with claims to the uniqueness of religious experience deny attention to and flatten the range of religious functions and uses within Hip-Hop culture. Derrida argues that the isolation of meaning (as presence) is an impossible possibility, as such an attempt requires a deferral of time, but pays acute attention to the kind of grammar and language such a project inherits. In a Derridian sense, the play with language within Hip Hop is unstable: not identifiable as coherent signifiers of existentialist meaning further requiring markers of intentionality on behalf of the subject. Thus, it is untrustworthy, by form unable to provide a coherence to meaning. Signs and symbols within Hip-Hop culture are much less stable than they appear, and this incoherence troubles the scholar's apprehension of a quest for meaning. Hip-Hop culture must be interrogated on its own terms. As Lynch argues, Sylvan's approach (which collapses popular music *as* religion)—and I would add, the work of the special issue journal (Hip Hop *as* quest for meaning which can be understood as religious)—"runs the risk of forcing cultural data about popular music into pre-determined religious categories—of community, transcendence, and theology,"[57] and further: of presence, meaning, and experience.

CONCLUSION: MOVING TO THE MATERIAL DIMENSION

This chapter has engaged and read the advantages and problematics of three general trends representative of the small discourse on religion and Hip-Hop culture. These trends enable possibilities of thinking religion and Hip-Hop culture together in varied ways—yet, religion is engaged in these faithful attempts in such a way that the *idea* of religion is maintained and relatively kept stable as an institutional, prophetic, or what McCutcheon would call "private" affair. While the works taken up in this chapter are notable for forging out academic space for such enquiry, common among them is a lack of a forceful engagement with the category of religion. Within each of the three trends, the religious is read as self-evident and used to unearth other social and cultural interests on behalf of the scholar. As represented by these trends, religion remains lodged within themes of morality and institutional religiosity, struggle and crisis, and ultimacy/orientation/presence and meaning. While each positionality maintains its own ideological commitments (i.e., church market maintenance, greater democratic political possibilities, and the persistence of religion in cultural forms), we are left with a thin analysis of religion's social processes.

Two tasks may be identified at this point as vital. One is a broadening of the field of enquiry into other material dimensions of Hip-Hop culture beyond rap music, to allow a back flow from lived reality—from the manifesting of Hip-Hop culture in the bodies of black youth—to wash into the discussion and facilitate the redescribing of religion beyond institutional referents and received theological categories. The present project works in the spirit of this sort of achievement, engaging Hip-Hop materiality even while reworking the rhetoric of religious studies thinking. The second task is, more specifically, a rethinking of inherited disciplinary traces. The next chapter extends the work of this one by engaging Pinn's theory of religion *complex subjectivity* using postmodern thought to rethink its phenomenological inheritance of religion.

4 Inside-Out
Complex Subjectivity and Postmodern Thought

"In the last analysis, what is at stake is . . . the privilege of the actual present, the now."

—Jacques Derrida[1]

"What is really going on in things, what is really happening, is always 'to come.'"

—Jacques Derrida[2]

Through detailed attention to particular rhetorical markers such as evil, pain, suffering, and the self, the religious exploration of Hip-Hop culture has often been figured as a quest for meaning. Such queries are considered religious insomuch as they address what scholars such as Anthony B. Pinn have called questions of ultimacy—hard questions of life that fuel a desire for the pursuit of greater life-meaning. Certainly, the construction of meaning (however conceived) is a human doing; it is not simply, self-evidently present, but rather a process manufactured and mediated through time, space, and practices. While we acknowledge its constructed nature, the task of apprehending meaning (as presence) and couching it as religious carries a complicated phenomenological inheritance often assuming privileged access to intentionality and consciousness by way of experience. Discourse centered on such thinking must be interrogated for the ways in which constructions of meaning in the world often retain dimensions and effects of unconscious commitments—unexamined ways of being in the world. Moreover, of further interest is what makes the construction of meaning in human activity a religious quest—or, what is decipherable about such a construction. I am not claiming that "meaning" itself doesn't exist; rather, we must clarify what the use of such grammar purports to mean, and why certain constructions of meaning are understood as religious among certain communities, groups, and practices.

I am persuaded that meaning incessantly remains in a process of deferral, thus making the search for meaning (as presence) ultimately what Derrida calls a grand transcendental illusion—in other words, utterly impossible. The method of this chapter will be deconstructive in nature—in a Derridian sense, an attempt to expose a particular *trace*,[3] to unearth a particular structure of thought embedded in metaphysics of presence. I refer to this *trace* as an *unintended* consequence of inheriting an intellectual genealogy within religious studies that privileges intentionality and consciousness (of the subject), apprehension of meaning, and the conflation of the desire that gives rise to religious activity grounded in affective faculties of subjectivity (inward feeling).

Further, the notion of a "quest for meaning" projects itself forward into the study of Hip Hop already crystallized and waiting to be retrieved. Similarly to the way the category of religion is apprehended at the moment of study as a unique, pre-existing essence, the religious-studies examiners of Hip Hop may be seen to be hampered by the pre-configuration of a "quest for meaning," equated with religious experience. I say "hampered" here because even those scholars who are seeking to bring a fresh eye to the analysis of religion and Hip-Hop culture may fail to notice the ways in which they are in fact constrained by such inherited equations. When the experience of or desire for meaning is pre-construed as religious, there is a narrowing of scope of inquiry. Further, such an approach fails to make allowance for the Derridian deferral of meaning within temporality; because the presence of meaning can never be seen as fixed or stable, meaning does not exist as a coherent, intelligible object to be found. Instead, the locus of supposed meaning is one of undecidability: *aporia*. The science of presence fails where there is no presence, and scholars setting out on a phenomeno-logical quest for meaning will find only phenomenology itself, as definitions double back on themselves and fail to connect with a lived reality.

This chapter redescribes the concept of religion in one such instance, seeking to remain faithful to its form and yet to expand three inherent problematics by tracing the positionality of its intellectual inheritance and offering new sources of theoretical engagement. Here, the idea of religion is approached as social process and formation: religion as non-unique human activity. The question is not what *is* religious about certain activity; rather, what are the effects of various uses of the religious? The redirection of this question has potential to yield interesting analyses beyond the simple citing of religion in cultural forms, without privileging certain activity more or less as religious.

By form, *complex subjectivity* (CS) as introduced in the preceding chapter offers an efficacious way to think of the religious, yet its sources seemingly constrain this potential. Here, we may find postmodern theory to be useful in introducing new sources to the articulation of the religious: that is, analyzing each problematic and then offering an alternative reworking through a different intellectual inheritance. This is not an attempt to jettison CS as a theory of religion, rather, a desire to advance it through critique and critical consideration of its limitations. Why take up CS as a theory of religion? Not only does it represent a push towards theory and method in the study of African-American religious thought, it is, to my knowledge, one of the few theories of religion that has seriously wrestled with charting the religious in Hip Hop. The deconstructive analysis of this chapter is an attempt to be *faithfully unfaithful* so that CS continues to live throughout/within discourse.

In the introduction, I argued that Hip-Hop culture has been an understudied topic of research within religious and theological studies. Chapter 3 charted the current trends and assumptions in the seminal work that explores the intersections of Hip Hop and religion. I argued that common to these trends is a thin engagement with the category of religion, the exception being the religious treatment of Hip-Hop culture in the work of Anthony B. Pinn. Yet there remains, even in these attempts to stretch the religious and theological complexity of Hip-Hop culture, a troubling *unintended* problematic: the reliance upon and inconspicuous *trace* of inherited phenomenological positionalities in approach to the category of religion. As scholars we remain seemingly trapped within a prison of presence, thus limiting the religious analysis of Hip-Hop culture to the search/quest for meaning as transcendental presence. Ultimately, this approach collapses religion *as* the search for meaning (read: coherence, presence, stability) and thus the religious pursuit of Hip-Hop culture *as* a quest for meaning. Again, the use of meaning for the explication of CS needs further probing, being left both illusive and vague. Is the desire for greater life-meaning in the world a religious pursuit—where do lines of distinction become made? Troubling the use of meaning in CS pushes us to reconsider its positionality of religion as "orientation" and "ultimate concern." The grammar used, as will be explored in some depth here, is derived from sources that privilege the category of religion as "experience" and search/quest for meaning as presence. Couching the taxonomy of religion within the affective—innate inner expressions, motivations, intentions, and behaviors— inevitably forces religion to be reliant upon these things, constructing a modernist (similar problematics can be seen in the work of Immanuel Kant and Friedrich Schleiermacher among others) framing of religion *as* feeling, unique, interior, and therefore universalizable (because it's dependent on the interior comportment of subjectivity). Ultimately, conceptualizing religion in this fashion—as the expression or feeling of orientation, stability, or that which is expressed within questions of ultimacy—fails to imagine religion in a way that remains faithful to the complexities of postmodern cultural productions. Grand transcendental claims and reliance upon phenomenological frames are too rigid to embrace the polysemy of functions and uses of the category "religion" within Hip-Hop culture beyond a modernist (almost Schleiermachian) "religion as feeling" approach.

Differing from other approaches within African-American religious studies, Pinn's theory of religion begins in and with subjectivity (rather than particular institutional referents, beliefs, and so on), an important point of departure for studying the life-worlds of everyday people. Equally important, it takes historical structures into account, one of the more interesting tensions in his work being the irreconcilable move from historical structures to an affective inner explication of desire and feeling. As such, Pinn's idea is to produce a generalizable theory of religion that helps describe black religious sensibilities, institutional and non-institutional. While this approach is commendable, it is also one of its problematic features. Pinn begins with a different question, one that interrogates what is unique about particular bodies that creates a yearning or desire for religiosity. In order to answer such a question, he has to consider the thoughts, feelings, intuitions, and desires of the subject themselves, data inaccessible to the method of his work. Attempting to chart desires and intuitions as data is a task that cannot fully come to terms with the postmodern stylings of Hip-Hop culture. Moreover, such a query limits our ability to understand the category of religion beyond a numinous-like consideration of the affective within subjectivity itself. This numinous-like postulation assumes conscious intentionality, ignores structuring structures (to what extent are subjects fully conscious of their own commitments), and lastly, bifurcates thought and action (conscious thought [intentionality]→leads to human [activity]).

This chapter is a critical examination of Pinn's theory of religion, using postmodern theory with the intent to make the concept of religion in his work less stable and coherent by offering new sources of engagement. This deconstruction re-imagines CS's core elements through postmodern theory in order to rethink its development of religion *outside* of the *inside* of subjectivity itself. Let us push ourselves to imagine the category of religion as human activity characterizable by particular social interests, rather than an interior *desire* for meaning within African-American religious thought. Let us rethink religion through various *assemblages* (multiplicity of forms) and positionalities of *play*. As Derrida reminds us through his idea of the *trace* (which holds the condition of possibility for meaning itself), possibilities are found in the "movement" of *difference* expressed in and through undecidability, ambiguity, and paradox. These things don't always reside in the interior comportment of consciousness, they are socially constructed through exteriorized structuring structures.

The argument of this chapter progresses in three sections. I begin by descriptively explicating Pinn's theory of religion and then move into a deconstruction of the phenomenological and inherited *traces* within *complex subjectivity*. Lastly, I re-read *complex subjectivity* through various postmodern lenses (Jacques Derrida, Pierre Bourdieu, Russell McCutcheon and James A. Beckford), engaging themes such as *play*, *habitus*, and *social formation/construction*. Each one of these concepts/themes is used to rethink a particular problematic of CS. The spirit of this chapter is largely deconstructive. My intention is to begin dialogue around a very important theory of religion with hopes that it sparks a robust conversation regarding theory and method in the study of African-American religious thought, with a focus on rethinking how we can conceptualize the religious by paying close attention to the intellectual traditions our suppositions inherit. This chapter makes space within the study of African-American

religious thought for theorizing religion outside of confessional and hermeneutical approaches which assume religion and religious experience to be
self-evident and unique (*sui generis*).

COMPLEX SUBJECTIVITY AND THE TRACES
OF ITS INTELLECTUAL INHERITANCE

> "For my purposes, religion will mean orientation—orientation in the
> ultimate sense, that is, how one comes to terms with the ultimate
> significance of one's place in the world."
>
> —Charles H. Long[4]

> "The religion of any people is more than a structure of thought; it is
> experience, expression, motivations, intentions, behaviors, styles and
> rhythms. Its first and fundamental expression is not on the level of
> thought. It gives rise to thought, but a form of thought that embodies
> the precision and nuances of its source."
>
> —Charles H. Long[5]

Charting the nature and meaning of religion more generally and black religion in particular is the intellectual query to which Anthony B. Pinn attends.
The constraints of fixity and terror produced within modernity, fixing black
bodies in time and space, is the starting point of Pinn's intellectual theorizing of the nature and meaning of religion as conceived for bodies read-out
of Western thought systems. Pinn suggests that in order to embark upon a
study of the institutions, thoughts, and activity that have comprised the rubric
"black religion," one must, in such archeological work, lift up the cultural
resources and artifacts that have been valuable for the thinking and doing
of religious activity and experience.[6] Pinn writes, "It becomes much more
necessary for the study of religion to include attention to a continually unfold-
ing array of cultural products,"[7] arguing that such an approach provides an
"archeology"—a way of investigating material culture through both structure and space. This approach, according to Pinn, allows for examination of
the "presentation" and "developments" of religion: "Material culture points
beyond itself to more fundamental modes of meaning and expression"[8] in
order to unearth the subjugated knowledge present in forms produced by a
historically unacknowledged cultural group within the Americas. With attention towards the cultural creativity in artifacts expressive of black life, it is in
and through these artifacts that Pinn articulates a push for increased agency
and life-meaning for subjectivities historically denied their own existence.

Unlike other articulators of black religion, Pinn does not find it necessary to explicate or theorize religion vis-à-vis a certain religious tradition; in fact, whether it be the Nation of Islam or the Black Church, he
argues that underlying *all* of these "historical expressions" is the pulse of

a greater move, desire, push, and concern—that which he calls *complex subjectivity*, understood as a religion-producing feeling, an "underlying impulse that gains historical manifestations in . . . institutional forms."[9] Furthermore, Pinn defines the experience of CS as "the *recognition of and response to the elemental feeling for complex subjectivity and the accompanying transformation of consciousness that allows for the histori- cally manifested battle against the terror of fixed identity.*"[10] It thus, as he argues, results in a push for greater life-meaning which necessitates and allows the possibility of continual struggle for increased agency and libera- tion of one's own subjectivity.

This definition requires some contextualization in order to be understood in the manner in which Pinn intends. He argues that the movement of CS retains a complexity that is open-ended and perpetual, allowing for a con- stant process of creativity. As already suggested, Pinn begins with the subject, describing subjectivity to be "complex in that it seeks to hold in tension many ontological possibilities, a way of existing in numerous spaces of identifica- tion as opposed to reified notions of identity that make dehumanization."[11] Thus, it is a process that is comfortable with *not* explaining away tension, but rather, one that embraces complexity. The subject, in Pinn's theory, is not figured as singular or fixed, but rather multidimensional and ambiguous, and whose humanity is not foreclosed. Further, with life options open-ended, the struggle to make sense of self is, for Pinn, a meaning-making activity con- structed through a perpetual process of becoming. And what makes this reli- gious? Pinn writes, "It is religious in that it addresses the search for *ultimate* meaning,"[12] thus, it is "the center of black religion."[13] Again, we must note the universalizing tendency of CS. Despite differences in (religious) expression, CS is explicated as the underlying cause/movement of the plurality of black reli- gion (or at least the ones Pinn attends to in *Terror and Triumph*). This is made possible in Pinn's theory because despite differences in expression, the (black) subject (regardless of religious difference) is universalizable through the shar- ing of similar cultural experiences of historical constraint and fixity. Again, the theorizing of CS begins with explication of the black subject, a strategy that runs the risk of essentializing difference.

The above explication is representative of the basic structure of CS, but just exactly how does it move in time and space? As an example, Pinn offers con- version as a lens by which to understand CS more fully. He asserts that there is something about the nature of conversion accounts that offers a window into the "why" of religious experience, or in Pinn's language, the "underlying motivation." He charts how CS would work through conversion, as one of many possibilities of its expression in the world, and writes that conversion is made possible by an *elemental feeling* which expresses the urge for CS based on a "triadic structure" of:

(1) confrontation by historical identity, often expressed in terms of existential pain and some type of terror; (2) wrestling with the old

consciousness and the possibility of regeneration, or in William James's language, a reconstitution of the soul; and (3) embrace of a new consciousness and new modes of behavior affecting relationship with the community of believers—those who have had a similar response to elemental feelings—and the larger community.[14]

The characteristics of how CS operates within the subject rely upon what Pinn calls the *inner impulse* (a deep stirring) and *elemental feeling*—ideas that find expression in and through affective internalized yearnings and motivations that assist in "consciousness" raising of the subjects themselves. This process assists in producing motivation to quest for what Pinn calls greater life-meaning (e.g., increased agency through the push against fixity of identity through open-ended processes of becoming).

To make clear, CS is an attempt to theorize the movement of religion and religious experience, taking subjectivity as its starting point, and historical struggle against the gaze of identity-fixation as its context. It is, as I understand it, described as a desired movement that can be generalizable for the plurality of religious expressiveness—beyond accounting for differences in religion. His project is tuned in to what makes humans quest for meaning, and further, how this can be, in part, understood as religious. While Pinn articulates and supports *why* this can be understood as religious, we are left to wonder what makes the quest for CS in the world, a religious one? In *why* this can be understood as religious, Pinn makes use of *sui generis* claims supporting the mode of religion as the par excellence of transformation. While allowing for the experience of religious affect within multiple traditions, he sets up a hierarchy of "life-changing experiences" in which only some are truly and entirely transformational, and not universally accessible. He poses the possibility of the "non-religious person," proposing that:

> not every person can speak of a religious experience, a recognition of and response out of the inner impulse. People may be able to outline the inspired embrace of a particular political platform, economic system and philosophy, or cultural formation, and these may be said to constitute life-changing experiences. However, they alone do not constitute the transformation of total being, the constitution of a new consciousness that sparks new meanings of life that are endemic to religion as feeling for complex subjectivity and to religion as historical manifestation of this feeling the form of institutions, doctrines, and practices.[15]

Accordingly, in order for a transformation of consciousness to qualify as *religious,* it has to transform the total being—something, Pinn argues, that is only accomplished through the mode of the religious. It is here that I find erroneous claims to the uniqueness of religion itself. According to Pinn, the total transformation of being is only partially accomplished in and approximated through dimensions such as economics, politics, or philosophy. Pinn is after a vision and doing of religion as recognition of something greater; he says, "It entails a recognition of deeper levels of being reflected in sociopolitical circumstances but is not fully captured through these circumstances,"[16] continuing that "this impulse is larger, more expansive, and it addresses the very meaning of our existence in ways that tie or bind together historical struggles."[17] Pinn is clear that religion understood as CS is concerned above all with "the very meaning of existence."[18]

It should at this point be clear that Pinn focuses attention toward the movement and shape of religion in history beginning with subjectivity itself. As such, the explication of CS is heavily dependent on describing feelings of the interior comportment (e.g., psyche, consciousness, inner stirring) of the subject to account for external modalities and experiences (e.g., conversion) that qualify as religious—and here emerge numerous problematics. Pinn shows the manner in which such movement is expressed in, and made possible by, conversion as one practice among others which gives shape to CS as prior movement to religious manifestation. In order to explain more fully the manner in which CS expresses itself, Pinn turns to the works of Charles H. Long and William James (among others) as intellectual interlocutors. He uses the epistemological frameworks of Long and James to discursively situate CS within the scholarly traditions of history and psychology of religion. By reading Pinn's intellectual *traces* and inheritances we can further chart how CS becomes constrained by the phenomenological baggage of its sources—thereby deconstructing its intended form and positionality, and creating an *unintended* consequence within its theoretical development.

THE TRACES OF WILLIAM JAMES AND CHARLES H. LONG

In form, Pinn gives articulation to the processes of religion-provoking circumstances by taking historical structures (as impinging) and black subjectivity (as oppressed yet not fully determined) into account. Furthermore, what makes CS give rise to the religious becomes dependent upon an inward turn of the subject—a rationale free of structuring structures grounded in full consciousness of subjects themselves. This inward turn is overtly evident; Pinn writes that CS is characterizable by "a common root impulse—a yearning or feeling for a new and complex subjectivity,"[19] turning to psychology of religion by applying James's work in *The Varieties of Religious Experience: A Study in Human Nature* (1902) to the idea of conversion. James argues that in and through the mode of conversion the subject is made whole (psychological health). The wholeness of the subject necessitates an existence that Pinn articulates as meaningful, grounded in a consciousness understood to be liberative. Through conversion, black people, according to Pinn, are enabled to practice their subjectivity with increased agency through their own choosing, with the "real self" becoming the "center of consciousness."[20] Although Pinn makes clear that he rejects James's "preoccupation with individuals and the importance of individuality," he finds James's understanding of conversion useful as a means by which to frame the "yearning for complex subjectivity as dominating one's consciousness and energy."[21] Vis-à-vis James, Pinn articulates the awakening of consciousness through a theory of regeneration (conversion).

In James, Pinn finds a way to ground and "center" his articulation of CS by describing its "transformational" sensibilities through James's articulation of conversion and regeneration. In the work of Long, Pinn finds a hermeneutical heuristic. With James and psychology of religion balanced on one hand, it's in the work of Long that Pinn finds a way to articulate the "depth" of human experience and consciousness by a turn to his "hermeneutic of the ontological dimension."[22] This heuristic begins its explication with "the presupposition that the sacred—the referent for religion—is manifest in the context of history and gives depth to all modalities of human consciousness and experience" and further "interprets the social as experience and expression to promote clearer vision regarding the issues of meaning and purpose that plague humans." With (Pinn's use of) Long's focus on the importance of both experience and the objects by which ideas of the sacred become interpreted in place, Pinn asserts that "the organization or structure of social reality is, in fact, an effort to communicate certain underlying impulses [and that] this hermeneutic probes cultural structures for what they say about their source," while being attentive and more sensitive to historical context. Important to note, Long's "hermeneutic of the ontological dimension" goes beyond the more obvious "structures of life" (e.g., churches, sports, etc.) towards that which Pinn calls "the elemental structure" (the impulse), that feeling which enables the desire for greater meaning and consciousness. Understood in this way, externalized practices and human activity reflect—in a causal manner—embedded intentional impulses and desires of subjects. Assuming full awareness (consciousness) and intentionality, this thought structure assumes (and bifurcates) thought→action.

Although more depth is required to fully situate James and Long, I invoke a small piece of how their work and thought become traced into and applied within Pinn's articulation of the religious. They are, by no means, the only interlocutors utilized by Pinn. I am persuaded, however, that they represent a particular kind of thought that produces a counterproductive tension within the framing of CS. This tension emerges within the move from historical structures to conscious, inward, intentional, universal desires and dimensions of subjectivity. When the affective is articulated in CS, little attention is given to structuring structures and the interrogation of consciousness itself. McCutcheon offers an important caution against over-reliance upon consciousness of subjects for social scientific analysis, pointing out that individual humans "go about living their lives" rather than continually reflecting on and putting forward a positionality for the record.[23] *Complex subjectivity* theorized as inward process assumes the subject to be fully conscious of the structuring conditions Pinn makes use of as a hermeneutic to uncover thoughts, intentions, and motivations of subjects—things that in reality are unobtainable and indecipherable. Next, I consider how James and Long understand the concept of religion in their respective work.

Concerned with the "mode" of religious discourse, Long laments that religion has seldom been seen as "a discipline that understood its task as the comprehensive study of meaning and nature of religion in the life of humankind,"[24] arguing that the problem in the study of religion is in fact one of hermeneutics. Relying upon and situating his work within the tradition of history of religions as he does, one is not hard pressed to spot the phenomenological *trace* in Long's emphasis upon and articulation of religion and religious experience as the quest for meaning and the nature and being of human consciousness. The self-evidence of religion for Long is expressed in and through the conceptualization of religion as an "authentic" mode of human experience, thus the center of meaning. Ultimately, Long privileges the "archaic" forms of religion, invariably essentializing that which he understands to be unique and subjugated forms of religious experience. Although Long stretches the limits of what has traditionally been understood as religious (beyond institutional forms) by expanding traditional ways of doing religion (as exemplified in the religiosities of "the oppressed"), he ultimately produces and thus collapses a discursive construction of religion as experience or search for meaning situated between "archaic" and "dominant" practices of religiosity. Moreover, Long unapologetically argues that the traditions of folks such as Otto, van der Leeuw, and Eliade (formative articulators of *sui generis* framing of religion) have "provided an interpretive schema that enables the investigator to study religion as religion,"[25] thus assuming there is a pure essence in what religion purports to be, something decipherable about its presence.

The use of the mode of conversion gives shape and meaning to the regenerative and transformational possibilities, according to Pinn. The use of conversion within Pinn's work gestures an ethic of liberation (whether configured as *future* hope or *actual* apprehension)—a renewed self. McCutcheon would caution here that "there can be no release from the historical,"[26] and as such, skepticism is warranted towards grammar that suggests otherwise. While certainly subjects struggle and survive under conditions of historical constraint, using the mode of religion or theological accounts of conversion to signal meaningful changes in the self, or possibilities of getting beyond such limitations, is indecipherable from a hermeneutical vantage point. In the work of James, among others, Pinn finds a way to explicate conversion as a "mode" of CS.

William James was no stranger to the *sui generis* trend that still dominates the academic study of religion today. Writing over a hundred years ago, James put forward that "any object that is infinitely important to us and awakens our devotion feels to us as if it must be *sui generis* and unique,"[27] and the subtitle of his work bears the trace of this tradition (e.g., Study in Human Nature). He figures the exploration of "religious experiences" as an investigation into "human nature"—the telltale rub of human consciousness. Along the same lines as Long's ideation of religion, James writes, "Religion, therefore, as I now ask you arbitrarily to take it, shall mean for us *the feelings, acts, and experiences of individual men in their solitude, so far as they apprehend themselves to stand in relation to whatever they may consider the divine.*"[28] Here we can see the *traces* of the "private affair" tradition of religious studies. The intellectual inheritance (of religion) traced into CS works within the phenomenological frame and places emphasis on the quest for religion as "impulse" and "feeling." Further, in Lectures IV and V of *Varieties* (1902), James refers to "the religion of the healthy-mindedness," asking, "What is human life's chief concern? One of the answers we should receive would be: 'It is happiness.'"[29] Against this configuration, James differentiates between what he calls "the religion of the healthy-mindedness and the sin sick soul."[30] Between the polarities of morality and deficiency, James writes that the "divided self" assists in acquainting "us in a general way with the phenomenon technically called 'Conversion.'"[31] James goes on to describe conversion in the following manner:

> To be converted, to be regenerated, to receive grace, to experience religion, to gain assurance, are so many phrases which denote the process, gradual or sudden, by which a self hitherto divided, and consciously wrong inferior and unhappy, becomes unified and consciously right superior and happy, in consequence of its firmer hold upon religious realities. This is at least what conversion signifies in general terms, whether or not we believe that a direct divine operation is needed to bring such a moral change about.[32]

James suggests that conversion is a process that occurs on the *inside* of the subject, thus altering consciousness and leading to something more positive (e.g., moral, inherently meaningful) in human nature. James understands consciousness to be *"the habitual centre of his personal energy"*[33] (similar language is used by Pinn), continuing: "To say a man is 'converted' means, in these terms, that religious ideas, previously peripheral in his consciousness, now take a central place, and that religious aims form the habitual centre of his energy."[34] Thus, it is the "divided soul" that becomes the candidate for conversion in James's work, where the "sick soul" undergoes conversion as a curative of its pathologies—a process resulting in what James refers to as the "twice born" soul. It has been argued that phenomenology, more specifically the existential philosophical strand, has been greatly influenced by James's emphasis on the structure of lived experience in general. One is not hard pressed to see the moralizing efforts of religion in James, evidenced in competing differentiations such as healthy and sick souls. This conflation collapses the experience and idea of religion (vis-à-vis conversion) as holy sanitizer of all things pure, good, and whole—in other words, religion as a moral "contraceptive" against threats of evil and contamination. The emphasis placed by both Long and James on religion (or the quest for its kind) as inner, unique, and meaningful helps frame and is further traced in Pinn's construction of CS. These traces constrain the kind of flexibility that Pinn has in mind for the movement of CS—again, the intellectual inheritances within CS often constrain and arrest it within a particular genealogy of the academic study of religion. In other words, the inheritance of Long and James (among others) must be interrogated given their central placement within Pinn's ideation of the religious. The inherited grammar of how the work of these interlocutors gives shape to CS in a manner unintended by Pinn himself deserves critical attention.

HIP HOP AND COMPLEX SUBJECTIVITY:
A QUEST FOR MEANING?

The unintended *traces* of CS's inheritances become more apparent in the 2009 special issue of *Culture & Religion* journal on "Hip Hop and Religion" co-edited by Pinn and myself. This special issue attempts to engage the religious density and complexity of Hip-Hop culture by using *complex subjectivity* as a guiding theory of religion. The issue shows the manner in which CS bears the *sui generis traces* of James, Long, and here, the explicit use of Paul Tillich. In the special issue, the sensibilities of Hip-Hop culture become understood as a "quest for meaning"; again, the (erroneous) emphasis on meaning figures prominently. Building from Long's Tillichian framing, the interplay between religion and culture is advanced, most especially when Pinn and Miller (again to switch to the third person) write that "culture is the form of religion."[35] Moreover, they argue that Tillich's conceptualization provides a way to understand religion as "orientation" towards those things considered "ultimate," usually couched within existential sensibilities. The use of the existential *as* religious is a discernable disposition also inherited by Long, who argues that religion is not a thought structure, rather, that it provides "experience, expressions, motivations, intentions, behaviors, styles and rhythms."[36] So conceived, culture becomes understood as the "stuff" from which meaning is made and apprehended—or in their language, "the 'housing' of our ultimate orientation."[37]

The authors attempt to broaden the understanding of religion configured as CS to account for the religious density and polysemy in Hip-Hop culture: "While some articles in this special issue make use of a Christian or Islamic orientation as the framework of analysis, the guiding theoretical arrangement points to a more expansive understanding of the nature and meaning of religion."[38] With such framing in place, here the religious exploration of Hip-Hop culture becomes figured as a quest for meaning. The theoretical underpinnings of CS attempt to account for a wide range of religious sensibilities in Hip-Hop culture as religious commitments. The "quest for meaning" motif (quest for meaning figured *as* religious) leaves the concept of religion vulnerable to inward, innate, and moral *feeling*, rather than taxanomical category. Understood in this way, religion is constructed as that which houses the *experience* of meaning, something purely affirmative which mitigates non-meaning, chaos, and the existentially absurd. Moreover, the Tillichian *traces* (and conflation) of religion *as culture* relativizes things assumed to hold a signification of "ultimate" as religious by nature. Positioning religion as a mode which secures meaning and escape from the existentially absurd overstretches its ability beyond social formation and human activity. The emphasis on meaning, lived coherence, and intelligibility privileges the realm of religion as that which provides transformation.

The redescribing of the religious in Hip-Hop culture cannot begin without first rethinking and de-privileging the inward turn of the category of religion. A new grammar and positionality is necessitated in order to turn from the causal *why* people are religious toward a critical consideration of the social processes and effects of its uses. McCutcheon says it best when he writes, "Simply put, I have no interest in what religion *really* is . . . instead, my interest has everything to do with *how* (i.e., description) and *why* (i.e., explanation) human communities divide up, classify, and ontologize their *ad hoc* social worlds in particular ways."[39] Persuaded by these suggestions, I propose a turn towards evaluating religious uses in Hip-Hop culture as effects of larger social, political, cultural, and economic processes, rather than the culmination of a shared uncaused underlying essence (→ inner impulse → elemental feeling → religious manifestation). While the special issue on "Hip Hop and Religion" attempted to highlight the robust constructions of meaning-making evidenced in cultural production, the essays in the journal transgressed the searching for meaning *as* religious motif. Certainly, shared ideas of the world are constructed in and through the exteriorizations of practices; however, we must utilize grammar that explicates meaning as something constructed on the exterior, rather than separating thought and action—considering thought as that which motivates action. The latter of these approaches doesn't account for unconscious and unexamined commitments that subjects often retain.

The "Hip Hop and Religion" special issue gave little consideration to what the manufacturing of religion in Hip-Hop culture accomplishes—and further, what structuring conditions structure such practices in the first place. In other words, it is necessary now to get beyond proving the manner in which Hip-Hop culture is or isn't religious (by using the construct of meaning as "proof" for verifying Hip Hop as a candidate for religious baptism), to give consideration to what poaching religious signifiers in Hip Hop does for localized cultural work. Does it provide a particular kind of capital, power, weight, or authenticity? It cannot be "proven" that the subjects making use of the religious do so in a fully conscious manner, which is why it defeats the purpose of such analysis to explain the underlying motivation of *why* subjects choose to be religious in the world, rather than examining the *effects* of such uses. The latter would guard against privileging the religious and invariably keeping religion within an arrested development of "presence" and "meaning." Future analysis must abandon endless hermeneuticist encoding and decoding, and turn its eye upon itself in a critical re-visioning. Redefining the public role of religion calls for a redefinition of the very category itself.

McCutcheon argues that the undefended assumption of religion as private affair will not suffice, asserting that the idea of a common inner experience (called religion) shared among people *qua Homo Religioso* is an indefensible universalization grounding a phenomenological approach to investigation.[40] Here, the necessity for the existential, phenomenological, and hermeneutical obsession with quests for meaning fades once the formulation of religion *as* the quest for "meaning" and "presence" is suspended as an unobtainable task.

In form, CS has much to offer, although its contributions are currently constrained in and through its intellectual inheritance. Despite some of its problematic formulations such as *inner impulse* and *elemental feeling*, I commend CS for beginning with an examination of historical effects of structures on subjectivity itself (e.g., fixity and constraint). The problematics inherent in CS bear the mark and disciplinary constraints of its intellectual traces. With that said, a change in grammar grounded in a range of intellectual traditions is necessitated if this theory of religion is to live up to its commitments as being located within human activity. How could the form of these ideas be rethought or redescribed in a way that remains faithful to the academic study of religion as human activity and social process?

CS as developed in *Terror and Triumph* bears an interesting tension between historical structures and existential subjectivity, in a way that becomes counterproductive and contradictory. The development of CS coincides with what Pinn charts in part one of his book as "Construction of Terror," practices of racial exclusion and marginalization such as lynching and slave auctions. It is in these practices, Pinn argues, that the enslaved black body becomes fixed as an "object." In the second part of the text ("Waging War"), Pinn considers responses to these dehumanizing processes: that is, how slaves "waged war" on the fixation, gaze, and violence of slavery. Here, the production of black religiosities is figured as "responses" to the crisis of fixity and terror, "archeologically" charting the Black Church and Nation of Islam as two examples among others. Among these institutional manifestations, along with modalities such as art, folklore, and literature, Pinn sites the pulse of what he calls "perpetual rebellion." This activity includes using raw materials and embodied sensibilities guided by a norm of liberation as a practice of fighting back. Finally, this leads Pinn to the third part of his construction, "Seeking Triumph," where he defines religion—more specifically black religion—as religious experience and the transformation of consciousness. Here, black religion is configured as a response to the historical trappings of terror as demonstrated in the first part of the book (the outward practices of social exclusion). He then, as others have critiqued, takes an unexpected existential turn from seeing religion as human response born out of historical trappings to analyzing interiorized motivations for seeking greater life-meaning understood as religious. This unexpectedness leaves CS wedged between historicity and existential subjectivity. In this triadic formula, one experiences crisis→ creates desire and push for agency→ resulting in pursuit of greater life-meaning→ hopes/experiences of transformation. This is representative of a thought structure caught in the irreconcilable interstices of crisis and liberation, despite Pinn's public admission that liberation remains in the temporality of the "to come" rather than an actual experience. Others have noted similar tension within Pinn's work:

> His talk of religion as an "inner impulse" sounds like an ahistorical essence, like the "souls of black folks," so to speak. The inner impulse is manifested in historical-sociological ways. I am not sure that the author has resolved this ambiguity in his own thinking. He vacillates between subjectivity as an artifact of historical-social-practical life. . . . and as historical-social-practical life as an artifact of an underlying subjectivity. Here we encounter a conflict between his inchoate pragmatism and his dominant existentialism.[41]

Moreover, fashioning a universal concept of religion based on "unique" experiences of racial minorities (who are assumed to all experience terror) not only racially essentializes "black religion" but also collapses religious differences into sameness. Moreover, this formulation keeps religion vulnerable to moral transformation. That is to say, fashioning the idea of religion as part of the "response" to "terror" continues in the disciplinary moralizing of religion as curative and salvific. Wedging concepts between polar opposites (terror and triumph) conceptually arrests religion in a formulaic manner—assuming one has access to *why* people turn to religion (e.g., a shared underlying motivation). This thought structure presumes that there is a "nature" to religion that can be apprehended and described in subjectivity. Above all, this ideological framing of religion ignores difference and remains vulnerable to perpetuating religion through a moral economy of order and resolve based on secular existential sensibilities.

Undeniably, fixity of structures can motivate subjects to quest for transgressive responses to their subaltern position. We are reminded that fixity, and humans' quest against it, end up reproducing structuring structures of different kinds. In other words, religion is not always seen as the curative salve, and to romanticize it as such is both nostalgic and ineffective. It's often the case that religion and the experiences of religion are the *effect* of fixity, not liberation from constrained life options. These are complex processes not always of our own choosing. We know "existential insecurity" to be one of the primary "religion-making" characteristics in modernity. In his essay "Existential Insecurity and New Religiosity: An Essay on Some Religion-Making Characteristics of Modernity" (2008), Anton van Harskamp asks, "Why do existential insecurities facilitate new religiosity?"[42] He argues that experiences such as evil "can provoke feelings of real existential insecurity, in the form of the so-called free-floating existential angst." This hypothesis can be seen within the construction of CS, most poignantly in how the quest for meaning emerges from the fight against historical terror and fixity. Understood in this way, the loss or threat to identity becomes a religion-making angst. The quest for religion is used as a way to regain that which has been lost, becoming a way by which identity is regained, apprehended, and (re)presented. Religion is thus situated within a realm of solution, cure, and response, and as an experience that struggles against "risk" and limitation. This logic leaves religion heuristically vulnerable to a formulaic hypothesis of loss→crisis→transformation.

I have suggested that the form of CS becomes constrained by its sources and intellectual inheritance. Accordingly, the next section attempts to rethink three problematics within CS through postmodern thought, more specifically the ideas of *play* (Jacques Derrida), *habitus* (Pierre Bourdieu), and *social formation/construction* (Russell T. McCutcheon and James A. Beckford), as an attempt to advance its form through an alternative rendering. A rethinking of each problematic through new sources and intellectual positionalities (beyond the tradition of Long, James, and Tillich) will assist in analyzing religion as human activity. I employ Derrida's concept of *play* to rethink emphasis on the "center" of consciousness, Bourdieu's *habitus* to rethink historical fixity as *effect* rather than *cause*, and lastly, I use McCutcheon and Beckford's *social formation/social process* to rethink religion's *sui generis* grounding.

DERRIDIAN PLAY AND PINN'S CENTER OF CONSCIOUSNESS

In the first section of this chapter, I argued that Pinn's articulation of CS bears the *trace* of its intellectual inheritance of the phenomenological and *sui generis* tradition inherited through modernist interlocutors of religion—James, Long, and even Tillich. Moreover, I argued that CS's over-reliance upon meaning assumes consciousness and intentionality on behalf of the subject. Thus, the quest for meaning becomes figured as a religious endeavor—motivated by an underlying impulse whose origins are un-articulated. I have suggested already that an over-emphasis on meaning not only assumes consciousness and presence, but likewise, collapses religion as an experience that is above all inherently meaningful, affirmative, and transformative. A focus on meaning is not necessarily what is at stake here;

rather, the *interiorization* of meaning and the *assumption* of meaning as the "actual" appearance of things provoked by inner essences and impulses grounded in intentionality need critical probing. A new grammar and intellectual inheritance are necessitated.

Phenomenological discourse places emphasis on the affective (emotions, feelings, etc.), and on the immediacy of experience, essence, and consciousness—things Derrida referred to as "grand transcendental illusions" grounded within and supported by a metaphysical frame (e.g., science of presence). Through the practice of deconstruction Derrida attempts to disrupt bifurcations and dualisms—problematics produced by metaphysics itself. Here, I re-read the first problematic of CS (center and consciousness) through Derrida's idea of *play*. This concept is applied to the problem of the center, what Pinn sometimes refers to as consciousness. This is the first step in "outing" the inside of the closet of subjectivity. Again, my approach is one of *faithful unfaithfulness*, described by Derrida as a way to affirm yet recast the heritage otherwise so that it can live. Derrida asks, "What does it mean to reaffirm? It means not simply accepting this heritage but relaunching it otherwise and keeping it alive."[43] He continues by arguing that one keeps a particular heritage alive, and avoids its putting to death, through the process of *reaffirmation*.

Derrida's 1966 Johns Hopkins University lecture "Structure, Sign and Play in the Discourse of the Human Sciences" became a destabilizing moment in interrogating the structuralist hegemony on stability and cogency of meaning. Derrida accomplishes this by decentering the center of the structure to allow for more room, flexibility, and play within structures themselves. In this lecture, Derrida gestures towards the instability and undecidability of signs—hence, why meaning can never be coherent and stable, but rather is theorized as infinite *play* of signification. Ultimately, there is a crisis of meaning at stake, for "the notion of a structure lacking any center represents the unthinkable itself."[44]

The center is never *really* the center. Emphasis placed on the new self becoming the "center of consciousnesses" in CS needs a new articulation. Reformulating via Derrida's decentering of the center through *play* allows the acknowledgment that there is in fact no center, no essence of consciousness itself. The "center" in Pinn's formulation of CS is consciousness—or put another way, intentionality based on a triadic structure (confrontation, wrestle, and embrace) as three actions that seemingly require and assume full intentionality on behalf of the subject. This triadic structure seemingly assumes a coherence towards a new self, but Derrida reminds us that "as always, coherence in contradiction expresses the force of a desire."[45] The idea of any center must be disrupted. Furthermore, the center masquerades as a signifier of presence itself, which gives the appearance of meaning. On this point Derrida writes, "It could be shown that all names related to fundamentals, to principles, or to the center have always designated an invariable presence . . . transcendentality, consciousness, God, man and so forth."[46] The absence of the center, the sign, the transcendental signified (however conceived), opens up space for *play* to be possible and to occur, both at once.

Without a center or triadic structure in place, the problem of "meaning" in CS can now be probed. As previously suggested, the articulation of CS relies upon the notion of intentionality. Given this problematic, the subject must be freed up from the expectations of intentionality—for apprehending pure consciousness or intentionality is impossible. In Pinn's articulation, the subject realizes the constraints of historical "fixity" which awakens something on the inside of subjectivity (inner impulse) thus causing movement through the triadic structure. But one is left wondering exactly how to account for such intentionality of consciousness, having to question why some people realize such fixity and others don't (and if they don't, how do we know?). Stated another way, are we ever (or always) fully aware of impinging structuring structures upon our own subjectivities? Can't it be suggested that the way we deal with fixation often entails a reproduction of the very inequality we recognize? Is not black religion, for example, an *effect* of such constraint, not always offering the kind of "triumph" Pinn assumes? Does it not become just another structuring structure of fixity for certain subjectivities who are "fixed" by its symbolic violence? One is left to believe that such reawakening in fact just occurs—that is, the underlying motivation is assumed to be self-evident. Unable to account for origins of this spontaneous motivation (e.g., is it cognitive, essence, psychical?), one is further confused by the situating of *inner impulse* and *elemental feeling* within the realm of consciousness. In order to rethink this type of phenomenological framing, its movement must first be acknowledged *not* as fueled by consciousness and intentionality, but rather, as *play* freed from the expectation that it accomplishes or holds within it some sort of ephemeral transformative potentiality and possibility. Derrida writes, "The absence of the transcendental signified extends the domain and the play of signification infinitely." He makes clear that the concept of *play* transgresses presence:

> Play is the disruption of presence. The presence of an element is always a signifying and substitutive reference inscribed in a system of differences and the movement of a chain. Play is always play of absence and presence, but if it is to be thought radically, play must be conceived of before the alternative of presence and absence. Being must be conceived of as presence or absence on the basis of the possibility of play and not the other way around.[47]

With the absence of a center and affirmation of *play* as that which disrupts presence and immediacy, we can rethink CS defined not by a center of consciousness but rather by the spontaneity of *play* whose future movement cannot be anticipated—rather, it remains in the temporality of the "to come." A triadic structure (the anticipation of movement) must be destroyed, if signification is to have infinite possibility; its "structure" mustn't be assumed beforehand, there is no totalizing intentionality (that such consciousness assumes), there can only be an element of undecidability with a polysemy of uses and functions. We often think of "a center" as that which binds together, the focal point of organization and activity. Derrida reminds us that the notion of the center undoubtedly means the absence of both *play* and *difference*, the absence of both the movement and the articulation that *play* provides.

RELIGIOUS HABITUS: BOURDIEU

What in fact shapes the types of social behavior that come to be described as religious? Any theoretical construction is vulnerable to relativism, universalization, and over-generalization when trying to account for such an expansive historical explanation of religious activity and motivation. As such, generalizations must have ability to hold in tension cultural particularities and differences. The construction of CS, as a theory of black religion, pays close attention to the historical "terror" forced upon black bodies— thus understanding the creative responses and movement by blacks in the Diaspora as a movement for greater life-meaning, some of which expresses itself as religious. I argued elsewhere that CS, described as a *response* to terror on behalf of the fixed black body, reflects a rather causal formula. The interiorized *inner impulse* and *elemental feeling* are explicated as the progenitor for movement towards greater life-meaning. In the process as developed in *Terror and Triumph*, however, it is assumed that these underlying motivations are fully conscious and give rise to activity itself.

These concepts need to be rethought in a way that binds together historical fixity and subjective agency with more cogency. Moreover, the effects of historical fixity and inequality must be rethought in a less causal manner than assuming that historical fixity upon subjects causes/motivates a quest for presence and meaning figured as religious. It is often the case that religion is the *effect* of social reproduction and inequality. That said, uses and practices of religion must be studied as such, rather than as manifestations of well thought-out intentions and motivations to subvert fixity itself. Although Pinn pays special attention to "racial" terror, the production of terror for marginalized group members continues in many forms.

The analyses of religious uses and activity cannot be fully dependent upon, nor assume, the subject's inner motivations. It is necessary to stay aware of structures and historical trappings, while granting agency to the subject in a way that doesn't separate thought and action. I propose turning to Bourdieu's concept of the *habitus* as a way to account for social reproduction without limiting the manifestation of practices as *response* to social inequality and constraint. Here, I want to rethink the concepts *inner impulse* and *elemental feeling* in light of Bourdieu's *habitus* (practice theory), which binds together social reproduction/inequality, agency, and structuring structures. In other words, binding the objective and subjective, Bourdieu's *habitus* allows one to account for the exteriorizations of social inequality (in practices) in a way that brings together thought and action. Comparatively speaking, while the *inner impulse* ignites movement within CS, questions remain about what it comprises, its point of origin, and so on. Similar problematics exist with a term such as "the sacred," which becomes impossible to explicate when described as an "inner feeling" or object of devotion that motivates certain practices. As theorized by Bourdieu, the exteriorizations of the *habitus* (in practices) retain a particular logic—yet remain, for the most part, unexamined by subjects themselves. Here, rethinking the location of consciousness and intentionality is vital.

Against frames of phenomenology and existentialism, the work of Bourdieu becomes extremely useful in clarifying the relationship between structure, agency, and subjectivity. The concept of the *habitus* makes room to account for social inequality as evidenced in cultural practices without the expectation of claims to full intentionality and consciousness. In *Outline of a Theory of Practice* (1977) Bourdieu develops a theory of practice accounting for both "incorporation" and "objectification" through the concept of the *habitus*—exteriorizations mirroring the effects of structures that are not fully determined to the conditions of its production. He further defines *habitus* as a system of "durable, transposable *dispositions*, structured structures predisposed to function as structuring structures, that is, as principles of the generating and structuring practices and representations which can be objectively 'regulated' and 'regular' without in any way being the product of obedience to rules."[48] As such, the *habitus* becomes a logical move away from intentionality-based arguments when theorizing the religious. Configuring religion as "quest for life-meaning" based on underlying motivations assumes total intentionality on behalf of the subject so conceived. *Habitus* allows room for historical inequality (in structures) expressed in and through practices, which mindlessly pick up and carry forward inheritances of all sorts. And thus: "It is because subjects do not, strictly speaking, know what they are doing that what they do has more meaning than they know."[49]

Key here is advocating for "transcending subjective intentions and conscious projects whether individual or collective,"[50] in order to get beyond intellectual projects grounded in, framed as, or oriented towards subjective intentionality. Understood in this way, exploring religious uses cannot only be figured as pure intentional "response" to terror and fixity, but rather, as products of durable inequalities tethered to structuring structures. The latter figures religious uses not as the solution, but also part of the reproduction and inheritances of inequality itself. Thus, the externalizations of practices offer a window beyond subjective quests for meaning, to consider complex dimensions of social reproduction, inherited externalized dispositions, and lived reality. To use Bourdieu's language, there is no "truth" within interaction and practice, no isolatable presence. It is for this reason that the execution of hermeneutical projects grounded in "meaning" and "coherence" is never quite successful nor fully plausible. The search for meaning and interpretation in practices themselves assumes an explicit intelligibility to what is in reality an inherent "taken for grantedness" on the part of subjects. Intentionality is not the archaic locus or "origin" of such practices. This is similar to what Antonio Gramsci calls *common sense*—the taken for granted, unquestioned, and unexamined assumptions evidenced in dispositions, taste, and practices generally understood to be natural or innate on the part of the subject.

Thus, exteriorization of the *habitus* becomes evident in cultural markers; however, Bourdieu reminds us that dispositions are always and at once multiple and able to change over time. Durable dispositions exposing stratification and social reproduction are thus understood through what Bourdieu refers to as *taste* and *distinction*. He writes, "Taste classifies, and it classifies the classifier"[51]; it is these structured "choices" which create the appearance of cohesion and coherence in what is, in reality, not of one's own choosing. Rather, choices evidenced in practices (taste) become, in part, the effects of durable dispositions.

Bourdieu's explication of the *habitus* accounts for power relations and social reproduction (expressed in cultural practices, choices, and worldviews), while providing a way to think about how historical inequality becomes inculcated in social behavior (providing a "logic of practice"). Again, mythical illusions of full consciousness and intentionality (in such practices) naively ignore the taken-for-grantedness and unintelligibility so often contained within the reproduction and maintenance of social inequality itself. Rather than focusing on explicit intentions (which denies a structuring structure of such choices) and mythical forms of liberation (religion as inherently meaningful), it is necessary to dig deeper into the invisible dimensions operating, structuring, and grounding particular actions and practices in culture more generally.

In Bourdieu, there exists a middle-ground between subjectivity and objectivity. More fully, between binding thought structures that assume agents to be radically free and able to make the world what it is that they fully desire (Sartrian existentialism and phenomenology more generally) and objectivism that appears to account for structuring structures to the point of excluding agency on behalf of the subject. Between these polar opposites, Bourdieu carves out a third way to understand social life and behavior. Here, practices are both constituted and yet constituting— not completely lodged in the ontological individualism of phenomenology yet not completely determined by relations of production. Cultural practices require a much more complicated stance, and one that must be maintained neither mystifying nor projecting coherence onto their complex dimensions.

Returning to the category of religion, Bourdieu provides a way to think about practices that come to be understood as religious. No longer beholden to causality, attention can now be redirected towards the kinds of effects produced and witnessed within cultural activity. Moreover, intentionality no longer becomes paramount, and what remain in view are the *traces* of historical inequality manifested in cultural practices as moments and possibilities of agency and change across various *fields* of interaction.

"CRITICS NOT CARETAKERS": RELIGION AS NON-UNIQUE SOCIAL FORMATION AND CONSTRUCTION

I have been suggesting a rethinking of notions of the center, over-emphasis on consciousness, presence, and meaning. Here, I focus on rethinking the last crucial element of CS—a privileging of the category of religion and religious experience, in other words its *sui generis* grounding. This third rethinking is crucial. It pertains to a disciplinary redefining of the academic study of religion in order to critically analyze religion's uses, functions, and negotiations in material cultural practices. Historically, scholars of religion have often classified the religious as a unique and independent experience, irreducibly different from and "other" than all other experiences of life. Anthropologist Malory Nye writes, "The uniqueness is what is referred to as the '*sui generis*' approach, that religion is a distinct element of human activity, that can be explained in solely human terms."[52] This stance has been more recently debated by scholars such as Russell T. McCutcheon. Taking a "genealogical" perspective, anthropologist of religion Talal Asad in *Genealogies of Religion: Disciplines and Reasons of Power in Christianity and Islam* (1993) forcefully argues that the concept of religion is always and at once the product of not only particular cultural and historical contexts but also, disciplinary imperialism. I have suggested that conceiving religion phenomenologically as unique and grounded in experience has limited and constrained the religious/theological studies analysis of Hip-Hop culture. Although the *sui generis* position continues to dominate the field of black religion, it becomes necessary more than ever to rethink ideas of religion using social theory. More recently, scholars have begun to take a different approach to the category of religion, in an attempt to become what McCutcheon calls better "critics" and not "caretakers" of the academic study of religion.

Influenced by scholars such as Michel Foucault, Jonathan Z. Smith Bruce Lincoln, and Noam Chomsky, McCutcheon has become one of the leading critics of the *sui generis* approach. In *Manufacturing Religion: The Discourse on Sui Generis Religion and the Politics of Nostalgia* (1997), McCutcheon suggests rethinking religion *not* as a category of unique inner and inward experience, but rather, as a manufactured conceptual tool and heuristic.[53] In other words, in a Foucauldian manner, McCutcheon understands the concept of religion to be discursive and "manufactured," and for pragmatic as well as intellectual purposes. He suggests that when religion is conceived of as "essential," "personal," and "unique" the category is foreclosed from critical examination—a discursive and political strategy that he argues is employed by scholars of religion to maintain the persistence of religion. The religious making of CS is grounded in interior essence, affective stirrings, and inner impulses which overgeneralize religion and deemphasize the "difference" characterizable by the multiplicity of actions within the black experience. In this sense, religion becomes a "private affair." In Pinn's formulation, the *inner impulse* and *elemental feeling* appear to be self-evident while religion's outer manifestations become the expressions (or response) of unique interior workings. These interiorized irreducible feelings are no different than the ways other words, such as the sacred, are understood.

Moreover, McCutcheon argues that *sui generis* approaches to the category of religion are representative of the field's dominant approach and disposition, from the work of Schleiermacher and Otto to Tillich, and that they isolate within subjectivity what otherwise might be seen to be in the realm of the public, the social. In other words, McCutcheon is made anxious by the widely used phenomenological method that dominates religious studies today. This method, in part, presupposes a shared "common essence" or impulse on behalf of subjects, and such affective sensibilities are assumed as self-evident. Citing Smith's use of Friedrich Nietzsche, McCutcheon argues that what we see evidenced in religious studies is a belief in the "myth of immaculate perception" solidified by "uncontestable" categories such as experience. It is this kind of privileging that entitles behaviors and actions *as* religious, thus obscuring the reality that there is nothing inherently religious about the manifestations under analysis, rather, they are actions and practices that come to be understood *as* religious by scholars and subjects themselves. McCutcheon writes that a *sui generis* stance grants weight and value not only to the abstraction of religion itself but to those persons who use the frame of religion to explain themselves and their actions. Privileging the interior and private (realms of subjectivity) creates the illusion of "essence" and invariably is grounded in the "ahistorical," and this framing allows religion to operate as distinct and autonomous. Charting the movement of CS within the realm of consciousness, inner impulse, and elemental feeling assumes the scholar of religion has access to the "nature and meaning" of subjects' consciousness. There is a particular kind of privileging at work here in this thought structure—and yet, questions remain, such as how exactly does the scholar discriminate certain feelings as giving rise to the religious? Why are certain bodies tuned in to such underlying impulses and elemental feelings? What exactly stirs up such feelings within individuals themselves? Because this underlying motivation is interiorized and appears to be ahistorical, there seems to be an invisible hand at work here. There is a type of "social privilege" at work. Rather than focusing on how historical terror produces and awakens an inner feeling within subjects that motivates a quest for the religious, perhaps we need to consider "how these ideas are related to, originate from, and lead to changes in the historical context in which human action takes place."[54] There is within the discourse on *sui generis* religion a characterizable yearning for origins made possible through the (re)activation of inner essences and feelings that work to recover or retrieve what has been historically lost. This positionality is evident in the formulation of CS—a yearning for the way something was (prior to "crisis" and "fixity"). There is, grounded in this discourse, a romanticizing of meaning and of consciousness, and a nostalgic mourning for origins.

Claims to uniqueness don't hold; they do however represent a type of scholarship, according to McCutcheon, represented by the traditions of Immanuel Kant, Rudolf Otto, Mircea Eliade, William James, and Paul Tillich, among others. These figures, in various ways, express a desire for understanding religion as obscure, hidden, and concealed yet made manifest in religious experience. They all share a purchase on the personalized and unique dimensions of the "nature" of religion—an idealistic desire and *a priori* illusion (there is nothing innate about religion). I am convinced that the "private affair" trend does little for the academic study of religion in culture. I propose a critical probing into terms such as *inner impulse* and *elemental feeling* by situating their form within a more critical theoretical discourse. Building on and borrowing from scholars such as McCutcheon and Beckford, I advocate for a social construction and understanding of the category of religion when analyzing Hip-Hop culture. With a focus on "social organizations," a social formation approach considers how practices and actions are maintained, contested, shared, manufactured, and negotiated. Such an approach loses the category of religion *per se* as a valuable construct; or at least, as a privileged one. Instead, those aspects and effects of social organization which have traditionally been granted religious status, and therefore fixed, are freed up to exist in their own right, leaving much more room for the sort of play I am advocating.

While religion may in fact provide a kind of anthropological salve for anxiety-produced feelings of insecurity, terror, fear, and the like, it is human 'doing' that comes to be understood or classified as religious experiences and practices. To situate and ground the category of religion as emerging from (what seems to be ahistorical) private and inner comportments makes it difficult to understand religion as social process in the outer world. It is more productive, as Beckford argues, to understand religion as a social construction rather than relying upon mystical definitions (e.g., similar to other social constructions in the world such as race and gender). Employing a social constructionist perspective to religion signifies that religion-making (or making that comes to be understood and classified by scholars as religious) is purely a human doing, *sans* essences. This perspective allows, as Beckford asserts, for the many ways in which "the meaning of the category of religion, is in various situations, intuited, asserted, doubted, challenged, rejected, substituted, re-cast and so on."[55] This perspective makes room for reflection on the doing of religion across various social contexts rather than being understood as a unitary phenomenon. Religion becomes a variable and contested process, and what exactly gets to "count" as religious is never fully agreed upon. There is no "transhistorical essence" to religion (as argued by Asad in *Genealogies of Religion*) and neither is it, as Beckford argues, a homogenous phenomenon.[56] There is an element of homogenization at work in CS in Pinn's construction of a generalizable theory of black religion that doesn't take into account other social-group differences within black communities. Instead, he classifies the many (institutional and non-institutional) manifestations of black religion as resulting from one larger movement (underlying impulse) that grounds these experiences of CS. It is this sort of privatized grand-narrative deployment of religion that folks such as McCutcheon see as confusing the study of religious essence, with the academic study of religion in general.

A social construction/formation approach to the category of religion takes a postmodern positionality, pushing beyond the "anthropological necessity" narratives that rely upon a phenomenology to account for the creation of meaning understood as, or through, the religious.

POSTMODERN COMPLEX SUBJECTIVITY

And so, back to the redescription of CS. In this chapter I have taken a theoretical assemblage approach that is primarily deconstructive in nature. With its starting point in subjectivity and human activity, CS is one of the few theories of religion that take seriously the historical experience of African Americans and their cultural productions as archeological artifacts. I have suggested throughout that there appears to be an *unintended* problematic within the thought structure caused by intellectual *traces* of modernist inheritances derived from its reliance upon the phenomenological tradition. This inheritance results in relying on interiorized affective feelings as behaviors that give rise to religious activity. In doing so, intentionality and consciousness are assumed, and a complicated tension between existential subjectivity and historical structures emerges as irreconcilable. Although Pinn is clear that religion is, above all, human activity, his formulation of *inner impulse* and *elemental feeling* make religious activity beholden to unexplainable privileged affective sensibilities, leaving questions about origins, location, and relationship to structuring structures unanswered. I have tried, with a theoretical assemblage of sorts, to read the problematics of CS through various positionalities. This deconstructive work is not suggesting a jettison of CS; rather, it is meant to create dialogue around reformulating the construction of CS in the service of examining cultural practices by suggesting a more forceful retheorizing of the "religious" in black religion. As a beginning of such probing, I have suggested as a first step rethinking the following problematics: (1) an erroneous focus on center of consciousness and intentionality, (2) collapsing the quest for meaning as giving rise to the religious, (3) redescription of what appear to be self-evident, uncaused, and ahistorical concepts of *inner impulse* and *elemental feeling*, and (4) a more complicated stance towards its inheritance of *sui generis* phenomenological sources which privilege the category of experience.

Above all, I suggest more engagement with postmodern and social theory to rethink the grammar and location of the religious. I have tried, in this chapter, to engage works that suggest critical examination of both religious *effects* and *causes* situated in human activity. McCutcheon reminds us that focusing on non-empirical "religious impulses" and "religious expressions" is indicative of a larger problem in the academic study of religion: assuming some sort of "common essence" that can be sought through examining phenomenologically the (secondary) religious expressions that manifest it—and, conversely, assuming these manifestations to have origins other than those that may be approached via historical and cultural rationales.

A new posture is therefore necessitated within African-American religious thought regarding what is "religious" about "black religion." Such work requires not a doing away with, but rather a redescription of the religious by shift in posture. It is my hope that this chapter opens critical dialogue in the field of African-American religious studies whereby a robust conversation regarding the formation of the religious in such work can take place. In this chapter, I have tried to rethink not the form of CS but rather its unexamined intellectual inheritances and positionality towards the religious by using postmodern thought and approaches. The articulation of CS, by form, is a plausible way into the life-worlds and contexts of many cultural practices; however, we must rethink its gaps and vulnerabilities so that it can live up to the what John Jackson would call the "paranoid" stylings of the postmodern condition. Beginning again, we must think it from the *inside*→out, exercising *faithful unfaithfulness* so that its contribution continues to live.

5 Youth Religiosity in America
The Empirical Landscape

This project sets out to explore the triad of Hip Hop, religion, and the demographic of youth in America, from a religious studies perspective. In the performance of this exploration it employs various lenses to see through and around these subjects individually and in relation to each other. The current chapter takes up the relationships between youth and the category of religion, as quantified through empirical studies, including my own recent examination of the changing religiosity of American youth over time. In so doing, it develops two main themes: To what extent is institutional religion still valued by youth in changing times? And in what ways has the empirical examination of youth religiosity been affected by narrowness of focus and narratives of mitigating deviance—what I have termed "buffering transgression"?

For the purposes of existing empirical studies on youth and religion, the construct of religion tends to be understood and measured as activity (such as reading scripture, praying, etc.) and involvement within institutional confines. Moreover, the subjective religiosity examined in these studies focuses on institutional religious participation with a traditional focus on belief within a Christian housing of descriptive theological markers. As such, religion in these studies is marked and measured by what is done *in* faith-based institutions, and beliefs are measured by traditional Christian ideas. While arguably useful in and of itself, this focus leaves uninterrogated the broader contexts of the lived experiences of youth, and especially the ways in which these experiences and subjective interpretations may be changing over time.

What is suggested by the empirical studies critiqued in this chapter is that institutional religious participation among youth mitigates and buffers deleterious social behaviors and crime. This narrative I refer to as a "buffering transgression" hypothesis, one which positions institutional religion as a moral disciplinarian of social ills—more on this later. While such studies point to the affirmative role of institutional religion among American youth in general, other studies have suggested that institutional religiosity is an important activity for black youth specifically. What such studies don't reveal, especially for marginalized demographics of youth, is the extent to which institutional religion upholds purchase and relevance in a changing cultural climate.

While the landscape of youth religiosity has been debated theoretically, and examined empirically, what this landscape in fact looks like—and more importantly, what it means for the shift of American religion—has yet to be critically examined among scholars.[1] Across works, a critical examination of religion and youth remains a seldom-engaged area of study. Little is known about how youth are constructing, negotiating, and making use of religion in culture.

This chapter calls into question the kinds of inferences and information empirical data provide, and what kind of privileged story of the religious is constructed and upheld. How is religion measured in such studies? What counts as religious when doing the work of social science, and what is left unexamined? In Chapters 3 and 4 I argued that granting a *sui generis* status to religion allows the category to remain largely uninterrogated, and here I want to continue the work of interrogation by holding up to examination the underlying assumptions that order and direct such works. So the movement of the argument is: seen as interior essence, religion is both taken for granted and granted a privileged status. Then, seen as bodies at risk, youth are juxtaposed against the category of religion and measured for fit. My position is that all along the line of this reasoning exist missed opportunities to apprehend and comprehend the lived realities of bodies in time and space. In his work on the study of belief in material culture, David Morgan argues that "the problem of belief qua prescription is that it reduces a religion to a body of assertions demanding assent."[2] He goes on to suggest that "rather than marginalizing belief, we need a more capacious account of it, one that looks to the embodied, material features of lived religion."[3] Those "material, embodied features of lived religion" are just the sort of stuff *Religion and Hip Hop* seeks to grapple with, coming at the subject from diverse angles and informed by layered sources and voices.

Where, then, shall we start in apprehending the experience of today's youth? Undeniably, compared to their European counterparts, American youth—sometimes by choice, perhaps constraint, or even familial obligation—are overtly characterized as religious. Youth in the U.S. affirmatively (and overwhelmingly) agree that religion, religious practice, and theological constructs such as divinity and salvation retain an importance and purchase in their lives. By contrast, it has been argued that in places such as Britain institutional religion is quickly "disappearing." Gordon Lynch writes:

> The Christian Church in Britain is going through an extraordinary period of change. The rapidly declining rates in church attendance lead some sociologists to suggest that it is entering a phase of near-terminal decline from which it is unlikely ever to recover to any significant extent.[4]

Using preexisting data, Lynch suggests that by the year 2030 mainstream Christianity in Britain could altogether disintegrate. Empirical research within the U.S. has barely begun to chart the changing face of religiosity among youth and their life-worlds in our shifting postmodern contexts. In *GenX Religion* (2000), Donald E. Miller and Arpi Misha Miller argue that "religion is still alive and well in this country,"[5] and while institutional church participation may be on a decline, this does not discount the fact that youth are producing and negotiating religion in very different ways. In the words of Miller and Miller, youth may simply be "seeking meaning and purpose while simultaneously avoiding what they perceive to be inauthentic attempts to mediate the sacred. Indeed, a new worldview is emerging, and it stands in stark contrast to the text-based, linear, rationalistic empiricism of the Enlightenment."[6] They go onto argue that what we see evidenced in the shifting religious cartography among youth is a break with Enlightenment metaphysics and teleological claims to truth. Thus, a generation which embraces difference and uncertainty, signaling a shift in knowledge production. This further shifts the shape and context of traditional belief.

Undeniably the religious terrain of American youth is varied, complex, and ever changing. Without a doubt, American youth, for the most part, participate in, engage, inherit, and make use of religion in one way or another. That is not to say such participation is always done in a confessional manner. Intergenerational familial transmission, peer effects, and effects of the internalization of traditional theological norms must all be accounted for. These are complicated problematics that require and necessitate a larger examination of the cultural and social life-worlds of youth in general. Beyond the inability of empirical studies to imagine worldviews, practices, and expressions of religiosity beyond the four walls, there lies a deeper, less explicit, and more ideological danger embedded in not only what such studies call for, but also, how the category of religion is empirically measured. As is often the case, religion becomes a variable of morality and social control that has social buffering effects. In other words, according to this trend, religious participation has the ability to produce social conformity in a dangerous and delinquent world where illicit, non-conforming social behavior (understood as teen sex and smoking), and criminal activity (soft and hard crime) are seen as factors that contribute towards decreasing life options for the affirmative advancement of adolescent development.

BUFFERING TRANSGRESSION AND THE ARRESTED DEVELOPMENT OF RELIGION

> "And now a day's things changed everyone's ashamed of the youth cuz the truth look strange"
>
> —Tupac Shakur, "Ghetto Gospel"[7]

"Such an assumption seems to ignore the central fact about deviance: it is created by society."

—Howard S. Becker[8]

In his song "Ghetto Gospel" late rapper Tupac (Pac) Shakur invokes the line quoted above, giving lyrical voice to expression of what he believes to be a moment in which youth are being socially misunderstood—a time where fears of youth are socially exaggerated and misplaced. After all, according to Pac, the "truth" of the Ghetto Gospel may vacuously be found in the strangeness of the outcast—youth themselves.

In a thematic continuation from Chapter 4, this chapter explores how the categories of religion and youth religiosity have been conceptualized in existing empirical studies on youth and religion. This exploration is important in two ways: first, it considers how the category of religion is figured in social scientific research on youth and religion—calling for an expansion of religion beyond institutional referents and participation; and secondly, it raises questions regarding the moralizing use of institutional participation as a strategy to combat what is referred to as delinquency in the literature itself. As such, this chapter calls for thinking the religious beyond institutional referents within empirical work and a critical examination of the *effects* of conflating religion within moral efficacy narratives. I refer to this conflation as "buffering transgression"—a heuristic conceptualization referring to the negative relationship (in a quantitative sense) empirically correlating institutional youth religious participation and levels of delinquent activity in everyday life. As we will see, empirical studies on youth and religion suggest that youth with higher rates of religious participation (understood institutionally) demonstrate lower levels of delinquency and crime. The problem with this construction is it collapses religious participation as activity that upholds moral and social norms (religion as technology of surveillance) by relying upon a narrow rendering of religion *as* institutional. Thought together, these problematic tendencies moralize the category of religion as a strategy to cleanse the crimes of society while denying critical attention to emergent cultural practices.

Empirical studies that perpetuate the "buffering transgression" hypothesis rely upon thin and traditional measures of "religiosity" defined by ancillary practices and institutional membership. This institutional housing is not expansive enough to embrace emergent cultural practices occurring beyond institutional spaces. One could argue that these empirical studies uphold religiosity as a notion of salvific purity that maintains its purifying transformative powers ("buffering mechanism") in and through the "difference" constructed upon and through categorical deviance. Moreover, these studies promote religious participation in faith institutions as strategy for social control. Often left unexamined are the symbolically violent effects that such institutions have on youth social group differences (such as gender and sexuality). Moreover, such hypotheses politically support the use of dominant institutions as quelling technologies and mechanisms of social control in processes of behavior modification. This chapter reads *how* religion is understood in empirical studies on youth and religion through a descriptive look at the work of two existing empirical studies. Here I offer attention to *how* religion is understood conceptually/empirically—and to what ends?

This chapter begins by engaging one of the largest data sets on youth and religion within the United States by considering the work of sociologist of religion Christian Smith. His empirical work emerging from the National Study of Youth and Religion (NSYR) employs extensive qualitative and quantitative methods to model the category of religion in relationship to youth participation. After a description of his findings, I focus attention towards empirical data (including Smith's) that perpetuate the "buffering transgression" phenomenon. Throughout, I suggest that while such studies chart an institutional portrait of youth and religion broadly, they not only remain confined to institutional renderings of religion, but similarly package religious activity as disciplining what is seen as "deviant" activity.

CHRISTIAN SMITH AND THE NATIONAL STUDY OF YOUTH AND RELIGION: AN OVERVIEW OF QUANTITATIVE LITERATURE

Principal investigator for probably the largest national sample on U.S. youth and religion, the NSYR, Christian Smith along with a number of colleagues sociologically considers the shape and influence of religiosity and spirituality among American youth. He empirically examines the texture, shape, and patterns of youth religiosity as a means by which to explore shifts in American religion more generally. In this sense, Smith's research is primarily an attempt to fill the void in research on youth and religion. Smith writes, "We know relatively little about the religious lives of American adolescents,"[9] continuing that "as a result, our social scientific knowledge of the religious affiliations, practices, beliefs, experiences, and attitudes of American youth is impoverished."[10]

The 2002 work of Smith, et al. makes use of preexisting data from studies such as Monitoring the Future (MTF; 1996), Survey of Adolescent Health (1995), and The Survey of Parents and Youth (1998), focusing attention on youth between the ages of 13 and 18. Based on their analyses, Smith et al. argue that the following eight trends are characterizable of American youth: (1) the majority of American youth are religious by way of institutional affiliation and identification; (2) the number of American adolescents within the Christian tradition has been gradually declining over the last two and one-half decades; (3) about half of American adolescents regularly participate in religious organizations; (4) about half of American youth are not religiously active; (5) religious participation of American adolescents declines with age; (6) girls tend to be somewhat more religiously active then boys; (7) religious participation of American adolescents is somewhat differentiated by race; and (8) religious participation of American adolescents varies somewhat by region of residence.[11]

The study measures and defines the religious participation among American youth according to traditional institutional referents. Empirically, the narrowing of what constitutes religious parameters makes measuring religiosity an easier task by focusing on behaviors generally understood as religious; however, such categorizations don't account for the uses of religion in cultural practices outside of institutional purviews.

Using preexisting data from MTF (1996), Smith and colleagues suggest that over the span of 20 years (1976–1996) there was a 10% decline among Protestant youth, with the identification of American youth with survey variables such as "other" religions and "not religious" each growing 5% over the 20-year period. These findings suggest that "although the vast majority of American youth remain within the Christian tradition, proportionately more youth both consider themselves not religious and are affiliating with non-Christian traditions over time."[12] In the study, activities connected to institutional housing are understood in terms of denominational affiliation, religious service attendance, and youth group participation.[13]

Smith, Faris, and Denton continue in a 2003 article, "Mapping American Adolescent Subjective Religiosity and Attitudes of Alienation Toward Religion: A Research Report," using MTF (1996) and Survey of Adolescent Health (1995) data to explore "three fundamental aspects of subjective youth religiosity" which they characterize by: (1) importance of religion; (2) frequency of prayer; and (3) born-again status, with "three measures of youth attitudes of alienation towards religion": (1) agreement with parents; (2) approval of churches; and (3) financial donations to churches.[14] They assert that impressionistic claims that American youth are alienated from traditional religion and are generally rebellious towards the idea of religion, are empirically invalid. They continue by arguing that these exaggerations are reflective of a lack of empirical data: "The problem, however, is that many of these works are journalistic, impressionistic, or semi-autobiographical. And those few that don't contain systematically-collected empirical data rely on research designs that are questionable."[15] They further claim, "Frequency distributions alert us immediately that the proportions of American 12th graders who express alienation from or hostility to religion are small." They in fact declare that empirical data show a reverse effect: "Evidence from 20 years of MTF surveys shows no such growth trend, in fact relatively little change at all."[16] They argue that despite claims to the contrary, youth do not feel isolated or unwelcomed by most institutions of religion. While the conclusions of this study rendered generalizations similar to those made in the 2002 report, what's interesting is the competing nature of two of the eight summary observations found in the 2003 report: (1) religious faith is important for the majority of American youth; and (2) religious faith is not really important for a large minority of American youth. Regarding the obvious tensions in these observations, the authors clarify that while nearly one-third of youth say that their faith is "very important" and another third that it is "pretty important," "four out of ten American youth do not find their religious faith to be even somewhat important in their lives,"[17] an historical trend that they argue is *not* growing remarkably over time. As already suggested, indicators of religiosity (religious faith, prayer, and born-again status) are understood institutionally for the purposes of this research, and what's considered religious practices and beliefs is drawn from traditionally recognized faith claims. Moreover, answers to survey questions regarding religious importance do not discriminate between rhetorical value of such claims and the actual performance of such belief in practices.

Interesting about the studies conducted by Smith and colleagues is the use of positivism (what's empirically evident) to counter impressionistic (non-data-supported) works that suggest the texture of American youth religiosity is represented by their assumed alienation from traditional religion and faith institutions. These impressionist works, according to Smith and Denton, assume that youth are "either opting out of faith altogether or are on quests to construct more authentic, postmodern versions of faith and spirituality."[18] Understood in this manner, Smith and Denton use empirical data to challenge the idea "that American religion generally is losing the coherence of historical religious traditions, as individuals increasingly create personal, bricolage spiritualities, eclectically mixing and matching spiritual practices from diverse faiths."[19] Here we see a more pronounced suspicious (ideological) disposition towards what may, in reality, represent syncretic postmodern religious practices whose texture is unable to be captured through survey data and in-depth interviews.

Interestingly enough, Smith and Denton's 2005 text *Soul Searching* analyzes first-wave (NSYR) data to consider *both* religious and non-religious youth (again, the distinctions are reliant upon institutional referents and traditional claims to belief). Regarding the "youth-as-spiritual-seeker" models, Smith and Denton argue that:

> Contrary to popular perceptions, the vast majority of American adolescents are not spiritual seekers or questers of the type often described by journalists and some scholars, but are instead mostly oriented toward and engaged in conventional religious traditions and communities.[20]

Again, how are such forceful claims made when practices outside of conventional religion are rarely taken into empirical consideration? Although they argue that "religious practices, in short, seem crucial to vibrant religious faith among American teens,"[21] one is left wondering just what kinds of practices may exist beyond the conventional.

In this text, the category of religion and its outward manifestations remain arrested within a privileged discourse of "excellence" and greater "good." According to Smith and Denton, these attributes are housed within "well-known religious practices" such as "prayer, scripture reading, meditation, and tithing."[22] The 2005 survey sample was specific to teenagers aged 13–17 grouped into six religious traditions and one nonreligious category, hence the consideration of institutional practices as privileged. It is possible, as others have argued, that traditional surveys often obfuscate complex answers that cannot be fully understood through the use of survey instruments. Although alternative practices are hinted at, the authors don't do much with "alternative" categories. Smith and Denton report that:

> the vast majority of U.S. teenagers identify themselves as Christian, either among the broad array of American Protestant denominations or as Catholics. Significant minorities of other U.S. adolescents are nonreligious, Mormon, and Jewish. The percentage of other minority faiths that often draw a great deal of public attention—paganism, Wicca, Buddhism, Muslim, and so on—remains at the start of the twenty-first century very small. Few U.S. teens appear to be dabbling with, much less switching to, such alternative faiths.[23]

And, while a large majority of American youth may be "dipping and dappling" in various syncretic forms of religion and spirituality, Smith and Denton collapse this "alternative" activity within one rubric they refer to as Moralistic Therapeutic Deism (MTD). They describe MTD as a:

> de facto dominant religion among contemporary U.S. teenagers. . . particularly evident among mainline Protestant and Catholic youth, but also visible among black and conservative Protestants, Jewish teens, and other religious types of teenagers, and even many nonreligious teenagers in the United States.[24]

Smith and Denton argue that there is largely represented in survey responses an inclination and posture towards this new ideology among American youth, which they describe as "inculcating a moralistic approach to life . . . that teaches that central to living a good and happy life is being a good, moral person,"[25] providing "therapeutic benefits to its adherents . . . feeling good, happy, secure, at peace,"[26] and devoid of traditional theological concerns such as sin, salvation, and divine sovereignty. Again, alternative practices and their "subjective" positionalities are here collapsed into one rubric, thereby flattening their differences. Smith and Denton observe that MTD is not fully Christian in texture, and that despite its historical connection to Christianity by way of thought structure, it has "morphed into Christianity's misbegotten step-cousin, Christian Moralistic Therapeutic Deism."[27] In more telling words, Smith and Denton write, "It is not so much that U.S. Christianity is being secularized. Rather more subtly, Christianity is either disintegrating into a pathetic version of itself, or more significantly,

Christianity is actively being colonized and displaced by a quite different religious faith."

Here, the exaggerated religious cost of this shift among American youth takes a moralizing turn. Continuing in this perspective, the authors want to suggest that the worldview of MTD could in fact be detrimental to the moral life of American youth. They suggest we consider its more vital consequences, that "there are consistent and impressive differences in outcomes between highly religious American teens and nonreligious teens."[28] In other words, differences in religion matter on life outcomes for youth. This observation leaves Smith and Denton to suggest that "simply because teenagers cannot see it does not make religion's influence any less real or important,"[29] going onto postulate that "in any case, it appears that religion does matter, even ironically, in the lives of religious believers who are not aware that it does."[30]

While *Soul Searching* used first-wave nationally representative data collected among youth aged 13 to 17, Smith's most recent text *Souls in Transition* (2009), written in conjunction with Snell, considers change in religiosity of the same sample of youth now 18 to 23 years old. Referring to the sample of youth, Smith and Snell assert that this book "examines them at the third measure point of their ongoing life trajectories,"[31] considering effects of life transitions on their religious participation and beliefs. This text stretches beyond the examination of mapping youth religious beliefs to consider mediating effects of the social context and macro social changes affecting emerging adulthood and their religious practices. Does religion still matter for these youth? If not, are there social consequences of changes in religious perspective?

Smith and Snell's study suggests a number of interesting findings. Their text concludes that there is an exceptional decline in institutional religious participation and that this necessitates an exploration of various representative cultural standards and trends. In sum, they suggest that the changing topography of American youth religiosity over time can broadly be understood through six major religious types among emerging adults: (1) committed traditionalists (embrace of a strong religious faith); (2) selective adherents (perform certain aspects of their religious traditions but neglect and ignore others); (3) spiritually open (not personally very committed to a religious faith but are nonetheless receptive to and at least mildly interested in some spiritual or religious matters); (4) religiously indifferent (neither care to practice religion nor oppose); (5) religiously disconnected (have little to no exposure or connection to religious people, ideas, or organizations); and (6) irreligious (hold skeptical attitudes about and make critical arguments against religion generally, rejecting the idea of personal faith).[32]

The 2009 text, which charts change in the same youth over five years, yields important empirical findings on the shape, texture, and flux of American youth religiosity. Yet, we are left knowing little about the population of youth who are declining in church participation, a consequence of confining the measure of religion/religiosity to traditional activities in institutions. For example, out of the six religious types, Smith and Snell's study tells little about those for whom religiosity changed over time. As will be seen in the next section, Smith extends his analysis beyond the simple critical mapping of youth religiosity, and argues that religious presence in the life of youth matters for its buffering effect.

A turn towards the buffering effects of institutional religiosity emerges at a point where empirical data verify changes in the pattern of youth religion over time. The shift in focus from mapping American youth religiosity to the politics of e/affect of institutional decline is an interesting one, as emphasis on the latter considers social *consequences* of church decline lodged within a causal discourse. This discourse is by no means disconnected from the politics of funding sources which privilege faith institutions.

"BUFFERING TRANSGRESSION": THE MORALIZING OF RELIGIOUS PARTICIPATION

The preceding section engaged the work of Christian Smith and NSYR data to map the terrain of youth and religion in America. Whether described institutionally or espoused ideologically (vis-à-vis intergenerational familial transmission and rhetorical pronouncements on surveys), American youth are indeed participating in religion in some way, shape, or form. No light is being cast, however, on religious uses in culture, outside of formal faith institutions. This gap in research is consequential of the ways in which religion is understood within empirical research. With a decline in institutional participation empirically confirmed in the 2005 text, the nature of the research seemingly turned towards social efficacy narratives. This move was not unconsidered. Towards the end of their 2005 text, Smith and Snell make extenuating claims regarding the differences in morality, perspectives on life, risk behaviors, mental health, and subjective well being according to the status of religious faith in emerging adulthood on the scale of the six religious types.[33]

The suggestion that participation in faith institutions serves as an "affirmative" space for youth developmental enhancement is not a new idea. Spaces such as black churches have been imagined as places that serve more than just religious needs for wanting and disadvantaged communities. Moreover, black church culture is often troped as a strategy to combat the perils of everyday social ills. Sociologist Mary Patillo-McCoy, in the essay "Church Culture as a Strategy of Action in the Black Community" (2008), argues that:

> in Groveland, the concrete concerns of curtailing youth delinquency and promoting neighborhood safety are addressed using the cultural tools of the black church. These tools—primarily prayer, call-and-response interaction, and Christian imagery—invoke the collective

orientation of Black Christianity and draw strength from the belief in a direct, beneficial relationship to God.[34]

The use of black church culture as social strategy in Groveland is representative of many places throughout America. There is no denying the important infrastructure that landscapes of faith (institutionally) provide, especially ones that serve marginalized communities as a whole. The fact that black people in North America espouse higher rates of religiosity and make claims to finding respite and socio-political advocacy within faith institutions across the board speaks to such impact. Although little is known regarding the changing relationship of black youth church membership, attendance, and participation over time, data confirm that more than their white and Hispanic counterparts, black youth continue to express higher rates of institutional affiliation and membership/participation. As reported in the Introduction, the Black Youth Project found that "black youth are significantly more likely than Hispanic and white youth to say that religion is 'very important' in their lives," with 67% of black youth agreeing with this statement compared to only 46% of Hispanic youth and 40% of white youth.[35] The study further indicates that black youth attend religious services more frequently and are "much more likely to engage in religious activities outside of their places of worship (e.g., praying at home, reading scripture outside of church, etc.) at higher rates." Overall, survey measures from this data regarding religion confirm that black youth are indicating importance and weight to the idea of and participation in religion in general.

The NSYR 2002 data suggest that "the Devoted and the Regular are much less likely to drink alcohol regularly and much less likely to binge-drink. More than four times the proportion of the Disengaged than the Devoted drinks alcohol weekly or more often, for example,"[36] thus drawing a relationship between the wellness of emerging adults and their subjective religiosity. The data further suggest that "the more religious emerging adults are generally healthier, happy with their bodies, and thoughtful about the meaning of life than the least religious." Interestingly enough, the authors are in fact arguing that religious presence (institutionally understood) in the lives of youth makes a social "difference"—in other words, religion matters. Smith and Snell see a connection between the group espousing "high end religious commitment and practice" and "higher scores on most multiple measures of positive life outcomes," yet these heuristics do not consider multiplicative modalities of religiosity beyond the four walls. Moreover, how does the measuring of subjective religiosity within rhetorical claims to faith represent, among other things, structuring familial inheritances rather than personal claims to belief? Do cultural practices outside of formal faith institutions merit similar buffering weight? Are other cultural practices done in collaboration with institutional activity, and if so, do they affect rates or changes in subjective religiosity and institutional membership?

And the "buffering transgression" configurations continue. Smith configures the construct of religiosity as a "protective factor" against events such as suicide, smoking, sexual behavior, and life-threatening calamities, demonstrating the manner in which the presence of religion in the lives of youth decreases nihilistic tendencies such as hopelessness and depression. Here, religion is understood within the paradigm of affirmative coping measures.[37] While data may confirm this validity, there is a privileging of religion in this assertion; Smith writes:

> A nonreductionistic sociological approach to religion is interested in understanding how the distinctively religious dimensions of the phenomenon of "religion" exert significant social influences. That is, this approach assumes there is something particularly *religious* in religion, which is not reducible to nonreligious explanations, and that these religious elements can exert "causal" influence in forming cultural practices and motivating action.[38]

As noted elsewhere in this project, religion so conceived within a *sui generis* framing ("something particularly *religious* in religion") maintains and perpetuates a disciplinary imperialism within the study of religion by privileging certain activity *as* distinctly religious. Because Smith understands religion to be an irreducible and self-evident phenomenon, his "nonreductionistic sociological approach" narrows both practices and the empirical examination of religion. While outcome-based empirical studies work hard to demonstrate negative and statistically significant relationships between positive life outcomes and religious participation, they ultimately contribute little information to examining the changing cartography of religion among youth in mediating social contexts. These studies and correlations ignore what type of hegemonic framing this gives institutional religion within the larger policy world. What do we make of Smith's findings that argue, "It is clear that American adolescents are gradually becoming more religiously pluralistic,"[39] continuing that "about half of American youth are not religiously active." In light of the changing patterns of youth religiosity over time, such studies in the future will need a more expansive way to conceive and test the idea of religion in a more relevant and multidimensional manner.

Moreover, couching religion as the main progenitor or causal mechanism for buffering what is seen or understood as "deviant" activity (teen pregnancy, sex, oral sex, smoking, and so on) keeps the idea of religion captive to a purely affirmative and positive moral construct upholding and maintaining notions of purity in disciplinary understandings of religion in general. Religion as moral category in empirical work puts religion in an antagonistic relationship with illicit social activity—ultimately leaving uninterrogated the manner in which religious social control has contributed much to both causes and effects of social pathology.

A brief consideration of another study reveals "buffering transgression" motifs reminiscent of those in Smith's work. Byron R. Johnson in "The Role of African-American Churches in Reducing Crime Among Black Youth" (2002) makes similar claims regarding black youth in particular. Like Smith and others, Johnson argues that institutional religious participation among black youth operates as a significant buffer against hard crime and other risk factors that occur in structurally disadvantaged neighborhoods that suffer deleterious effects of urban decay. Here, Johnson argues that the black church, while historically important, has been a space significantly understudied by criminologists. Viewing the church as an important "agency of social control" in the promotion of "pro-social" behavior, Johnson argues that more empirical exploration is needed. In his study, Johnson makes a clear distinction between the buffering merit of religious and non-religious variables; his data (on religious participation) distinguish "variables for non-religious social control and social learning . . . to control for spuriousness"[40]—in other words, Johnson wants to make a clear delineation between the manner in which religion (understood institutionally) affects delinquency apart from what he understands to be more secular social networks with similar buffering effects (such as sex, family, and conventional attitudes among others).

For the purposes of his study, Johnson understands religious participation and the idea of religion to be the extent to which one is involved within a church or religious institution. He uses a 3-point Likert scale to measure how often subjects had participated (in church) during the previous year. Overall, Johnson conceptualizes and statistically measures the practice of (institutional) religion as: (1) occurring within institutional confines; (2) an agency of local social control; and lastly (3) that which not only socially controls but likewise becomes a variable that configures "religiosity as a protective factor" from the disorder, chaos, and disarray produced vis-à-vis structural disadvantage. He writes, "To address this neglected area in the literature, I examine whether black youth's involvement in religious institutions mediates or buffers those individuals from the effects of neighborhood disorder,"[41] further stating that "in methodological terms, and consistent with prior research, neighborhood disorder is expected to promote youth participation in crime, but that this deleterious effect will decrease when religious involvement is included in the analyses." Thus, Johnson asserts that "religious involvement is expected to significantly mediate and buffer at-risk youth . . . in that religious involvement facilitates the development of bonds and social networks that are likely to dissuade individual youth from engaging in deviant acts." As we can see, an institutional definition of religion becomes necessary for Johnson's claims related to social bonds and network theory, a discourse that for the large part relies upon formal institutions.

Ultimately, Johnson's study pushes for more criminological assessment of the role religious institutions play in decreasing hard crime among the demographic of black youth. In his study, the idea of religion is narrowly measured as "institutional," privileged as unique in social transformation and control (among other non-religious variables) while being fashioned as a moral category that buffers illicit activity.

TRANSGRESSION AND THE ARRESTED DEVELOPMENT OF RELIGION

Conceiving of religion as what is practiced *in* institutions ignores both the role of dominant institutions and the complex life-worlds of youth. This narrow perspective arrests the cultural play with religiosity to the prison of institutional limitation. In the foreword to *Everyday Religion: Observing Modern Religious Lives* (2007), edited by sociologist Nancy T. Ammerman, Peter L. Berger writes:

> Of course churches, synagogues, and other religious organizations continue to play an important role in contemporary society. But much of religious life takes place outside these institutional locales. To limit the study of religion to these locales would be like, say, studying politics by only looking at the activities of organized political parties. As far back as 1967, in his influential book *The Invisible Religion*, Thomas Luckman insisted that sociologists must be attentive to religious phenomena that are institutionally diffuse.[42]

Ammerman argues that religion is constantly and continually being reshaped and redefined in very different ways, yet scholars continue to lack "better definitions and indicators"[43] that can assist in a broader and more relevant understanding of how religion is used in everyday life. More pointedly stated, Ammerman argues that investigating lived religiosities in everyday life does not bifurcate traditional ways of doing religion with current manifestations; rather, she pushes for increased attention to emergent forms of religion that are unconventional and alternative yet coexist and cross with older traditions. The arrested development of religion to institutional referents ignores what I alluded to earlier, the reality of the overlapping social and cultural worlds of youth. Complex and multiple belongings blur boundaries and appearance of certain faith practices often practiced together without contradiction in thought or form. Despite rhetorical answers to survey questions that suggest traditional theological beliefs are being held in place among American youth, a deeper look into everyday social and culture practices may reveal a bricolage and syncretic styling of religion among this demographic.

While conceptual slippage (of religion) may be consequential to issues of operationalization in empirical studies (issues of measurement), Smith's work positions itself over and against "impressionistic" claims of bricolage and syncretic uses of religion among youth. Although Smith confirms that some of the NSYR data suggest a growing population of spiritual seeking youth, he chooses to categorize the religiosity of these youth into six rubrics that are segregated over and against institutional religion and traditional theology (Committed Traditionalists, Selective Adherents, Spiritually Open, Religiously Indifferent, Religiously Disconnected, and Irreligious).[44] In other words, these categories only differentiate between varying degrees of (institutional) religiosity. They tell us little about how such categories hold, change, or are affected by the social and cultural life-worlds inhabited by American youth. This disconnection is powerfully reflected in what Flory and Miller argue when they write:

> Traditional definitions of reality are fuzzy for this generation. Their failure to commit to traditional religious and denominational structures does not signal their lack of interest in questions of meanings and values. Instead, it signals that new institutions are being birthed, and that current ones must be reinvented if they are to survive within this environment.[45]

That is to say, more traditional ways of theorizing and conceptualizing the category of religion must be consistent with and relevant to changing dimensions of culture that youth consume and produce on a daily basis. While the arrested development of religion to institutional definitions limits its analysis for the relevance of contemporary youth culture, equally troubling is the use of religious participation as a moral and protective variable—what I have referred throughout as "buffering transgression." History tells the tale of the complicated role faith institutions play in society—they are the cause and effect of harm and advancement, concurrently. The types of moral code promulgated in and by such empirical claims include ideological agendas such as abstinence-only programs and gender-specific activities. This may reduce legal and behavioral "waywardness" (in terms of disciplining bodies toward normativity) while perpetuating dangerous ideological structurings of hegemonic codes.

Thus, the category of religion must be freed from its institutional referent and chains; the blanket of morality and social control must be pulled back to allow for a more robust theorizing and an expansion of its conceptual and pragmatic realities beyond plastic distinctions. Thin in analysis, and plastic in distinction, grouping youth religiosity according to their relationship to institutions and traditional theological beliefs obscures the vigorous terrain of religious uses in cultural forms and practices. In sum it fails to capture the complexity and multidimensionality of youth cultural and social contexts in a postindustrial age.

The "buffering transgression" motifs construct religion as a social and moral discipliner, creating order and stasis to what is in reality in-process. The "buffering transgression" hypothesis imagines religious institutions as mode of moral transmission and thus situates the larger world, particularly areas of urban decay where neighborhood disorder abounds (as suggested by Johnson's article), as dangerous. As Mary Douglas reminds us in *Purity and Danger*, "The ideal order of society is guarded by dangers which threaten transgressors. These danger-beliefs are as much threats which one man use to coerce another as dangers which he himself fears to incur by his own lapses from righteousness."[46] Douglas helps us to think more deeply about the constructionist nature of what is called danger (or delinquency) within the social body of society. Or, turning to Jacques Derrida, that religion at times can function similarly to an immune system, where the body (here understood as the institution of religion) is kept safe from the contamination of the foreign antibodies of the larger world (deviance), and thus, the social body (such as the church) must continually work to "immunize" against the threats that pose the risk of contamination from the outside (neighborhood disorder and urban decay). This maintains the hegemony of religion without freeing it to the exuberance of "play," thus enabling it to be used, consumed, and produced in a multiplicity of ways free from the expectations of "buffering" motifs. Derrida, among others, asserts that religion carries a sort of imperialism with it, and that at the core of its structure it is grounded in, solidified by, and characterized as that which "rejects"; when the alterity of "otherness" (that which is "foreign") attempts to break forth, religion rejects the foreign antibodies in order to remain pure and *indemne*—without harm. Lastly, Michel Foucault would add to the argument that any narrative about morality is thus implicated by larger issues of power and that the policing of behaviors in relation to these codes is more usually comparable against something larger, something more transcendent. Understood in this way, the measuring of religion in these empirical studies remains beholden to a Durkheimian frame of social control, as a protective agent with unique "buffering" effects. This process disciplines the bodies of deviant and wayward youth while ignoring the many-ness of youth religious subjectivity.

RELIGION IN/AS CULTURE

The first part of this chapter has offered a window into the religious patterns of youth in American society; what is evidenced in such data is that there are in fact cartographical shifts occurring among American youth. However, these cartographical shifts only tell a partial story. Less institutional definitions and measures of religion are needed within empirical (social science) work to account for the messiness of cultural uses of religion that blur lines and distinctions between belief and social interests.

Johnson's study confirmed that black youth (among others) continue to find an affirmative space within institutional religion, but what happens "within the four walls" of the church does not tell the whole story. Beyond the institution lies the larger whole of the cultural sphere, and in this realm, belief and religiosity are in dynamic interplay with other elements of social interaction. While Smith conjectures subjective religiosity as a meaningful construct, and while youth have indeed inherited and continue to reaffirm confessional belief both inside and outside the religious institution, the broader social and cultural contexts in which these same youth live their daily lives and which they help create suggest more complicated and less distinguishable facets. This is what sociologist of religion Gordon Lynch is getting at when he draws attention to the gap between the concept of belief retained and promulgated by scholars, and the experiences and understandings of those individuals to whom such beliefs are ascribed:

> In my own discipline of sociology of religion, such narrow conceptions of belief persist both in terms of the emphasis on survey data measuring respondents' attitudes to creedal statements . . . and the use of interviews to try to elicit the core beliefs and spirituality of those within and beyond institutional religion. The persistence of such propositional understandings of belief—even in the face of evidence that they make little sense to research respondents—makes David Morgan's grounding of belief in socially shared practices and aesthetic regimes a welcome corrective.[47]

Such a corrective is not entirely unique to such academics as Lynch and Morgan, and fits within a set of newer academic approaches across disciplines that seek to ground understanding and interpretation within material practices. While traditional approaches to the study of religion take a creed-based path of investigation, starting from the lived realities of the people themselves reveals more complicated iterations of belief.

Quoting my own voice in the introduction to the 2011 article "Habits of the Heart," which presented the results of my study on youth religiosity over time,

> Among various modalities of youth culture today, rap lyrics have replaced sacred scripture, CDs are played in place of old-time religion humming, sagging pants and skinny jeans are worn underneath or without the choir robe, and clubs, bars, and corners have transformed into ecclesiastical spaces where the watchful eye of god is replaced by technological surveillance of cameras and effervescent blue lights. The rugged, edgy, and gritty terrains of youth culture are growing realities in our world. They don't compete with more traditional ways of "practicing" religion, as impressionistic work assumes; rather, they reflect the myriad ways religion is being used in forms that challenge confessional and apologetic postures.[48]

Where the church is popularly seen to be in massive decline, a slide complemented by a pathological increase in deviance and disorder, a "market maintenance" paradigm is activated to rescue and redeem youth from secularization. Hence Smith's construction of MTD as individualized postmodern bricolage-like spiritual quests among youth today—causing unnecessary alarm among churches, parents, and youth workers. One aim of the current chapter is to give speculative popular imagination an empirical face, and based on such findings to set directions for exploring the changing texture and geography of youth religiosity.

The academic, popular, and political fuss over the loss of traditional creedal religion among youth forces a distinction where one does not naturally exist. With youth being categorized dichotemously as either churched or dechurched, as either religious or secular (and further, religious or deviant), the messy cultural syncretism that is actually occurring is flattened and fractured before it has a chance to perform its work. Let me again quote from Smith and colleagues, who provide a window on the anxieties that motivate such distinctions:

> A series of high-profile events—including multiple school shootings and local epidemic outbreaks of sexually-transmitted diseases among youth—have heightened broad public concern about problems in youth culture. There appears to be a growing awareness of and interest in religious, spiritual, and moral influences in the lives of youth among not only religious leaders, but also educators, social service providers, public policy-makers, philanthropists and journalists.[49]

A more gentle and less worried approach might reveal the changing expressions of religiosity in a postmodern society to include full and fertile manifestations and iterations that, while overlapping with and reinventing traditional beliefs and themes, also perform the work of freshly mediating between the self and all that is other.

An approach that was less motivated by concerns over church decline, secularization, and the equating of loss of traditional religion with pathological behaviors might instead engage the altered religiosity of youth as a rich and instructional source of knowledge on alternative uses of elements of religion traditionally apprehended as confessional and personal. An examination of these uses of religion holds much promise for their contribution to theory and method in the academic study of religion. As youth change in their experiences, expressions, and creations, so too must empirical work shift its emphasis beyond institutional referents and motifs of buffering transgression, beyond an inherent meaningfulness and usefulness of the construct of religion.

SOCIAL DIFFERENCES AND RELIGIOUS ATTENDANCE

The problematics explored herein notwithstanding, the empirical studies investigated in this chapter have been solid in mapping out the extent to which the church continues to matter for American youth and, more specifically germane to the current inquiry, for black youth in America.

Earlier in this chapter sociologist Patillo-McCoy described the historical role of the black church in supporting and promoting black communities. Consistent with this historical figuring of the role of the church, social scientists have reported narratives and statistics on the institution of religion as a significant space for black youth, and have cited religious institutional involvement as countering influences of urban deviance. And, I would add, and as will be illustrated in Chapter 6 of this work, outside of the four walls of the religious institution similar effects are produced by other social manifestations as church rituals are recast and played out on the streets. However, says Cathy Cohen in a 2007 research summary of the attitudes and behaviors of black youth in America, "while African American religious institutions are possibly the most significant institutions in Black communities, some raise the question of whether their role as social regulator and political mobilizer has waned in recent years."[50] Writing somewhat earlier, Johnson and colleagues addressed such questions empirically and found that:

> Church attendance tends to buffer the effects of neighborhood disorder on serious crime among black youth: that is, the linkage between a disordered neighborhood and serious crime is not as great when black youth are actively involved in the church. The same cannot be said for minor crime.[51]

And more specifically:

> The severity of the effects of neighborhood disorder on an individual's behavior depends on the level of that resident's religious involvement (i.e., the effect of neighborhood disorder decreases as an individual's religious involvement increases).[52]

These and other works confirm the buffering role of institutional religious involvement for black youth, as indeed for other youth in America. Delving into these demographics more deeply, *Soul Searching* details how various social differences affect the religiosity of American youth, as understood through six measures including belief in God, attending religious services weekly or more often, recognizing faith as extremely important, participating regularly in youth religious groups, praying, and reading the Bible regularly. Working from data compiled in the NSYR, Smith and Denton found social differences such as age, race, gender, and regional location to be significantly associated with rates of youth religiosity, as were also parent religiosity, relationship with parents, and parent education.[53] Although religious involvement among teens showed some decrease with age, the difference was not significant. Girls were more likely than boys to score highly on all six measures of religiosity, and black and Hispanic teenagers were found to be more devoted than white teenagers on many of the religiosity measures. More specifically, according to NSYR data on religious service attendance, 20% of black youth attend more than once a week, compared with 16% of white youth, 12% of Hispanic youth, and 9% of Asian youth,[54] although black and Hispanic youth are less likely to belong to religious youth groups. Parenthetically, these findings on race revealed in the NSYR data are consistent with those of other studies, including Cohen's Black Youth Project.

Turning to other social factors uncovered in Smith and Denton's analysis, strong parental bonds and affirming relationships between teens and their parents were found to be significant, as was having parents who themselves attended church more frequently. Teens whose parents were married were found to be more religiously inclined, as were teens who were involved in organized activities. For social class, defined by a number of factors including parental education, the results were mixed, but teens from low-income families were shown to be less involved in youth groups and in attending services. While family income per se was not found to be a predictor of youth religiosity, interesting results emerged from analysis of 2002 U.S. Census data that grouped counties into quartiles by median family income. There was an inverse relationship between youth religiosity and median family income, with an increase in county median family income being associated with a decrease in youth religiosity measured by five of the six variables, with the exception again being religious service attendance. In relation to regional location, NSYR data revealed that while rural–urban differences were insignificant when all demographic variables were controlled for, there was a broad geographic difference, with a continuum from the more religious South through the least religious Northeast. Finally, Smith and Denton's analysis showed the most significant social predictor of difference in of youth religiosity to be, in fact, denominational affiliation.[55]

TEMPORAL CARTOGRAPHY: YOUTH RELIGIOSITY ACROSS TIME

In charting the known terrain of youth religiosity in America, this chapter has identified a number of possible avenues of inquiry left unmapped by current research, among them the dimension of time. While studies such as Smith's and Johnson's are useful in demonstrating the affirmative role of religious institutions among youth, they don't provide a *trajectory* of youth church attendance over a long period of time, or at least, significant periods of time (Smith's is specific to five years). In other words, while the "buffering transgression" hypothesis may in fact prove to be empirically valid, these studies don't show rates of change in religious attendance over an extended trajectory. Quantitative longitudinal measurement of such rates of change provides a more dynamic view of institutional religious participation than the static "snapshot" approach of the studies thus far discussed in this chapter.

This section will report at some length on a quantitative research project I instigated to begin to address this lack, using data from the National Longitudinal Survey of Youth (NLSY) 1979 and subsequent follow-up surveys to chart the level and rate of change in youth religious attendance from 1992 to 2006. Latent class growth modeling was used to map trajectories of rate of change in religious attendance for the individual youth surveyed. We further examined the data for meaningful covariation with relevant social predictors. The results were published in a special issue on "Race, Religion, and Late Democracy" (2011) of *The Annals of the American Academy of Political and Social Science*, to which publication the reader is referred for a full report of our findings.[56]

The picture built up so far in this chapter shows that the church does "still matter" as a space of participation, helping buffer participants against the worst of the effects of social disorder; and also, that there is still considerable interest among many, if not all, youth in retaining some degree of religiosity. It is also clear that the religiosity of youth is changing as the cultural context changes, likely in form as well as content. Among narratives of declining attendance vying with socially positive buffering effects, as well as alarming speculations of nihilism and moral panics, it would seem useful to investigate the existence and extent of such decline, examining religious engagement among youth in a shifting topography. Fortunately the twenty-first century inquirer into this matter is served by the foresight of the NLSY79 in initiating and continuing to compile data on, among other things, the religious inclinations and practices of a particular sample of youth over time. We were able to make use of these existing data to statistically and longitudinally examine church attendance over time, thus adding to the thread of research specifically addressing institutional religiosity among youth, broken down by demographics including race. While numbers do not tell a whole story, and while the choice of *which* numbers will be compiled determines the plot of said story to a considerable degree, as argued throughout this chapter, quantitative research certainly holds a place in the quest to relate thinking to reality and thus to meaningful response.

Let us return at this point to the 2009 findings of Smith and Snell, who did in fact address this very question, albeit using just two moments in time as reference markers to measure changes in various aspects of youth religiosity over a period of five years. Returning to the same sample of youth surveyed in the first wave of NSYR data collection and now aged 18 to 23, they compared the responses of these emerging adults to the same questions they had been asked five years earlier. The picture that emerges from their findings is one of a relatively small degree of declining church attendance, roughly 11% of those who at ages 13 to 17 had attended once a week or more, leaving just under half of the population studied attending religious services. But the data analyzed by Smith and Snell did not use attendance as the only measure of religiosity. Youth were also asked questions about the value they place on faith, with 44% affirming that faith is "very" or "extremely" important in their lives, and at the other end of the scale 26.8% saying it is not important. Smith and Snell argue that these numbers reflect a substantive difference, in that while church attendance itself may be declining among youth, these same youth profess faith to hold a key role in their everyday lives. Here, there are differences also among social demographics, with 72% of black Protestant emerging adults professing faith to be extremely important in their daily lives, compared to the national average of 44%—and this in spite of a decline in church attendance among this same demographic of 17% for those who had attended once a week or more at ages 13 to 17.[57]

The dataset engaged by Smith and Snell enabled the compilation of valuable information on the changing life worlds of teens in America, but was limited in that it accessed only two points in time, thus affording only a rather jerky plotting of movement. Visualizing information as a graph, the more points there are available to map, the smoother and more accurate the curves and projections based on them, and the more accurate the correlation with lived reality. More useful, then, will be longitudinal data that track the rate of change in youth religiosity over a longer period of time. The study reported on in this section considers change that occurred over a period of fifteen years, from 1992 to 2006, from data collected every other year. "Habits of the Heart" set out to find out, through latent class growth modeling applied to data from the NLSY79, whether there was significant change in church attendance among youth between these years, and if so, the social demographics that predicted such change, assessing such factors as race, gender, social class, and urban–rural differences. As well as charting these rates of change and demographic predictors of differential rates of change, the study aimed to consider the implications for the "buffering transgression" hypotheses this chapter has been situating. Institutional religion has been posited to mitigate the effects of negative cultural change and urban decay, but if for some groups of youth such practices become increasingly irrelevant, and their interests and expressions lie largely beyond the four walls, does empirical research need to rethink its focus on more traditional manifestations of religiosity?

These, then, were the questions and context that prompted an examination of the NLSY79 data using growth mixture modeling to ascertain the level and rate of change of youth church attendance. The NLSY79 surveyed a nationally representative sample of 12,686 youth aged 14 to 22. Seven years after this initial study, a new survey was launched to study the population of the 11,469 children of the female respondents to the NLSY79. This new survey, which was then repeated biennially in a longitudinal project, was called the National Longitudinal Survey of Youth 1979 Children and Young Adults (NLSY79-Children). In the NLSY79-Children, the mother's NLSY79 information was linked to a new set of data collected for her children, including demographic information as well as responses from the child and/or the mother on such issues as child–parent interaction, attitudes toward schooling, dating and friendship patterns, religious attendance, health, substance use, and home responsibilities. For my study, the demographic information and responses on religious attendance were accessed, for the years 1992 to 2006. Earlier years were unfortunately not able to be included in my study because there was too much data missing for the years 1988 and 1992.

The NLSY79-Children recorded religious service attendance, which became the dependent variable in my study, through a self-reported Likert scale of 1 to 6 on how often the child/youth had attended religious services in the past year, where 1 was not at all and 6 was more than once a week. For independent variables we used data on race/ethnicity, gender, age, urban/rural (captured for 1996 and again for 2006), and three social class proxies: family permanent income, family wealth, and parental education. Family permanent income is a more stable indicator of lifetime economic status than is annual income; for this study permanent income was averaged over six years, 1988 through 1993. The family's net worth in 1988 as taken as an estimate of family wealth. Parental education was measured over a range from high school diploma to professional degree. The sample consisted of 48.9% females, and included white (43.7%), black (34.3%), and Latina/o (22%) youth, with age being measured in years from 10 to 22, beginning in 1992.

The modeling technique used in the study was able to provide information about 1) the level of church attendance; 2) the direction and rate of change of attendance (i.e., steady or sharp increase or decrease); and 3) how the demographic data predict both of these. Similarly, the same technique was used to provide information about urban/rural residence and migration in either direction, and then to interact this information with the attendance information. To do this, trajectories of change were modeled for each of the individuals, and these trajectories were compared to find meaningful clusters that could be grouped into what are termed latent classes. For attendance there were found to be two latent classes. One included those who attended frequently (47% of the sample), and this class showed a steady decline between 1992 and 2006; the other was composed of infrequent attenders, and this class showed a sharp decline over that same period. For residence, one latent class included those who in 1996 resided in rural or urban areas and in 2006 resided in rural areas; and the other latent class included those who in 1996 resided in rural or urban areas and in 2006 resided in urban areas (83% of the sample). When these two sets of latent classes were interacted together, the final results were as follows.

Half of the sample (49.6%) were now urban residents, and were in the group "frequent attender, steady decline." A further 23.3% were now urban residents, and were in the group "infrequent attender, sharp decline." A similar number, 20.4%, were now rural residents and were in the group "frequent attender, steady decline." Finally, a small number (6.7%) were now rural residents and were in the group "infrequent attender, sharp decline."

A number of meaningful effects came to light when these results were examined in terms of the demographic variables. Considering race/ethnicity, the highest level of religious attendance was found among black youth, followed by latina/o youth, with white youth having the lowest level, and this held for each of the latent classes; and notably, each of these groups showed a decline in attendance over time. Black youth were two and a half times more likely be in the "frequent attender, steady decline" latent class than were white youth, and latina/o youth were one and a half times more likely than white youth to be in this latent class. Age was found to predict both level and rate of change of religious attendance, with increasing age decreasing attendance and also increasing the rate of change in attendance. Family wealth (but not parental education and family income) was found to be a meaningful predictor, with an increase in wealth corresponding to a higher level of youth religious attendance. Finally, and in contrast to findings of other studies, gender was not shown to be a meaningful predictor, perhaps because of overlap with race/ethnicity effects.

So, stepping back from the intricacies of this statistical analysis, what do these results tell us about how much the church still matters for youth? And further, how much do race, social class, and urban/rural context matter in situating youth in relation to church attendance? The most striking and consistent feature of the findings was the cross-the-board decline in religious service attendance for all three racial/ethnic groups comprising the study sample. Because data were not collected on faith affiliation, the study was not able to address whether there were differences in rates of change in attendance among the different denominations. Race was, however, found to matter in that there are still higher levels of church attendance among black youth than either Latina/o or white youth. Beyond confirming an overall shift in America's population from rural to urban (corresponding to similar contextual shifts worldwide), these analyses specified that youth who live in urban situations, including those who migrate to cities from rural areas, are somewhat more likely to see a sharper decline in church attendance over time. While wealth was also found to matter, gender was not found to be a significant predictor in these analyses, in contrast to existing literature, a discrepancy which may point to the role of gender being masked here by the more powerful effect of race/ethnicity.

THE STUDY OF RELIGION BEYOND INSTITUTIONAL AND "BUFFERING MOTIFS": CONCLUSION

Reading the mapping of youth religiosity in the largest empirical study on youth and religion in the U.S., the early sections of this chapter chart the social implications of institutional participation and empirical findings. While such mapping makes clear that American youth are indeed practicing, thinking, and inheriting religion, some in a more traditional manner and others less so, the category of religion becomes deployed within studies focused on efficacy narratives, resulting in "buffering transgression" motifs. While the religious terrain of youth is vast and converging, few empirical studies (on religion) have explored the cultural milieus and repertoires that youth inhabit. An examination of what youth are up to necessitates a different posture regarding the measuring and operationalization of the category of religion—and the ends such study serves. Framing research in terms of the institutional referent rather than youth everyday practices, leaves the idea of religion in an arrested development grounded in nostalgia and a politics of religious respectability. These narrowed ideas and uses of religion challenge empirical research to consider rethinking context, grammar, and lexicon in order to explore the creative uses of religion in a rapidly changing cultural topography among youth in America.

Among these topographical changes that affect youth is the shifting of populations to urban areas, where they are particularly exposed to the influences narrated here as nihilism and moral panics—or more positively framed as spaces of creative manifestation and inventive re-positioning, as Chapter 6 of this book will witness. Such reshaping lies at one edge of what Smith and Snell (2009) sought to engage in making a distinction between the declining institutional religious practice among youth, a trend which was also confirmed in my longitudinal study cited here, and these same youth retaining their theological beliefs more or less intact. According to Smith and Snell, institutional participation is not to be seen as the only measure of the importance of religion in the lives of youth, for the decline in institutional religious participation among youth does not signal a corresponding decline in the salience of belief, which in remaining resilient fulfils the same function in buffering youth from harm. Granted the affirmative workings of the religious in the lives of youth, does this affirmative effect have to do with institutional practices, or with the more inculcated salience of belief, or both? Such careful distinctions must be made in future empirical research that seeks to uncover the actual workings of (the category of) religion in the lives of youth, with survey instruments designed to capture effects and affects beyond narrow and traditional understandings.

Belief and practice, then, although they may go hand in hand in a more traditional manner, may also be reshaped and combined in complex positionings, with either or both being reinvented as they interact with other changing influences and experiences. Institutional ideations of the religious are only one starting point for inquiry into this vast and postmodern-like territory, which can usefully be visualized in three dimensions if not four. Seen this way, all kinds of spaces of construction and action emerge, over space, psyche, and time. What is actually occurring in the space between professed belief and everyday practices, between inherited family belief structures and vibrant cultural manifestations and de-manifestations? The sites of such practical manifestation are multiple and unexpected, encompassing those aspects of human experiencing that are categorized as religious as well as some that are embodied otherwise.

Amid narratives and empirical documentation of decline in institutional participation, whether sharp or steady over time as variously indicated by the findings of the "Habits of the Heart" study, what remains untold because unasked is, to quote again from that study,

> what may alternatively be taking place as unconventional affirmative infrastructures that potentially hold similar buffering effects beyond institutional religiosity. Moreover, it could be found that activities conceived as "deviant" in buffering transgression literature serve affirmative capacities in the lives of youth; and if this is indeed the case, then such studies need to rethink the labeling of deviance.[58]

This perspective may be taken further in a commitment to not foreclose options through such restrictive constructions as:

- Religious practice buffers transgression so decline in religiosity plus increase in social decay leads to increase in deviancy.
- Or alternately, retained interior belief buffers transgression so in spite of decline in religious participation and increase in social decay, there is hope for a slowing down of deviancy.

Instead, the inquirer into the world of youth and spirit may engage with an array of unique and interacting uses and effects clustered around the (previous) category of religion, as youth dynamically relate to self, family, peers, and society.

Beyond empirical findings and the institutional marketplace, then, material youth culture and their everyday practices hold much promise for the scholarly investigation of religion in everyday life. While faith institutions hold the supportive legacy of the past for communities affected by disadvantage and deleterious effects historically, popular culture and its everyday practices hold the promise for the future of more robust and invigorating investigations into the shape-shifting uses of the religious in the lives of youth in general. The final chapter, "Faith in the Flesh" takes up one instance of such shape-shifting, embodiment in the dance form Krump.

6 Faith in the Flesh

"There is a spirit in the midst of Krumping. We don't have after school programs when you don't want to do football, because that's pretty much the only thing that you can do in the inner-city. . . we're all thought of to be sports players. . . . Is there something else for us to do? So what we did is a group of us got together and we invented this [Krump Dancing] . . . A lot of people think it's just "Oh, they're just a bunch of rowdy, you know, just ghetto, heathen, thugs." No, what we are . . . are oppressed."

—Dragon[1]

"When you catch the Holy Spirit, it's an indescribable feeling that enters your soul," says Miss Prissy. "When the spirit is ready to exit, it leaves a mark on you and that's what you saw in the film. The Holy Spirit entered [Daisy] in a dance form and used her as a vessel."

—Behind the Scenes of RIZE[2]

"The idea that we act as social agents from the center of our belief-systems fails to do justice to the more complex motive-forces that shape the conduct of everyday life. These include the unconscious, desire, habit, the logics of local practices . . . our need to maintain acceptable performances of self-presentation, cultural norms, and the ways in which our material environment shapes our imaginations and actions."

—Gordon Lynch[3]

Nestled between two abandoned stores and neighbor to a bustling establishment called Payless Caskets in South Central Los Angeles, Tommy Johnson, known to his community as "Tommy the Hip-Hop Clown," helped transformed a poor, urban, and gritty neighborhood forty-five minutes from Hollywood into an aggressive, artistic, raw never-seen-before Hip-Hop production. Tommy's Hip-Hop Academy provided an artistic safe haven as well as a space for a new style of Hip Hop to emerge. Tommy the Hip-Hop Clown has set the stage for the emergence of what would be described as one of the rawest forms of dancing to ever be seen, with faith based roots, Krumping (sometimes referred to as K.R.U.M.P which means: Kingdom Radically Uplifted Mighty Praise) emerged. Venturing from Hollywood to what one of the mothers in the documentary RIZE called "Hollywatts" (combination of Hollywood and the Watts ghetto), renowned fashion photographer David LaChapelle unexpectedly encountered a gritty, raw, and un-captured dance form embodied by marginalized black urban youth. LaChappelle became transfixed—or as he says, obsessed—with documenting exactly what this was and what these youth in Watts, LA were up to. After invigorating conversation and observation, LaChapelle took a leap of faith beyond his formal training and began capturing this urban phenomenon that was taking South Central, LA by storm.

Beginning in 2002 and utilizing his own financial resources ($500,000), sandwiched into breaks from his regular job as a Hollywood photographer, LaChapelle embarked upon a three-year journey that would transform not only his life, but also the lives of many youth who were, until then, a diamond in the rough on a desert ghetto planet not far from the place where dreams come true. Taking the genius of Hollywood to the ghettos of Hollywatts, LaChapelle chronicles how a certain style of dancing, originally called Clowning, has not only provided a cathartic embodied release, but also an artistic medium of survival for many youth who otherwise would end up in one of those caskets that Tommy's academy shares walls with. The youth in this documentary, RIZE, say where they are from: either you belong to a set (a gang) or a dance crew, either you bang or you get Krump, and these youth in RIZE choose life—they choose to get Krump.

While chapter 5 may have painted a bleak future for institutional religious participation among youth, this chapter, based on visual ethnography of the documentary RIZE, provides one example of how a group of urban marginal youth surrounded by churches, caskets, liquor stores, death, and run-down schools, have been able to survive a landscape of death through the use of one important element—their bodies. Using the spontaneity of their flesh through dance, these youth have been able to survive and channel social anxieties that come along with life on the underside of capitalism.

This chapter begins with a brief synopsis of the documentary RIZE, and then moves into a material analysis of various themes that run across this film; each theme will simultaneously be put in conversation with previous theoretical chapters, more generally Chapter 4, using the material data as a way to engage and call into question earlier theoretical suppositions and frameworks such as "buffering transgression" and "postmodern *complex subjectivity*." That is to say, this chapter uses material data of a documentary to enhance, challenge, and expand earlier theoretical and conceptual claims within a social scientific method. This is offered in counterpoint to the empirical work carried out in Chapter 5; through patient charting of the terrain and the use of multiple lenses, a process of looking through one window after another and then doing away with the whole concept of windows only to take it up anew, a more rounded sensibility may emerge as the stuff of religious study.

Methodologically, then, this chapter does not perform a religious or theological analysis of RIZE; rather, it explores and investigates themes of significance within RIZE and considers social processes situated in particular cultural life-worlds. Sometimes religious grammar is used by the subjects to describe aspects of this dance form, and in these instances I consider what such grammar accomplishes for the workings of Krump culture. While it would be easy to dub RIZE a new religious movement, there is something more fascinating about its practices beyond narrowing it to yet another religion. The complex (social, political, and cultural) dimensions of RIZE exemplify a particular sort of "faith in the flesh"—not faith in a theological sense, but faith understood as emphasis and importance in and on the corporeal body. The body: the object that remains in threat given these youths' social conditions of living, a material reminder of their social constraint and fixity. While their bodies remain fixed by the constraints of ghetto death, they are not fully determined—their bodies also represent the site and mode of human possibility. The creation of possibility through the body is not synonymous with the concept of regeneration in a religious sense; rather, the body as demonstrated in RIZE occupies multiple significance: ingenuity for the lack of means (e.g., lack of dance studios, no extracurricular sports offered in schools), mode of release for particular social anxieties, and a visceral social critique of structural constraint. That is not to say, however, that particular uses of religious experience (such as being slain in the spirit) are not comparatively used in the film; overall, the subjects of RIZE make clear that before "they started this dance thing" there was nothing made available to them to express the affective range of their ontological pain. Lastly, RIZE is an artistic battle against oppression—here saving grace abounds in one sole resource: the Body, and one type of place: the Urban Ghetto.

RIZE: A SYNOPSIS

After spending time in prison for selling drugs and against the backdrop of the Rodney King Riots that shook the racial foundations of Los Angeles, Tommy "the Hip-Hop Clown" Johnson embarked upon a journey to keep the youth of South Central off the streets while generating some income in the wake of no employment. After having been invited to be a Clown for a kids' birthday party in 1992, Tommy, also referred to as a ghetto celebrity on the streets, began building up his entertainment enterprise. With no materials but some face paint, a Clown outfit, and a "tricked out" green car with rims and bass, Tommy began frequenting the streets of the his neighborhood to make his presence known. He would pull up to a hood, get out of the car, and start "Clowning" around. In the film, Tommy notes that unlike other opportunities and resources afforded to entrepreneurs starting a business venture, he started out with nothing but Clown materials, a bucket and a sign, and very little cash. Beyond hustling, Tommy, who states he was changed for the better in jail, pleaded for a second life, a second chance. It would be his second chance at life that connected him back to his community and "at-risk" black urban youth. Tommy turned his business venture into a space that provided an alternative to gang and drug life in a place where choices and life options are scarce.

While performing at birthday parties, Tommy began noticing something different about how kids were "moving" their bodies—how they were dancing to the music. Noticing something new on the Hip-Hop horizons, Tommy began adding dancers to his Clown business as additional entertainment. Over the years, Tommy became more than a boss; he served multiple roles as mentor, friend, big brother, father figure, and confidant. Tommy's dance crew and academy would provide smiles, entertainment, and happiness to a neighborhood filled with pain—but once again, something more was emerging on the ghetto horizons beyond entertainment. Again, Tommy noticed the dance form was changing; something a bit grittier, edgier, and subterranean was forming. A style of dance called "Krumping" was birthing—a more forceful style exemplified by aggressive movement, struggle, and tenacity for survival. Clowning provided smiles and happy faces to a bleak situation—but Krumping would remind the world that being down-and-out doesn't kill a will to survive and learn things such as art and culture even in the absence of formal training. Headed by former Clowners Lil C and Tight Eyez, the evolution of Krumping began. In something similar to a denominational split, groups began to splinter and merge culminating into between fifty and eighty Clown and Krump groups. They donned names that characterized their different styles—like Rice Track Clowns and Stripper Dance, among others. Krump dancers range in age from four years old on up, and appear to be gender inclusive. Tommy the Hip-Hop Clown began something that could not be taken away: smiles for kids and the beginnings of a cultural mode of release for the expression of struggle and pain. With so many different groups in place Tommy embraced the change and fostered a healthy environment for competition by creating a forum called The Battle Zone, a place that Tommy says "is like fighting, getting out your anger, but on the dance floor with creative moves . . . we got the Lil Mama Match, the Big Boy Match, matches on the inside of a ring and the crowd . . . you be the judge." Here the Clowners and the Krumpers face off in a "battle" motif without rage, violence, and shooting—only a healthy and perhaps an anger-filled dose of competition.

MAKING A DOLLAR OUT OF 15 CENTS: HISTORICAL FIXITY AND MAKING DO

The constraint of life options and everyday struggle is a constant theme throughout RIZE. Make no mistake about it, this film highlights how a group of youth destined for social and physical death way too early, made something out of nothing. Shortly before LaChapelle embarked on his journey to film this dance subculture, this part of LA was still trying to recover from aftershocks of racial and class tensions emerging from the Rodney King Riots of 1992. This film is about dance, and its emergence in relationship to the historical and social struggle against rage, poverty, class, race tensions, and lack of resources. The technical artist and editor of the film, LaChapelle, contextualizes RIZE within the historical trace of the LA Watts Riots of 1965—we see a burning city in the background, pain-filled streets, while the lyrical guidance of gospel music is played to motivate reflection. The film fast forwards to 1992 showing a similar scene—outraged residents of LA after the Rodney King incident, and now instead of gospel music guiding our reflection, a voice narrates saying, "This is where we grew up, we were kids, we grew from this. And this is where we still live."

The play with historicity is an attempt to root this film in structures themselves, not that the emergence of RIZE is causally linked to these structuring structures of constraint, but rather, it wasn't produced in a vacuum—a fact that many participants, or at least the ones in the video, are aware of. We are reminded that *complex subjectivity* (CS) is situated in the movement of social anxieties that rise from terror and fear of historical fixity and constraint. I suggested that what remains unique about Pinn's theory of religion is its starting point in subjectivity and attention to historical structures. Situating Pinn's emphasis on the feeling and movement of the marginalized (*inner impulse* and *elemental feeling*) within Pierre Bourdieu's concept of *habitus* offered a way to think about structures, practices, and social inequality, a way that doesn't overdetermine consciousness and intentionality. Themes of crisis and struggle are clear and evident within RIZE—subjects highlighted in this film are persuaded that Krumping is in part a "response" to constrained life choices.

The youth in RIZE are aware, to some extent, of their conditions of existence. For example, Krumper Dragon states, "Basically we from the inner city or what you would call the ghetto, you know the lower parts of Los Angeles, Watts, Eastside of LA, Compton, Long Beach, and we don't get the best of everything so what we do, we come together and dance." In another segment, Dragon goes onto mention that "we don't have after-school programs, when you don't want to do football," and Lil C adds, "In better neighborhoods they have performing arts schools. . . it's nothing like that available when you live where we live." Some of the youth in RIZE describe Krumping as being birthed in the womb of oppression—fixity and constraint. Understood in this manner, Krumping becomes the ingenuous *effect* of social reproduction as well as the mode of agency. The social realities of fixity and constraint frame this film from the very beginning—in one sense as a true reflection of the conditions from which RIZE emerges, but equally as a constructed biased story created through technological editing. The narrative is mediated in such a way as to create coherence of this motif. Throughout the film, survival is articulated through the means of the flesh, as described by one participant. In other words, it doesn't provide transcendence from such social conditions, rather, the bodily comportment becomes a material mode by which aesthetics of survival become expressed.

There's no coherent triadic structure (confrontation by historical identity, wrestling with the old consciousness, embrace of new consciousness)[4] evidenced in RIZE—no clear decipherable delineation of the movement by which these subjects garner increased modes of awareness of their social reality. While full consciousness of social constraint is indeterminable, Krumpers highlighted in this film offer an articulation of the relationship between structural fixity and the evolution of Krumping—namely that of social crisis. There is a level of consciousness present here. I would argue however that while the motivation for the production of Krumping may be social crisis, there are elements of its form, such as spontaneity, that are exemplary of *play* in emergent cultural forms. The overall movement of Krumping suggests against placing this dance form within a causal frame of *cause* and *response*. As an emergent dance form, it's grounded in the soil of struggle and pain, what Pinn dubbed the historical terror of fixity, but yet boasts dimensions beyond a narrative of resistance. With Krumping come many codes: as some of the subjects in the film declare, "Not everybody can be Krump." There is a construction of authenticity that allows one into the Krump space. Stated otherwise, there is a particular experience that one must endure in order to create the conditions of possibility—being Krump. In this sense, Krumping becomes a partial response to the terror of fixity, a creative cultural form emerging in a very particular cultural and social geography.

MAKING DO: SURVIVAL AS MEANING-MAKING

> "Our struggle is what makes us special."
>
> —Lil C[5]

> "Sly as a fox and twice as quick: there are countless ways of making do."
>
> —Michel de Certeau[6]

Scholars of religion might suggest we think about the activity of Krumping *as* a quest for meaning. This, however, is dependent upon how meaning itself is understood. If the idea of meaning is invoked as a fully aware, conscious, inherently good, moral, essence then I would have to answer no to this question based on a nostalgic rendering that is not scientifically verifiable. However, I would like to suggest an alternate framing to how the construct of meaning is used in formulations of the religious by shifting emphasis away from meaning *behaviors* to focus on meaning *systems*. The former has its point of departure in attempting to apprehend decipherable behaviors and actions as "meaningful" while the latter places emphasis on (accounting for) structures and context by which meaning is produced. The recovery and explication of meaning, in the affective sense, is important within a particular tradition of religious studies that, according to

Russell T. McCutcheon, is exemplary of the theological and liberal human-ist strand. He argues that for this strand:

> the object of study—variously termed God, the Sacred, the *mysterium tremendum*, ultimacy, religious experience, or simply Human Nature, the Human Spirit, or the Human Condition—cannot be grasped by the usual epistemological techniques and must therefore be deciphered by studying its varied expressions (e.g. myths, rituals, symbols).[7]

He continues by suggesting that this tradition takes up such things as "non-historical truth, value and meaning" rather than grounding scholarship in "an examination of the thoroughly historical—and thus negotiable and contestable—structural conditions that make things such as truth, value and meaning items of discourse."[8] According to McCutcheon, a distinction should be made between the role of the scholar of religion and the liberal religious theological thinkers, who are at liberty to speculate on "ultimate meaning" and the "inexpressible essences" in "human nature," specula-tions that have no place in the (rigorous) academic community. While many will find McCutcheon's perspective debatable, he does however, raise a poignant point regarding what constitutes verifiable data for the academic study of religion. He is correct, I believe, that situating religion within the study of affective emotions, behaviors, and impulses, offers little to the pub-lic study of religion within the academic setting. That is not to deny, as I argued in Chapter 4, that the idea of meaning doesn't exist, rather, we mustn't act as if such data are self-evident and accessible: i.e., that mean-ing itself exists, separable from our ideations of it. A way forward would focus less on proving the meaningful merit of cultural activity, and more on exploring the *contexts* that house the production of meaning.

Krumping is about survival and the mediation of social anxiety through the body. In other words, Krumping does not become a mode of rizing *out-side* of the real; rather, Krumping becomes an artistic expression of living *with* the real, that is, the circumstances of everyday struggle (e.g., lack of resources, few materials, and little infrastructure). What we see expressed in RIZE is similar to what Michel de Certeau referred to as the "poetic ways of 'making do' (*bricolage*)"[9]—the appropriation and production of everyday mundane activities and raw material into a strategy of survival. This kind of making do both reflects and critiques structures of constraint while showing the tenacity, resilience, and agency of subjects to survive, by making meaning out of what seems like nothing.

In the beginning of the film, Dragon, articulates this art or perhaps war of making do when he states:

> If you're drowning and there's nothing around for help but a board floating, you're gonna reach out for that board floating, you're gonna reach out for that board and this was our board. We floated abroad and

we built us a big ship and we are going to sail into the dance world, the art world, and we are gonna take it by storm . . .

In a June 22, 2005 interview with Charlie Rose, Krump participant Lil C articulates a similar sentiment when he says, "The youth gravitated towards this because it was, it was an alternative to what was being offered to us, spoon fed to us, so I was like you know I gotta get into this, ended up joining the crew."[10] Realizing constrained life options, the lack of resources, and little access to structures such as art and dance academies, the youth in this film use language of invention and ingenuity to describe the logic behind the creation of this dance phenomenon. There is a sense of "making do" here with materials that such a life can afford them—some face paint, their bodies, and a spirit of tenacity and survival.

These youth are akin to contemporary *bricoleurs*—artisans of their trade with a resourceful and creative inventiveness. This is reminiscent of what Claude Levi-Strauss articulates in his seminal work *The Savage Mind* (1966) when he describes the spontaneous characteristic of *bricolage*—the ways in which objects are manipulated for alternative purposes. In a Straussian sense, these youth become the makers of their world by creating something out nothing, in what seems like a Jedi mind trick—a playing of the structure's hand. Krumpers recall what Strauss described as "the scientist creating events (changing the world) by means of structures and the 'bricoleur' creating structures by means of events"[11] in a "handy-man" style of construction. It is the use and manipulation of the body in the temporality of the urban ghetto that allows Krumping to not transform or liberate such subjects—but rather to survive against all odds.

In Chapter 4, I argued that inherent to both Pinn's and Miller's formulation of religion was an erroneous purchase placed on "meaning"—in other words, the quest for meaning became explicated as and grounds for a religious quest by positing quests for meaning as "orientation" and "ultimacy" and therefore religious. Moreover, I argued that formulating religion *as* the quest for meaning was synonymous to the search for what Derrida called grand transcendental illusions—a metaphysics of presence. Noting similarities between the work of Clifford Geertz and Paul Tillich and their influence within religious studies within North America, McCutcheon writes:

> Geertz's enduring contribution to the study of religion was to assist his peers to shift the ground from disputing *truth* to ascertaining the *meaning* of cultural acts by means of a nuanced, or what he called thick, description of practice. His goal, then, was not to explain these assorted practices, but merely to chronicle them and recover their meaning *as it was believed the participants themselves understood them.*[12]

The Geertzian and even Tillichian emphasis upon concern with meaning in culture continues to dominate cultural exploration within religion and theology. Again, I am suggesting here a turn from exploring the "meaning" of practices to considering the construction of meaning-making environments. The latter mitigates against isolating the essence of meaning in a way that is unobservable. That is not to say that practices of Krumping do not represent structures of meaning-making; however, considering the production of meaning in relationship to the context by which such activity emerges mitigates false assumptions of apprehending the intentionality and consciousness of subjects.

A constant theme throughout RIZE is reference to the practice of Krumping as a cathartic activity. Contrary to the anxiety-producing angst of historical fixity, the youth here are not, as some theories of religion would suggest, searching for identity. In other words, identity—as exemplified in RIZE—was not lost or destroyed through historical fixity. The anxieties produced within social inequality and everyday struggle did not fully determine a sense of self. Throughout the film, the youth make clear that they know who they are, and focus more specifically on the lack of resources for the channeling of emotions: rage, anger, pain, and so on. The production of Krumping does not assist in regaining the identity that has been lost through the fixity of terror, for the identity remains intact, though perhaps altered. Krumping becomes a space-within-no-space to "free one's mind" from the struggles of life. Understood in this manner, Krumping does not become a "solution" or curative to social reproduction as often theorized about religious experience; rather, it offers a space to rise "in contradiction" to the *real*—defying the limitations of social inequality.

When Dragon explicates the art of making do by using the metaphorical analogy of Krumping as a "board"—a raw material from which they would sail—he continues by saying, "This is our belief, this is not a trend, let me repeat, this is not a trend." The use of "belief" here calls our attention to the "weight" that Krumping holds within Dragon's life. Dragon wants the world to know through his use of "belief" that Krumping is not just another commodified Hip-Hop trend to be marketed and mass-produced on TV and around the world. Juxtaposing the word belief here with the word trend is a telling comparison: while Hip Hop may, as some have argued, become a global and transnational trend, Dragon makes the differentiation that Krumping is a belief. The social capital of "belief" endows Krumping with power. Through definitional alliances it gives Krumping a cosmological authenticity, demanding significance that would separate it from other Hip-Hop dance trends.

The activity of Krumping provides meaning through a mode of survival; Dragon states:

> We don't have after school programs, when you don't want to do football, because that is pretty much all you can do in the inner-city—there's always a football team, because in the inner-city we all thought of to be sports players. Everyone is not a sports player, everyone does

not play basketball, and everybody does not play football, is there something else for us to do? So what we did is, is a group of us got together and we invented this.

Another cast member, Tight Eyez, gives voice to the significance Krumping holds for him when he states, "Our only outlet is music, and a lot of the times dancing comes out," to which Lil C adds, "In better neighborhoods they have performing arts schools, they have ballet, they have modern, you have jazz, you have tap, and just all those prestigious academies you can go to, it's nothing like that available to you, when you live where we live." And so, these youth make do with what they have, and they learn how to survive through creative uses of their bodies. Dragon argues that many people get Krump because they are oppressed; he says, "You know, a lot of people just think it's, you know, oh they're just a bunch of rowdy, you know, ghetto, just heathen and thugs, no, what we are, are oppressed." Oppression houses the motivation for these youth getting Krump, and the manner in which they get it. In RIZE, Krumping becomes marketed as something that grew from oppression, as well as an art form that performs the theatrics of oppression. The survival element here doesn't transcend such oppression, rather it becomes a way to creatively cope, to create manufacturing zones of agency.

Lil C articulates the cathartic dimensions of Krumping—he puts it in this way:

> Say if people have problems, you know, didn't get this, didn't get that, short on this bill, short on that bill, the fact that you can get Krump, you can channel that anger, anything negative that has happened in your life, you can channel that into your dancing, and you can release that in a positive way because you are releasing that through art—the art of dance.

Dragon adds, "This is our ghetto ballet, this is how we express ourselves, this is the only way we see fit of storytelling, this is the only way of making ourselves feel like we belong." The cathartic release provided by this dance modality not only performs life's hurts and pains, it offers a cultural channeling of hurt in a rather productive way. Reflecting on his own life struggles, Lil C tells the story of what losing his dad (who committed suicide) was like, describing how he felt like people were judging him because he didn't cry at the funeral. The youth in RIZE are all, for the most part, no strangers to broken families, drug use, crime, and jail. Tight Eyez recalls how he had to go into a crack house to rescue his own mother from the hell of drugs. He says, "It was not a pretty sight, it still hurts, but that's why I got Krumping for—that's why I get Krump." Poignantly, Lil C adds that "Krumpness is the closed chapter of your life of hurt, sorrow, anguish that people don't know about." Here LaChapelle offers a vivid picture of what the expelling of pain through Krumping looks like.

Lil C, no shirt on, black sweaty body facing the calm peaceful waters at a beach—just him, his life, and the waters. Lil C begins to get Krump while beckoning the water. Through non-verbal gestures, he beckons one of earth's most serene yet forceful masses, eyes closed. The voice of his mother narrates softly over this scene, saying, "Kids these days have a whole set of anxieties, maybe he's angry that he seen me work all my life. . . . Maybe he's angry that he doesn't have a dad, he'll say, I just never envisioned that dad wouldn't be here."

The vignettes highlighted above offer a narrative of social struggle that becomes worked out in the body. We are reminded that experiences such as struggle and pain are part of conditions and circumstances are often understood as "religion-making characteristics."[13] I earlier raised the point that often questions of evil, pain, and the self/human are understood to be "religious" questions—an error of thought produced by the theological inheritance and dominance within the academic study of religion. Experiences often understood as existential aren't, in RIZE, dealt with through traditional means such as the cosmological pursuit. For example, death is a reality that many of these youth witness on a daily basis; they know it, live it, and have a keen and sharp sense of the fragility of life. While death is one of the experiences that can provoke such existential insecurity, this assertion is not validated by the data in RIZE. Rather than angst creating existential insecurity, these youth, with no options left as they say, use the art of dance as a means to channel rage and anger. They are not, as has been frequently theorized about religion, attempting to "regain" something that has been lost, or searching for "answers" to why they have been dealt such a terrible hand in life—or looking to be regenerated into something 'new' as William James's work would assert. They simply want to release anxiety produced from the pressures of ghetto life and realities. Religion often becomes thought of as a curative for social anxiety—here Krumping doesn't cure, it isn't the final solution, it's a means to create and survive.

The art of Krumping heavily relies upon the affective—feelings of anger, rage, sadness, and so on. The ways in which subjects attest to Krumping as a vehicle by which to express these sentiments are akin to Pinn's attention to what he called *inner impulse* and *elemental feeling* as described in Chapter 4. The channeling of rage in Krumping can most certainly be understood as a dimension of these concepts. I would suggest, however, that the affective range in RIZE is historically situated and manifested in the exteriorization of practices themselves. As such, the movement of feelings in RIZE is given a material housing in ways that push these concepts towards the outside of the inside of subjectivity itself. This is particularly why I made use of practice theory (vis-à-vis Bourdieu) in Chapter 4 to give *inner impulse* and *elemental feeling* a structural housing manifested in materiality itself.

THE METAPHYSICS OF KRUMPING?:
"THERE IS A SPIRIT THAT IS THERE"

Earlier in this chapter we heard Dragon describe Krumping as a "belief" and not a trend, thus endowing Krumping with a particular kind of power that cannot be duplicated nor commodified like other "trendy" Hip-Hop forms. In Chapter 4, I conjectured that perhaps characteristic of Hip-Hop cultural practices were *spontaneity* and *play*, and these elements are certainly evidenced in Krumping, grounded in and given shape by particular ritualistic codes. In this sense the movement of Krumping is spontaneously exerted from the body, yet there are what may in fact be unconscious and unwritten codes that give it what Bourdieu would call a logic of practice. For example, Dragon says, "When you know that there is a Krump session, me myself, and I know a lot of the people will stop whatever is going on if there is a gathering because it's the spirit that's there, there is a spirit in the, in the midst of Krumping there is a spirit there." Lil C also makes note of a particular kind of kinetic authenticity inherent in Krumping when he states, "The style changes every day, if you haven't danced in two days and come to a Krump session, we're gonna know. You're gonna be like, oh, that has to be the real thing because I will never see anything like this again." There is a certain way of knowing that is endemic to the Krumper's style, and that cannot be forced nor manufactured.

We have already established that the ethos of Krumping is about releasing social anxiety while creating access to resources otherwise unavailable. Krumping is a socially constructed dance form that allows participants to express their emotions and feelings through aggressive battling-styled movements. Earlier in this chapter we heard Lil C mention how youth gravitated towards Krumping because there were few options left for them. After learning what they needed to learn from Tommy the Clown, he says,

> before you know it we were dancing to much more aggressive music, we were experiencing turmoil and anguish in our lives, and the dance style began to change, became more aggressive, we would just turn the music on real loud . . . just real rugged music . . . we would just hype each other up and feed off of each other's kinetic energy, and it was crazy, before you know it, three people in a room, seven people in a room, ten people in a room, fifteen, thirty, sixty . . . then you have a Krump session, we called it Krump it just came to us. . . . You feel so serene after you get it all out, it's nothing like it, nothing at all.[14]

Here, language of "kinetic energy" is invoked to describe what these youth *feel* when dancing. Producer LaChapelle captures a vivid scene of one youth participant, Daisy. Uncertain of what is occurring in this Krump session, against the noise of youth screaming, cheering and clapping, LaChapelle asks, "What's happening?" but still the picture isn't clear. Daisy, one of

RIZE's cast members, is participating in an outdoor Krump session, with lots of people around. What we see next is someone hugging Daisy. Baby Tight Eyez tells the camera crew, "She just struck," some more words from the background that cannot be deciphered are exchanged, and he continues by saying, "That's what we all been waiting on, yup, that's what we all been waiting on." Overcome by emotion, the participants in this Krump session tell the camera that Daisy was "wilding out." Others, such as Miss Prissy, suggest that we witnessed Daisy catching the Holy Spirit; she says, "When you catch the Holy Spirit, it's an indescribable feeling that enters your soul," continuing, "When the spirit is ready to exit, it leaves a mark on you and that's what you saw in the film. The Holy Spirit entered [Daisy] in a dance form and used her as a vessel."[15]

While we remain uncertain about other Krumpers' religious commitments, Miss Prissy and Dragon are no strangers to institutional religion. They both agree that their form of dance cannot be rehearsed or pre-planned, it just happens. Other film segments show both of these youth dancing, albeit less aggressively, in the church (what some call praise dance). The youth make clear that before they "came up with this Krumping thing" there were no alternatives—this would, I suspect, even include institutions of faith. While religious language is at times invoked in the film, there is no mention of Krumpers' religious views or perspectives. A detour from this silence comes from Krumper Miss Prissy when she mentions how the space of the church enhanced her appreciation and embrace for her gift of Krumping: "If you go to a Christian church these same movements can be found in church. Dragon bought me back to Christ. One day we were getting Krump in my garage and he told me you know you would be a lot better if you start going back to church . . . it was God telling me my child this is your gift, use it." We are then shown a segment of both Miss Prissy and Dragon in church praise dancing (a similar yet different style of dancing commonly practiced in churches).

Beyond the youth themselves, parents gave praise for and recognition of the affirmative dimensions of Krumping. Dragon's mom says:

> The first time I saw Dragon get Krump, I thought he was on drugs, or maybe somebody had given him something, he was just like running around, screaming and tearing off his clothes and I didn't know what happened to him. Then he explained to me there was a new form of dancing that kinda too 'em back to their roots. I love it now, I get Krump too. I get Krump for Christ, but I get Krump.

When the producer LaChapelle asks, "Is there a difference?" she answers, "I don't think there is a difference. When they dance, they dance from their spirit, and uh, when I'm, when I'm at church I dance from my spirit." With the exception of Missy, no distinction was made in the film when referring to the signifier "spirit." Made clear however is that something "happens"—an event of sorts—in the midst of Krumping.

The transformational effects (understood as releasing and channeling of social anxiety) of participating in RIZE suggest a rethinking and retooling of how liberation and conversion motifs are explicated in theories of religion. On one hand, the element of "experience" is key here in the production of Krumping—yet there is also a sense in which this "experience" is part and parcel of the manufacturing of this dance modality itself. In order to receive the cathartic release that Krumping promises its participants, one must participate—and not just participate, but participate authentically. This cathartic release however challenges *sui generis* frames in the sense that the therapeutic dimension of Krumping is manufactured through rituals of gathering, battling, and so on. There is no renewed self (e.g., conversion) nor is there evidence of an essence or object of orientation encountered. In other words there is little emphasis on the privatization and interiorization of the release provided by Krumping—rather the feeling of letting go is for the most part manufactured through exterior practices (i.e., face painting, large numbers of people, a battle circle, a specific type of clothing style, the space of urban concrete, etc.). One must "experience" Krumping in order to understand it (one will simply not benefit by just watching) and in a prerequisite manner, understand the angst and pain of the struggles attached to social inequality. There is a communally shared feeling exemplified in the narratives of these youth. The feeling is produced and manufactured when the conditions and contexts have been created—from the outside, *not* the inside. There is no genie in the bottle here; the deployment of "spirit" language when describing the affective qualities of Krumping allows certain subjects to socially endow this art form with a symbolic-like capital, therefore constructing authority of its significance and power. Religious uses of words such as belief and spirit establish Krumping as something that's more than *just* dancing. The troping of "belief" language sets Krumping apart in the Hip-Hop world.

Here, the term 'belief' does not connote a phenomenological reductionism of cultural practice *as* belief—or something religious in nature. Rather, its usage defines the social construction—the manufacturing of a certain kind of authenticity of the practices of Krumping themselves. It both warrants and garners a kind of attention that distinguishes it from the more popularized mass appeal of Hip-Hop culture—grounding Krumping in a form of necessity that arises out of a specific kind of *habitus*. If anything, Krumpers do not come together for fun, games, and entertainment (as exemplified by the Clown groups), rather Krumping becomes a battle-like cipher and production of survival against all odds. Here, the metaphysics and social processes of Krumping take place at the site of human activity to construct and endow Krumping with symbolic weight in the world by using grammar that delineates significance and importance. Moreover, codes are socially constructed to house Krumping as something set apart from commodification and marketing of Krumping as just a commodified Hip-Hop trend. Krumping is just as much about the construction of authenticity and "street credibility" as it is a narrative about cathartic release and coping.

BODY AS SITE OF SIGNIFICANCE

Above all, Krumping is about the body as site of significance—an altered ethic of faith in flesh. The same black body that struggles to survive in a landscape where social and physical death lurks before its time—is the instrument used to not *transcend* social conditions, but rather, to *perform* a theatrics of struggle and pain in a meaningful way. Here is a performativity produced within the structures of social inequality, using raw materials and the body to perform agency and constraint. While the body is the site of significance in RIZE, I have not done full justice to these bodies. Fleshy dimensions of these bodies become disembodied and obscured through theorizing and explication. While I attempt to use voices when necessary, the flesh of these bodies is limited by way of discourse. The presentation of these bodies in RIZE is multiply mediated through the editing of LaChapelle as well as technological production of media in general to construct a narrative—a story. Furthermore, these bodies become the ocular object of the ethnographer's gaze. That is to say, the fleshiness of Krumpers' bodies is doubly and triply mediated in ways that suggest a binding of the material (e.g., real bodies) and the discursive. This chapter is a discursive analysis of fleshy bodies that by way of their form and production in RIZE are already discursively presented. I already acknowledged in Chapter 1 that there is tension within this project between material and discursive analyses of bodies themselves—perhaps a productive tension, or perhaps one that reduces the body to pure text to read. Perhaps, that's all we can do. Susan Bordo, whose work I used in Chapter 1 in relationship to the body of the materiality of the "nappy-headed ho," argues, "I consider postmodern culture, poststructuralist thought, and some aspects of contemporary feminism as embodying fantasies of transcendence of the materiality and historicity of the body, its situatedness in space and time."[16] It is worth noting that by "materiality," Bordo doesn't mean material in the sense of isolatable physical matter; rather, influenced by Michel Foucault and Karl Marx, she's referring to the ways in which culture has a "direct grip" on the fleshy body.[17] That is to say, the ways in which culture structures the habits and practices of the body itself. Yet, as mentioned in Chapter 1, Bordo doesn't resolve the tensions between (cultural) construction and the material (bodily matter). Her analysis of materiality is at times confused—sometimes located within the discursive and at others, on the outside. This ambiguity remains un-interrogated in her work. On the other hand Butler makes clear that the body *is* text—and never transcends the discursive. This chapter approaches the bodies of Krumpers as real yet structured and mediated—I can see their fleshiness presented in the film, yet my apprehension of their materiality is through my own discursive rendering. By the structuring of the discursive, I can offer no essential "meaning" to what these bodies "mean" outside of virtual mediation and text.

The necessity of Krumping has already been established as a 'belief' and not a trend—a belief that is grounded in and given shape by various ritualistic codes of authenticity and performance. I suggested in Chapter 4 that a postmodern rethinking of CS would, in part, be distinguished by elements such as *play* and *spontaneity*. The data from RIZE suggest that these elements exist, however they operate within more rigid codes and rituals than I had initially anticipated. That is to say, the movement of a Krump session is not complete free "play"—nor is it fully "spontaneous." Its movement is spontaneous, unpredictable, and unrehearsed, yet grounded in more structured elements of conduct. There is a certain kind of authenticity to Krumping as suggested by some of the data already recorded here. Subjects noted that they could decipher if a Krumper had been out of the Krumping element for only a few days' time. The ritualistic styling of Krumping houses its shape and form, and this styling is continually and communally updated. Krumping utilizes as its main instrument the materiality of the body; the body is the site of significance of this dance phenomenon. As such, I suggest that the body—the flesh of the participants—becomes the tool of utility. Here, faith (as in hope and the release of social anxiety) is dependent upon the participation and presence of the body.

The comportment of the body carries within it intentionality as well as dimensions of unconsciousness—it is, as we have seen, the angst of struggle that motivates the body to participate in a Krump session. The stylizations of the body cannot be and are not rehearsed beforehand—they are however, in each Krump session, endowed with a uniqueness that cannot be replicated or duplicated by others in a different space and time, perhaps a buying into claims of cultural uniqueness. Notwithstanding, I caution against a plastic distinction and overemphasis placed on *intentionality*—or the type of "thought" that brings one to perform a particular kind of practice. Ritual and practice theoretician Catherine Bell, by utilizing theorists such as Bourdieu, argues that the divide between thought and practice has for too long dominated the field of ritual studies. In other words, it has often been theorized that practices become the expression of a pre-existing belief—the performance of a certain kind of ethos and/or cosmos.

Bell's fusion of ritual (beyond thought, action, and belief) with social theory highlights her critique of thought/action dichotomies. She finds an interesting way to use practice theory as a dimension of ritual—or what she would later come to call *ritualization*. She writes:

> Since practice is situational and strategic, people engage in ritualization as a practical way of dealing with some specific circumstances. Ritual is never simply or solely a matter of routine, habit, or the "dead weight of tradition." . . . The strategies of ritualization are particularly rooted in the body, specifically, the interaction of the social body within a symbolically constituted spatial and temporal environment. . . . Ritualization is embedded with the dynamics of the body defined within a symbolically structured environment.[18]

In RIZE, the body retains the utmost significance—it is the main tool by which Krumping becomes manufactured by the participants as both the site and field of social inequality (*habitus*) where disadvantage unduly becomes inscribed *upon* the flesh, yet the flesh is not fully determined. Here, the flesh seemingly becomes the vessel of release, that which secretes the angst of the social struggle. The body here holds in tension both peril and promise—a reminder of the past as well as the agent of coping.

From the outset, it is made known that the movement and stylization of the body exemplified in Krumping will blow your mind—with lightening speed; one has to wonder if the producer of the film has made this dance form appear faster than it really is. But make no mistake—a qualifier is made before the film even begins stating that "the footage in this film has not been sped up in any way." In other words, what you see is what you get.

In the 2005 Rose interview, RIZE cast member Lil C pointedly describes how the comportment of the body becomes the seminal instrument whereby Krumping is manufactured:

> . . . aggressive in a physical sense . . . it was a physical battle within our-
> selves, our bodies would become the instrument, the chest would be the
> base, we would stomp, we would just hype each other up and feed off of
> each other's kinetic energy. . . . A Krump session is a group of kids gath-
> ering, in a vicinity, wherever, the street . . . wherever, usually the street
> because its real organic, music blastin, big circle, and you just go out, and
> you just get Krump and you just release all your frustrations on the dance
> floor because you become an artist when you enter the Krump circle the
> dance floor is your canvass, and you become an artist, and your painting,
> but it's more of abstract art . . . it's crazy . . .[19]

Whether it's talk of a "spirit that is there" from one participant or the sharing of "kinetic energy" as expressed here by Lil C, what we can infer from such data is that something happens—an event takes place in the midst of Krumping. This something, as I have suggested throughout, is the cathartic release of social anxiety in a shared space of community. In Krumping, the physical body in a theoretical sense represents both the question and the answer: it is that which holds the inscription of inequal-ity—and yet, the body becomes that which provides an artistic release of stress. I would argue however that the placement of the body in Krump-ing culture and ciphers does not represent liberation or increased agency, or what Pinn has theorized as the push for greater life-meaning vis-à-vis open ended processes of becoming. Rather, what Pinn has explicated as the *inner impulse* or *elemental feeling* as a deep stirring—the motiva-tion for increased agency—is exemplified in Krumping yet in an altered manner. Taking the basic theoretical structure of inner impulse and ele-mental feeling understood through a Bourdieuian *habitus*-like structure (as structuring dispositions that reflect in some ways the social relations of production and inequality), the compelling motivation for Krumping is struggle—that which begins on the outside of the subject and throughout time interpellates the subject from the outside in, thus constricting and stratifying the body and life options in a fixed manner. It is the shared environment of struggle that motivates these subjects to use the body as the instrument of release.

The film does not suggest that Krumping provides a modality of consciousness raising or liberation. On the contrary, if just for a moment, an impossible possibility occurs within the space of social struggle: an altered space of release is created—not a place where burdens are laid to rest, but rather, a ritualization where the burdens of life are come to terms with, face to face. Social difference is both the cause and the effect of the underlying motivation to get Krump. This acknowledgement guards from the interiorization of meaning as inward and privatized in a manner explicated by scholars such as James and Rudolf Otto. Rethinking the experience of Krumping through the lens of social constructionism leads to the acknowledgement that "experience" in Krumping is manufactured through cultural and social practices. In a push away from modernist perspectives of the sacred by embracing paradigms and approaches in media, religion, and popular culture, Gordon Lynch reminds us that:

> religious experience is not something that takes place prior to cultural practices and expressions, but that religious experience is constructed precisely through engagement with particular cultural practices and resources—whether through popular religious iconography, music, dance or other media. The sacred is encountered in and through culture, not in some privatized, mystical space that is separate from it.[20]

In addition to the primary emphasis on the body, there are accompanying elements that assist in making Krumping effective. I would call these supplementary codes rituals of *combat*. Everything about Krumping performs struggle and war—from the underlying motivation to get Krump, to the theatrics of Krump, survival is about war. The participants, as I will explicate more thoroughly in the next section, describe Krumping as their only alternative to joining a gang in South Central LA. As such, Krumping draws from the raw and enticing elements of gang culture—and baptizes them through the dimension of art thus producing an affirmative and safe way to be "hard core" in a less harmful manner.

The subjects throughout RIZE are painted as warriors of combat—an element that originated from Tommy's Clown group and was later incorporated into the Krump groups. Both Lil C and Tight Eyez explain that "we look like we are fighting somebody, but we're not fighting anybody, like you can push somebody, and they see nothing of it, fighting is the last thing on our minds when we're dancing. It is the last thing." In comparison to the Clown groups, Lil C explains that Krumping is a league of its own:

> It's more of like the, not the black sheep, but it's a raw version, like you have organized ball and you have street ball. Krumping is the street ball, you have a boy who gets Krump and just coincidently his girl-friend gets Krump. They face off, it's the classic battle of the sexes and that what makes like, "oh my god, the females do this too?"

In the Krump session/circle/cipher an altered ethic takes shape that is only valuable within the Krump session. If behaviors such as aggression are taken out outside the Krump circle in the gang-infested streets of "Hollywatts," the altered ethic literally disappears. These Krumpers know how to code-switch. What this further suggests is that the codes of Krumping (forming a circle, bringing your problems to the Krump session, face painting, spontaneous movements of the body, and so on) create a space-within-a-space where street ethics are stylistically incorporated yet ethically renegotiated.

And what's more—some of the youth articulate an innateness of Krump-ing from birth. Dragon cautions, "This is just not a bunch of people acting wild, this is a art form, this is as valid as your ballet, as your waltz, as your tap dance, except we didn't have to go to school for this, cause it was already implanted in us, from birth." While Dragon doesn't further explain what he means by this, I suspect he is referring to something inherent in the "style" of black culture. This not only gives Krumping historical and cultural origins by way of racial essentialism and inheritance, it's a way to maintain the authenticity of Krumping as something not everyone can do (e.g., participation is specific to race, class, and geographical location). There are certain experiences, environments, and circumstances that both *bring* and *allow* one to get Krump.

Back to the problems of constructed significance. LaChapelle uses Dragon's statement regarding the genetic predisposition of Krumping as an entry into a three-minute comparison between African tribal war-rior dances and the movements found in Krumping. In one sense, the comparison is highly compelling, in some cases showing almost exact duplication of moves found in both tribal African dances and the rituals of Krumping—however, it is important to stay cognizant that the simi-larities are not *real*; they are the compelling brilliance of LaChapelle's editing work to construct a cultural narrative that has purchase within the African-American community (e.g., retentions and cultural memory). African drumming guides this very compelling and intriguing compari-son of two African warrior men—the similarities are persuasive. From the depictions of sweaty black bodies, tribal face painting, pushing, shoving, and battling, one begins to wonder if Dragon is onto something when he states, "You're born with it" (the knowledge and know-how of Krumping). While enticing, this manufactured comparison must remain wholly in the brilliance of editing—there is no further evidence of a trans-historical African essence embedded in the art form of Krumping. This digital manufacturing endows Krumping with racial and ethnic significance. Fueled by the testimony that the stimulus for Krumping is *inside* of the subject—LaChapelle grants historical authenticity to this dance modality. In a fashion similar to that of religious scholars and theorists, LaChapelle puts the story of Krumping together through a mediated lens of his own construction.

CODES OF COMBAT: RITUALS OF THE ART OF WAR

The physical war raging within the social environments of the subjects in RIZE becomes an outward artistic expression in the form of *battle*—activity that mitigates constricting forces of historical circumstances, gang culture, and the lack of resources. Having the film open with the historical reminder of the Watts riots of 1965 followed by scenes of the Rodney King Riots of 1992, frames and constructs Krumping as a *response* to social disparity—as well as a testament to the tenacity of human will and strength to rise up above the circumstances of the real. The codes of Krumping—that which I have called *rituals of combat*—signify not only retaliation and revolt against historical and current conditions, but also shape Krumping as an art form that defies the commodity fetish of Hip-Hop commodification. Thus the art of Krumping can be envisioned and understood as *effect* of urban struggle and survival. The voices of youth in the film similarly support this notion.

The *style* of Krumping exemplifies the warrior/street soldier narrative that is portrayed in the film: faces are painted in a tribal-like manner, clothes are ripped and torn off in the Krump circle, participants come face to face in a battle-like format, fatigues and militaristic artifacts are worn with power, and what's more, the music narrating the film signifies battle and competition. For example, the song "Break It on Down" played in one set of the film goes: "you wanna battle with me?/you wanna battle with me?/you wanna battle with me?/don't start nothing/won't be nothing/don't start nothing/won't be nothing/Krump Clown break it on down/Krump Clown break it on down."

It is not only the aesthetic *style* of Krumping that gives it street- and warrior-type authenticity—it is the *look* of the Krumper that distinguishes it from more trendy dimensions of Hip-Hop culture. This style adorns Krumpers with the hardness that comes with both *being* and *getting* Krump. For example, Miss Prissy in the film says, "Some of us may look gritty, some of us may not have the prettiest smiles, you know what I am saying? But, we are Krump, and that's the part that makes us Krump." In Krumping culture there is a deep recognition of *differ-ence*—in other words, these participants both know and understand that despite purchase placed on distinctions between "high" and "low" culture, Krumping (whose creation was birthed from lack of resources, and pain and anguish) is no different from tap, ballet, and more "recog-nized" forms of art. And yet, there remains a difference—something sets Krumping subjects and lifestyle apart from what they may encounter forty-five minutes down the street in Hollywood.

In his 1984 landmark book *Distinction: A Social Critique of the Judgment of Taste*, Pierre Bourdieu makes a correlation between taste and social stratifi-cation. Inherited and learned from early on, stratification produces particular aesthetic preferences within various social groups, producing a *difference* in various dispositions. It is through the accumulation of various forms of capi-tal (such as social, economic, cultural) that tensions of class are produced and seen through particular practices of *taste*. It is thus the *taste* of particular social groups that produces differences in style, preferences, and so on. The *difference* produced between the differences of different social and cultural preferences (such as music, architecture, clothes, art, food, etc.), is where class differences are most evident, what Bourdieu would come to call *distinction*.[21]

The warrior-like codes of RIZE hold within them their own "logic of practice"—a particular kind of *habitus* that is specific to a particular social/cultural group. These codes are both the origin and the consequence of Krumpers' social positionality. If everyday life on the streets of South Central LA is characterized by strife, struggle, and pain, it is logical then that the culture produced within such conditions would represent these elements. Krumpers are indeed street warriors—Krumping to deal with struggle, face to face.

The theme of difference plays an interesting role in RIZE. In one sense the youth in RIZE argue that there is no *difference* between Krumping and jazz for example, and yet throughout they tell a story about how Krumping *is* different. One must "go through" what they live in order to both *get* and *be* Krump. These youth know the difference, these differences are inscribed into Krump culture. They also know and feel a sense of *difference* with respect to the cultural codes of Hollywood. This is best articulated by Miss Prissy, who says:

> Some people don't feel safe outside of this place, I mean I've seen a lot of people come from Hollywood come and visit my home and be like, "How do you live here? You live in South Central, oh it's so, it's so dangerous." It's not dangerous, it's life, a lot of the kids out here they don't have that, they don't have that push or that drive to go and be in Hollywood because so many people have knocked them down already so their comfort level is the hood, it's scary to go to Hollywood com-ing from the hood, for the simple fact that everything is so intimidat-ing. When I first got my first glance of Hollywood everybody seemed

like this to me [throws head up in a bourgeois fashion] and I felt like
this [throws head down], like everybody is so uppity, everybody has so
many things going for themselves and here I am, and that's how the
kids here feel. We're just some, some gutter kids.

Miss Prissy gives expression to the hardened reality of these youth bodies. Their body, disposition, preferences, and so on bear the mark, the
trace of social disenfranchisement; again, the body is central and key in
understanding the complex dimensions of Krump culture.

While Clown groups often perform for entertainment purposes,
Krumping is described as something that reflects pain and anguish. With
over fifty different Krump groups, each group has its own style and fla-
vor. For example, one group that goes by the name of Stripper Dance
(and whose youngest member is five years old) self-describes as ". . . like
when you open both of your legs, you bend like this, then you be making your butt bounce like that, but it really be bouncing." When some
Krumpers criticized that the age of five years was too young for such
provocative moves, a member of this group retorted back, "She's having fun, not being sexual. What's wrong with poppin?" Yet, Krumpers
make an ethical distinction. Lil C says, "You have stripper dance which
we do not do, you have Clown dancing, then you have Krumping." Tight
Eyez jumps in to say (referring to Krumping), "Like hygiene, it's either
you smell good or you don't, either you Krump or you not." Shown here
are not only internal distinctions between the splinter groups, but also
varied ethical dimensions among them as well.

The physical battle of everyday life becomes acted out artistically
in Krump culture—in this sense, Krumping becomes at once a critique
(of society), a performance of inequality, and a mode of social release
more generally.

A BLOOD OR A CLOWN? THE "BUFFERING EFFECTS" OF KRUMP/CLOWN CULTURE

Throughout RIZE, Tommy the Clown is depicted as a role model, a
mentor, a father, and an example to the youth of the community he
serves. In Chapter 5 of this project I critiqued what I suggested was an
underlying theoretical disposition within scholarly work that explores
youth religiosity—that which I referred to as *buffering transgression*.
In this model, institutional religiosity is constructed as a moral necessity by using empirical data to demonstrate the affirmative effects of
youth church participation. It is theorized that youth who participate
in institutional religion have increased and greater life options and
chances, while suggesting that faith institutions provide a "buffering"

effect in the lives of marginal and "at-risk" youth. Throughout, I have critiqued this model of engagement. I have also suggested that a measuring of religious effects be extended beyond institutional referents to consider if non-faith-based cultural practices hold similar buffering merit.

Interestingly, data from RIZE incorporate similar "buffering transgression" sentiments by validating Krumping as having analogous social efficacy effects. Larry, the oldest Clown member and Tommy's right-hand man, is typical of Krumping's buffering merit. Larry's mother describes how before meeting Tommy, her son was "off the ringer." In fact, she goes as far as to say that Tommy had more control than she did. She further states, "I want him to be a Clown, that's how he separated himself from all the bullcrap out here in Hollywatts." Describing "Hollywatts" as a "lion's den," she paints a picture with "gangs on one side and Clowns on the other." Another RIZE cast member, Lil Tommy, says, "They [the gangs] gonna ask you who dance with or they gonna be like what set you from [set=gang], so that's why it's either a gang or a Clown group. If you say Clown group, they'll go about their business." Making an obvious distinction between "gangs" and "Clowns," parents and youth alike articulated the affirmative dimensions of Krumping in the lives of these youth (e.g., a decipherable change in behavior). One mother testifies, "Larry is over here with the Clowns, I thank God for that, I am so glad they came out with this Clown thing cause ain't no telling where the kids would be or what they be doing. What else is there to do?" These narratives highlight the bifurcated life options of South Central LA as either/ or, not both/and. Not only does Krumping and Clowning mitigate gang involvement, it seemingly provides various forms of access that would not traditionally be afforded. Another cast member, Termite, states that being a Clown has meant opportunities to "get away, travel out of the neighborhood, meet new people, make a name for myself, doing something positive . . . I would have been a bad person." Lil C adds that "Clown groups are in a real sense like families," and Tight Eyez continues, "We laugh together, we cry together, we go through whatever one person go through that whole group goes through."

Krumping and Clowning may provide an alternative to more violent life options such as gang membership, but also these cultural groups act as familial stand-ins, as expressed by Lil C. In fact, the film shows the story of how Tight Eyez, an older Krump member, takes a younger member, Baby Tight Eyez, under his "brotherly" wing. Tight Eyez becomes a positive influence and physical protection in the life of his mentee. Sitting on a stoop reflecting on his life in the company of Tight Eyez, Baby Tight Eyez says with much pain and regret, "My mom she in jail, she in jail 'cause she don't wanna live right, she just smoking dope for as long as I know since I was a baby, before I was born."

In the 2005 interview, Lil C describes how Krumping became an alternative to what was being spoon fed to them by society. In this interview, Charlie Rose asks a few cast members, "Where would you be today if you hadn't started dancing?" Lil C responds:

> I have no idea. Um, I came from a single parent home, due to my father committing suicide, my mother was always my, uh, mother and my father . . . living in a very tough neighborhood, South Central LA, crime ridden, violence, drugs, police. . . If not for her I don't know what would have become of me, but because of her . . . Tommy, David [the producer of RIZE], I learned through all of them that I have a gift and there's no need for me to let the statistics and stereotypes infect my mind."

In the same 2005 interview, Tommy reflects back on his life before Clowning when he was in jail, recalling how the judge at his parole hearing facetiously said, "Oh you'll be back, you'll be back." Tommy says with a smirk on his face, "But I proved him wrong." When he first fell in love with the entertainment side of Clowning, with "creating smiles" as his main intention, Tommy began to receive emails from distressed mothers pleading with him for his assistance in helping keep kids off the street. This reality was part of Tommy's motivation for wanting to open the academy, providing a space where the kids could participate in a more productive option than what they were being dealt.

The story, message, and tenacity of Krumping and Clowning on one hand buys into the "buffering transgression" motif that I have challenged. On the exterior, Krumping may appear to be deviant—as Dragon said, "a bunch of people acting wild," or what Lil C termed "ghetto heathen thugs"—but a deeper peek into the worldview of Krumping demonstrates its subversive social efficacy merit.

While Krump culture may provide motivation for wanting more out of life, sparking an ethos of continued survival as exemplified by Dragon's sentiments when he states, "We have the belief that we can be somebody and that we are gonna be somebody. We're gonna rise no matter what"— the reality of death is not too far away. Lives of the young are still being snatched too early from this neighborhood. Clowning and Krumping may provide a protective alternative to the dangers of street life and gang participation, but there are no guarantees. During the filming of RIZE, a fifteen-year-old female named Qualisha Ford, a member of the Clowns, was gunned down by gang members for no reason—she was at the wrong place at the wrong time—and LaChapelle dedicated RIZE to her memory. Austin Harriss, the owner of Payless Caskets, reminds the youth in the film, "I know ya'll some good Clowns but you betta Clown right, unless I know where you gonna end up. Right here with me," while encouraging them to come in and take a look at the caskets—the physical holding place that has claimed too many, too early in the streets of South Central, LA.

AND SO . . .

Earlier in this chapter, Dragon reminded us that Krumping is a belief and not a trend and though exactly what he meant in the deployment of the word "belief" remains opaque, the words of LaChapelle nicely sum up what may have been going through Dragon's mind that day. In that 2005 interview, Rose probes LaChapelle, Tommy, and Lil C regarding how we (the public) are to know that Krumping is not just another trendy Hip-Hop production. LaChapelle responds, "It's not a trend because it's their lives."[22]

My intention in this chapter was to use the data, life stories, and worlds highlighted in RIZE to make sense of earlier theoretical formulations in this project. On one hand, there is much room here to create a religious scenario out of RIZE, albeit theoretically manufactured, of course. The rich data of RIZE will tempt many in constructing a religious story based on experience—and yet, there is also another challenge lurking. RIZE portrays the life-worlds and actual voices of youth in South Central LA—yet these voices and life-worlds are also mediated and doubly constructed. The story available to be seen in RIZE is an edited story. As highlighted earlier in the chapter, some connections in the film are questionable, such as the (constructed) comparison between African tribal dancers and the movement of Krumping, a manufacturing that stylistically tries to support the comment by a Krumper that one cannot learn Krumping, rather one is born with it. Despite the mediation of the portrayal of Krumping, this film, I believe, gave a genuine look into urban youth subcultural practices and the logic that guides one among many cultural forms. Although the youths' voices were mediated through editing and LaChapelle as the producer, I also believe that these voices were presented in a reliable manner. The words of Lil C exemplify LaChapelle's spirit: "He's [LaChapelle] never tried to water us down, commercialize us, exploit us, anything, he wants us to always keep it raw."

I have tried to put the material of RIZE in conversation with earlier theoretical suppositions, trying where necessary to use the data as a means by which to enhance and/or push back on the theorist's imagination. While RIZE both confirms and challenges earlier theoretical possibilities, it is also reflective of some of the critiques I have been constructing throughout this project. Overall, I would argue that social inequality is in one sense the stimulus for getting Krump, while Krump reflects the very social inequality of its participants. While Krumping reflects the *habitus* (the bodily social reproduction) of Krumpers—it also becomes an artistic mechanism to deal with anxieties and tensions from the hardships of everyday life. By form and structure, Krumping represents a kind of faith in the flesh—however, the body is not transformed into a new consciousness, an altered self. The Krump session doesn't provide a new perspective on life; rather, it alleviates and materially channels the pain of life.

Apparent throughout this film—and as poignantly theorized by Pinn's theory of religion, *complex subjectivity*—Krumpers are, to some extent, conscious of the historical fixity of their urban ghetto. They make clear that they live their lives in an internal colony-within-a-colony. Moreover, Krumping testifies to the reality that, as Pinn has suggested, their subjectivity is not fixed, rather through a process of what he refers to as "perpetual rebellion" Krumping emerges in tension with historical terror.

Krumping begins and ends in subjectivity—the materiality of the bodily comportment. And yet, while the body becomes the instrument of release, the reality of death continually lurks—that is to say, Krumping does not provide a protective shield, it is a celebration of "ghetto" art forms at the least and a survival mechanism at best. There are no data to suggest that Krumping provides an altered conversion, transformation, or liberation, rather its production becomes an expression and critique of the social reproduction of inequality.

Krumping is likewise characterized by both spontaneity and various logics of practice—that which I have referred to in this chapter as codes of combat. Rituals (i.e., face painting, clothing style, and aggressive movements) of conduct that give shape and form to Krumping as an art of war, are exemplary of social conditions marked by a tenacity for survival. Krumping displays everyday life—struggle, pain, anger, and hope. Within Krumping, there is an indigenous cultural capital formed. That is why participants make clear that Krumping cannot be practiced as a trend; rather, it has to be lived on a daily basis. Likewise, it is these codes of combat that endow Krumping with a particular kind of authenticity, a street authenticity that demarcates it from other trendier Hip-Hop cultural productions. This allows for a certain kind of significance that keeps Krump culture comparable to analogous spaces such as the church as well as what is classified by dominant culture as high forms of art (i.e., jazz, ballet, tap, modern dance, etc.). Again, the body is central in the rituals of combat—the *style* of Krumping, the warrior paint, and aggressive bodily movements endow Krumping with a narrative of origins. Some of this is supported by the Krumpers themselves; but some is mediated and manufactured by the producer.

Lastly, Krumpers and their families testify to the "buffering transgression" motif I critiqued in Chapter 5. Krumping takes elements of deviance (e.g., the familial style of gang culture, the aggression of the streets, and the rawness of the ghetto) and incorporates them something more acceptable, productive, and affirmative. In one sense, Krumping buys into the very ideological positionality that I argued was evident in social science literature on the affirmative buffering merits of institutional religious participation, and yet, it also confirms that perhaps more attention can be given to the potential buffering merit of non-institutional cultural forms that at first glance are assumed to be "deviant" and devoid of such potentiality. However, the "buffering transgression" motif that was lifted up in RIZE by both parents and youth differs in its ideological posture from the social science literature discussed in Chapter 5. In other words, while social science literature embraces the positive attributes of the morality of institutional religious participation (which in turn assists in disciplining bodies to act according to societal rules and norms), Krumping does not boast a privileged posture of "morality"—rather, it provides another "alternative," it becomes a cultural *resource* that assists in giving the youth something else to do, even while providing and embracing the "deviant" elements that one may search for in gang culture.

The Krumping culture highlighted in RIZE provides a challenge to the scholar of religion on the quest for new cultural religions. Rather than a subjugated religiosity evidenced in Krumping culture, what has become clear is that Krumping provides an alternative cultural sphere that highlights not only faith in the flesh but an aggressively therapeutic way to express and perform daily struggle. In Krumping can be observed subjects who are in every way complex—Pinn's *complex subjectivity* embodied—yet a pulse can be sensed of elements that push back on this intellectual formulation. Like a splayed-out postmodern hand of cards, Krump embodies *spontaneity* with structure and codes, historical *traces* (albeit manufactured and mediated), a hint of Derridian *aporia* (a complexity and awe in Krumping that there may be a "spirit that is there"—for although it remains uncertain whether there is in fact such a spirit, it can be inferred that the language of "spirit" provides Krumping culture with the potential power of a religious form), the creative ingenuity of *making do* and *bricolage*, a structured disposition of *play* and performance, all undergirded by a Bourdieu-like *habitus* inculcated and inscripted onto the body motivated by social *difference* itself.

The culture of Krumping constructs meaning grounded in survival and making-do. There is no search for grand illusions of truth and coherence; rather, the in/coherence of Krumping reflects the complexities of urban ghetto life. The materiality of the body in Krumping becomes both the question and the answer—a testament to the relations of production and poverty only forty-five minutes from opportunity (Hollywood), and also a faith that the flesh will get you through another day in the ghettos of Hollywatts.

Perhaps there is no rising above the *real* here in Krump culture—more accurately reflective of the this cultural production is rising to *deal* with the real. There is here no real escape from or of the *real*, only a moment, an impossible possibility of survival and hope—for the culture of death continually lurks and no "real" protective shields are formed, only a will to survive.

Conclusion
When the Religious Ain't So Religious, After All

"I'm the religion that to me is the realist religion there is. I try to pray to God every night unless I pass out. I learned this in jail, I talked to every God (member of the Five Percent Nation) there was in jail. I think that if you take one of the "O's" out of "Good" it's "God", if you add a "D" to "Evil", it's the "Devil". I think some cool motherf**ker sat down a long time ago and said let's figure out a way to control motherf**kers."

—Tupac Shakur[1]

I opened up this project with two very different quotes, disparate ways of thinking that among them hold in tension the dimensions of this project of inquiry—to them I add here the voice of rapper Tupac Shakur, who, as cited in Chapter 3, expresses a confusing explication of his religious perspectives. Queer theorist Judith Butler proclaimed there can be no construction of a "proper object" of a discipline without doing violence to the object so conceived, and lastly religious studies scholar Russell T. McCutcheon theorized that despite the popular approach and consensus within religious studies, "religion" is not an inner object of meaning and experience—it is not a "private affair." In fact, what we as scholars have come to call the religious, really ain't so religious after all. Rather, religion is a taxonomical way by which a particular discipline picks and chooses what human behavior and social activity should come to be understood as "uniquely" religious. The category of religion, most often left un-interrogated, is used in various ways to accomplish particular social, political, and religious interests on behalf of the scholars themselves—indeed, echoing the ways in which religion has been seen elsewhere in this work as being used to achieve certain *effects* in the lives of human subjects, among them the youth manifesting Hip-Hop culture in America.

Hip-Hop cultural practices retain within them an "anti-proper" sentiment—a cultural posture that marks and perpetually calls into question the "proper" search of the scholars' "object" of inquiry—mine included. I set out to use Hip-Hop cultural modalities to investigate the category of religion—and yet, the varied social and cultural interests of Hip Hop would always and at once call into question the "proper object" of my study. I expressed a hope at the outset that investigating the materiality of Hip Hop would offer the opportunity to explore an understudied area of research in religious studies, while using such exploration to focus outside-in on the central "object" of investigation—the category of religion itself.

I have conducted this inquiry from the position that the category of what scholars have come to call "religion" is in fact a human doing, production, and manufacturing with a particular social and political history. Seen thus as an act of imagining and doing, religion eludes the theoretical and taxonomical category that has often privileged particular practices and experiences as "religious." For the duration of this project such claims have been suspended, the category of religion thus emptied. My method throughout has been what McCutcheon has called a "critic not caretaker" approach in order to investigate religion in a critical manner.

There is no need here to ask the question: "What is religious?" Rather, as scholars of religious studies we can approach cultural practices with the understanding that there is nothing in and of itself unique about religion. Of greater interest is the exploration of *why* certain social processes come to be understood and classified *as* religious, and furthermore what these classifications accomplish among particular groups across time and space. The second chapter of this work demonstrated three very different uses of the religious in Hip-Hop material cultural practice, revealing how religion can be used aesthetically to garner a certain kind of *power, authorization*, or *authenticity*. In other instances we saw the troping of religion and philosophy as a means by which to create *tactics* and *strategies* for alternative purposes. Overall, the exploration revealed that approaching Hip-Hop cultural practices with a critical eye lends itself to a more robust exploration of complicated dimensions of social life.

This project set out to refashion a religious studies approach to Hip-Hop and youth culture, in so doing laying out a groundwork that can serve as a foundation for future engagement. While the use of the empirical here functioned as a window into the life-worlds of youth and Hip Hop cultural workers, in this project only visual, virtual and quantitative methods were used. There is much room for extended qualitative research in such under-engaged spaces, where voices upon voices are speaking, for those who care to listen. That is not to privilege the face-to-face as more authentic than the ethnographic imagination approach taken in this project, but that expanding the empirical under formal ethnographic methods will offer more insight into particular life-worlds. All empirical analysis is marked by the bias of the researcher's own narrative and frames of reference, and that is of course also the case here. Advocating for empirical methods and social science approaches is not to say that this methodology allows access to purer forms of data. Rather, I am simply saying that qualitative data such as interviews and participant observation offer a larger window into the life-worlds and human activity of subjects themselves, in a way that is less mediated than mere hermeneutical analysis of purely textual sources.

One of the book's starting points was the exploration of three knowledge productions within Hip-Hop culture, and its final chapter analyzed the documentary RIZE, which could also be seen as fitting within this grouping. Taken together, this material reveals important insights for future work in this area. The data from both chapters indicate that what often *appears* as religious is in fact not very religious—if religion is being understood as a confessional, coherent, decipherable inward essence that is self-evident. Rather than searching for the essence of *meaning*, taking a postmodern informed critical approach allows a shift of focus.

The data from RIZE yield pertinent insight into the *logic* of Clowning and Krumping and what the organization and social processes of this dance culture provide for its participants. Rather than constructing Krumping and Clowning *as* a religion, I approach zones of significance within Krumping as both *causes* and *effects* of constrained life options. In other words, survival is the mode of constructing meaning in RIZE. In instances when traditional "religious" or "theological" language is used by the subjects, I approach these uses as products of human construction used to accomplish a particular task. For instance, I've suggested that the use of "belief" endows Krumping with a means by which to separate itself from market trends within Hip-Hop culture. Even so, one remains cognizant that significance in RIZE is continually being mediated and manufactured by the film's producer. This mediation assists in constructing a mythos endowing Krumping and Clown culture with a narrative of origins and historicity. First and foremost, however, the materiality of the body remains central in Krump and Clown culture as *site* and *mode* for the releasing of social anxiety as "faith" is made manifest in the flesh. This embodiment exemplifies what this project has been trying to arrive at: a religious rhetoric that starts not with the category of religion, but in and among the lived lives of human subjects.

It is my hope that religious studies analyses of Hip-Hop culture can *begin again*. In each moment through this project, Hip-Hop culture in various manifestations represented a dimension of "anti-properness"—more specifically, I see Hip-Hop culture by form and content to represent altered ways of knowing in the world. In other words, while the religious studies scholar may have a "proper object" of study in mind (religion), Hip Hop cultural practices seemingly call this "properness" into question by challenging the very epistemological structure by which our field of analysis is developed. Here, I have offered a new approach to engaging Hip Hop in specific and popular culture in general. The postmodern stylings of Hip-Hop practices are indeed, as anthropologist John Jackson reminds us, paranoid by form. Hip Hop is tricky, witty, and more often than not words and appearances are not what they seem. This multi-positionality forces a new perspective to our intended "object" of inquiry—Hip Hop's paranoia, to use Jackson's language, forces a redescribing and new lens of analysis. A shift in disposition and approach is required to do justice to the stylings of popular culture.

This project borrows the language of "rethinking" and "redescribing" from Russell T. McCutcheon as set forth in his work *Critics Not Caretakers: Redescribing the Public Study of Religion* (2001), where he argues that redescribing the category of religion invariably calls for a redescribing of what the field of religion purports to do by such work. *Religion and Hip Hop* has attempted to redescribe the category of religion for future work in the intersections of religion and popular culture while also expanding engagement with Hip-Hop cultural material beyond the more common approach of reading and analyzing rap lyrics. Among Hip-Hop culture, religion is figured as many things, but rarely is a singular confessional approach taken. This very multiplicity is a indicator of the fractured life-worlds of the postmodern condition, for when the image is kaleidoscopic, to try to contain and make sense of the picture within a single rectilinear frame is an exercise in distortion. Instead, it may serve as a clue that many forces are at work, that may require the deployment of multiple lenses and perspectives, for when the Word becomes flesh in the material dimension, how is that word to be read, and by whom? The stylings and uses of religion within the living-out of Hip Hop material culture are cutting back through the dimensions, and the scholar setting out to locate religion may find that 'religion' has reposited the locus of study.

Notes

NOTES TO THE INTRODUCTION

1. Judith Butler, "Against Proper Objects. Intro duction," *Differences: A Journal of Feminist Cultural Studies* 6.2, no. 3 (1994): 6.
2. Racquel Z. Rivera, *New York Ricans from the Hip Hop Zone* (New York: Palgrave MacMillan, 2003), 15.
3. I have in mind scholars such as Michael Eric Dyson, Anthony B. Pinn, Mark Anthony Neal, Tricia Rose, Imani Perry, bell hooks, and Cornel West among a host of others.
4. Stanley Cohen, *Folk Devils and Moral Panics*, 3rd Edition (New York: Routledge, 2002 c1972), 1.
5. For an extended conversation on the ways in which religion has often been theorized as a phenomenon that both maintains (order) and legitimates, see Peter Berger's work, *The Sacred Canopy* where, in part, he argues that there is something unique about the ways in which religion has the effective capacity to "maintain" reality and mitigate forces of chaos and disorder. He goes onto argue that one of the "prime functions" of religion is the very idea of "world-maintenance." See: Peter Berger, *Sacred Canopy: Elements of A Sociological Theory of Religion* (New York: Anchor, 1990 c1967).
6. bell hooks, *Outlaw Culture* (New York: Routledge, 1994), 5.
7. Gayatri Spivak, "Can the Subaltern Speak?" in *Marxism and the Interpretation of Culture*, ed. Cary Nelson and Lawrence Grossberg (Urbana: University of Illinois Press, 1988).
8. Gordon Lynch, *Understanding Theology and Popular Culture* (Malden: Blackwell, 2005), 26.
9. hooks, *Outlaw Culture*, 5.
10. Russell T. McCutcheon, *Critics Not Caretakers: Redescribing the Public Study of Religion* (Albany: State University of New York Press, 2001), 9.
11. Russell T. McCutcheon, *Manufacturing Religion* (New York: Oxford University Press, 1997) and Talal Asad, *Genealogies of Religion: Discipline and Reasons of Power in Christianity and Islam* (Baltimore: Johns Hopkins, 1993).
12. Stewart M. Hoover, "The Cross at Willow Creek: Seeker Religion and the Contemporary Marketplace," in *Religion and Popular Culture in America*, ed. Bruce David Forbes and Jeffrey H. Mahan (Berkeley: University of California Press, 2000), 148.
13. McCutcheon, *Manufacturing Religion*, 3.
14. Malory Nye, *Religion: The Basics* 2nd Edition (London: Routledge, 2008 c2004), 19.
15. Nye, *Religion*, 20.

16. James A. Beckford, *Social Theory and Religion* (Cambridge: Cambridge University Press, 2003), 2–3.
17. Beckford, *Social Theory and Religion*, 4.
18. McCutcheon, *Critics Not Caretakers*, 60.
19. McCutcheon, *Critics Not Caretakers*, 27.
20. Gordon Lynch, "Object Theory: Towards a Mediated, Dynamic and Inter-subjective Theory of Religion," in *Religion and Material Culture: The Matter of Belief*, ed. David Morgan (London: Routledge, 2010), 4.
21. Lynch, "Object Theory," 40.
22. Jasbir K. Puar, *Terrorist Assemblages: Homonationalism in Queer Times* (Durham: Duke University Press, 2007), xv.
23. Puar, *Terrorist Assemblages*, 212.
24. The mid to late 1990s saw an explosion of cultural criticism by African-American scholars in the wider academy, which among other things not only forged a sustained engagement with Hip-Hop culture specifically, but also legitimated the academic and scholarly study of Hip Hop as a viable arena of critical discourse. Earlier focus on social criticism from a pragmatic philosophical and existential posture can be found in Cornel West's *Race Matters* (1994) and *Democracy Matters* (2005) among others, which pushed for a "necessary engagement with youth culture" in general. West's engagement goes beyond the disembodied disinterested critic: he continues to occupy multiple spaces of reflection, embedding himself within the broader culture in which he engages (this is also exemplified in the release of his rap/spoken word CDs). Specific engagement with rap music and the lives of rappers is evidenced in Michael Eric Dyson's *Between God and Gangsta Rap: Bearing Witness to Black Culture* (New York: Oxford University Press, 1996) and *Holler if You Hear Me: Searching for TuPac Shakur* (New York, Basic Civitas, 2006), among numerous others. See Cornel West, *Democracy Matters: Winning the Fight Against Imperialism* (Reprint, New York: Penguin Books, 2004); *Race Matters* (New York: Vintage, 2001).
25. For example, see the following works: Dyson's *Between God and Gangsta Rap* and *Holler if You Hear Me*, Bakari Kitwana's forthcoming work on Hip Hop and the Black Church *Get Your Soul Right: Ministering to the Hip Hop Generation*, Cornel West's *Democracy Matters* and *Race Matters*, John Michael Spencer's (defunct) journal on Theology & Music: *Black Sacred Music: A Journal of Theomusicology* and the Special Issues of *Black Sacred Music* (1991 and 1992). There is also a growing amount of scholarship that looks at the varied Islamic sensibilities of rap music, such as Felicia M. Miyakawa's *Five Percenter Rap: God Hop's Music, Message and Black Muslim Mission*, and Samuel Thomas Livingston's *The ideological and Philosophical Influence of the Nation of Islam on Hip-Hop Culture*. Anthony B. Pinn's *Noise & Spirit* also looked at, among other religious expressions, the Islamic (Five Percent) dimensions of rap music.
26. Anthony B. Pinn, *Noise and Spirit: The Religious and Spiritual Sensibilities of Rap Music* (New York: New York University Press, 2003), 2.
27. For example see the following: Tommy Killonen *Un.Orthodox Church. Hip Hop.Culture*, Eric Gutierrez *Disciples of the Street: The Promise of a Hip-Hop Church*, Ralph C. Watkins *The Gospel Remix: Reaching the Hip Hop Generation*, Ronald Charles Hemphill *Church Based Strategies to Reach, Reclaim and Redeem Young African American Males within The Hip Hop Generation*, Efrem Smith and Phil Jackson *The Hip-Hop Church: Connecting With The Movement Shaping Our Culture*.
28. Pinn, *Noise and Spirit*, 14.

29. For one such example, see Anthony B. Pinn and Paul Easterling's article, "Followers of Black Jesus on Alert," *Black Theology: An International Journal* 7, no. 1 (2009), 31–44.

30. Anthony B. Pinn, "On A Mission From God: African American Music and the Nature/Meaning of Conversion in Religious Life" in *Between Sacred and Profane Researching Religion and Popular Culture*, ed. Gordon Lynch (London: I.B. Tauris, 2007), 146.

31. See: Robin Sylvan *Traces of the Spirit: The Religious Dimensions of Popular Music* (2002), *Trance Formation: The Spiritual Dimensions of Global Rave Culture* (2005), Richard W. Flory and Donald E. Miller's *Finding Faith: The Spiritual Quest of the Post-Boomer Generation* (2008) and *MySpace to Sacred Space: God for a New Generation* (2007).

32. Here, I take the theoretical position articulated by Michel de Certeau in *The Practice of Everyday Life* (1984) when he gives a detailed explication of the relationship between consumers and producers. That is to say that while mass culture relies on the creativity of everyday "consumers," consumers likewise have the agency to "individualize" mass culture and make it their own. This perspective mitigates against an over-determined relationship between structure and individual agency, and shows that structures in fact parasitically poach everyday creativity, relying upon the ingenuity of everyday people who often become estranged or alienated from the very object that they create, only to be re-appropriated in a new way by the "consumer." For an extended discussion, see: Michel de Certeau, *The Practice of Everyday Life* (Los Angeles: University of California Press, 1984).

33. See for example one such study: Center for Civic Innovation, Manhattan Institute, "The Role of African-American Churches in Reducing Crime Among Black Youth" by Bryon R. Johnson; available from (http://www.manhattan-institute.org/html/crrucs2001_2.htm); Internet; accessed 12 January 2010.

34. See: Black Youth Project, "Black Youth Project: Research Summary," by Cathy J. Cohen, available from: http://blackyouthproject.uchicago.edu/writings/research_summary.pdf; Internet; accessed 12 January 2010.

35. See: Black Youth Project, "Black Youth Project: Research Summary," by Cathy J. Cohen, available from: http://blackyouthproject.uchicago.edu/writings/research_summary.pdf; Internet; accessed 12 January 2010, page 2.

36. de Certeau, *The Practice of Everyday Life*, xi.

NOTES TO CHAPTER 1

1. For a detailed analysis of the role of (black) moral panics and the scapegoating of Hip Hop and youth culture, please see the chapter, "Gangsta Rap Made Me Do It" in *Democracy Remixed: Black Youth and the Future of American Politics* (London: Oxford University Press, 2010).

2. Bill Cosby quote, available from http://www.eightcitiesmap.com/transcript_bc.htm, Internet, accessed 25 February 2010.

3. Cathy J. Cohen, *Democracy Remixed: Black Youth and the Future of American Politics* (London: Oxford University Press, 2010), 23.

4. Nas quote, available from http://www.youtube.com/watch?v=Mfz7wVxzuoE, Internet, accessed 3 February 2010.

5. Don Imus quote, Available from; http://www.youtube.com/watch?v=RF9BjB7Bzr0, Internet, accessed 3 February 2010.

6. KRS One, *The Gospel of Hip Hop: The First Instrument* (Brooklyn: I Am Hip Hop, 2009), 132.

7. Cited in KRS One, *The Gospel of Hip Hop*, 129.

8. I use the word "elite" here to signify voices that were privileged enough to be given public air-time to speak for and on behalf of the whole of the black community. The groups given such space in the Imus controversy were folks (mostly black men) with access to various forms of dominant capital, and they ultimately became the authorities on such commentary and analysis.

9. Mary Douglas, *Purity and Danger: An Analysis of Concepts of Pollution and Taboo* (New York: Routledge, 1966), 2.

10. Douglas, *Purity and Danger*, 6.

11. Douglas, *Purity and Danger*, xi.

12. Michael Eric Dyson, *Is Bill Cosby Right (Or Has the Black Middle Class Lost Its Mind?)* (New York: Basic Civitas, 2005), xiii.

13. Douglas, *Purity and Danger*, xix.

14. Available from; http://www.youtube.com/watch?v=zIUzLpO1kxI, Internet, accessed 3 February 2010.

15. Available from; http://www.youtube.com/watch?v=RF9BjB7Bzr0, Internet, accessed 3 February 2010.

16. Cathy J. Cohen, *Democracy Remixed: Black Youth and the Future of American Politics* (London: Oxford University Press, 2010), 23.

17. Here, I use the trope "multiplicity" to signify identity configurations that exceed the grasp of numerical logic that constricts the diversity of identity in general. I follow the ways in which theologian Laurel C. Schneider pushes for conceptions of the divine within a trope of "multiplicity"—that which exceeds what she calls the "Logic of the One." For Schneider, multiplicity "is not a mathematical statement"; rather, it is as she states, "limitation and possibility, constituted, not opposed." See Laurel C. Schneider, *Beyond Monotheism: A Theology of Multiplicity* (London: Routledge, 2008).

18. Available from http://www.youtube.com/watch?v=bmF8iIeOVEo, Internet, accessed 3 February 2010.

19. Media Matters, "Imus Called Womens Basketball Team 'nappy-headed hos'" available from http://mediamatters.org/items/200704040011, Internet, accessed 10 February 2010.

20. "Don Imus on Al Sharpton's Radio Show," *New York Times* 9 April 2007, Media and Advertising Section, available from http://www.nytimes.com/2007/04/09/business/media/09imus_transcript.html, Internet, accessed 10 February 2010.

21. Racialicious, "Oprah's Town Hall Meetings on Misogyny and Hip Hop," available from http://www.racialicious.com/2007/04/20/oprahs-town-hallmeetings-on-misogyny-in-hip-hop/, Internet, accessed 20 February 2010.

22. "NAACP Buries Symbolically Buries N-Word" *Washington Post* 9 July 2007, available from http://www.washingtonpost.com/wp-dyn/content/article/2007/07/09/AR2007070900609.html, Internet, accessed 10 February 2010.

23. Available from http://www.tmz.com/2006/11/20/kramers-racist-tirade-caught-on-tape/, Internet, accessed 25 February 2010.

24. Judith Butler, *Gender Trouble: Feminism and the Subversion of Identity* (New York: Routledge, 1999), viii.

25. Butler, *Gender Trouble* , xvi.

26. Laurel C. Schneider, "What Race Is Your Sex?" in *Disrupting White Supremacy From Within* (Cleveland: Pilgrim Press, 2004), 143.

27. E. Patrick Johnson and Mae G. Henderson, eds. *Black Queer Studies: A Critical Anthology* (Durham: Duke University Press, 2005), 5.

28. Johnson and Henderson, *Black Queer Studies*, 6.

29. Johnson and Henderson, *Black Queer Studies*, 7.

30. Butler, *Gender Trouble*, xvi.

31. Cathy Cohen, "Punks, Bulldaggers, and Welfare Queens: The Radical Potential of Queer Politics," in *Black Queer Studies*, 22.
32. Cohen, "Punks, Bulldaggers, and Welfare Queens," 23.
33. Cohen, "Punks, Bulldaggers, and Welfare Queens," 25.
34. Iris Marion Young, *Justice and the Politics of Difference* (Princeton: Princeton University Press, 1990), 127.
35. See Cathy J. Cohen, *The Boundaries of Blackness: AIDS and the Breakdown of Black Politics* (Chicago: University of Chicago Press).
36. Judith Butler, *Bodies that Matter: On the Discursive Limits of Sex* (New York: Routledge, 1993), xii.
37. Butler, *Bodies that Matter*, 8.
38. Susan Bordo, *The Flight to Objectivity: Essays on Cartesianism and Culture* (Albany: State University of New York Press, 1987), 283.
39. Butler, *Bodies that Matter* , ix.
40. Butler, *Bodies that Matter*, 8
41. Young, *Justice and the Politics of Difference*, 137.
42. Cohen, "Punks, Bulldaggers, and Welfare Queens," 33.
43. Butler, *Undoing Gender* (New York: Routledge, 2004), 179.
44. Young, *Justice and the Politics of Difference,* 152.
45. Butler, *Undoing Gender*, 223.
46. Judith Butler, *Excitable Speech: A Politics of the Performative* (New York: Routledge, 1997), 1.
47. Butler, *Excitable Speech*, 2.
48. Butler, *Excitable Speech,* 23.

NOTES TO CHAPTER 2

1. Lupe Fiasco, "Hip Hop Saved My Life."
2. Nasir Jones, "Hip Hop Is Dead."
3. http://brooklyntheborough.com/?p=1003, Internet, accessed 15 November 2009.
4. http://www.examiner.com/x-10853-Portland-Humanist-Examiner~-y2009m8d25-Rap-religion-KRSOne-to-release-HipHop-Bible, Internet, accessed 5 January 2010.
5. http://www.mtv.com/news/articles/1542740/20061009/nas.jhtml, Internet, accessed 6 November 2009.
6. http://tmagicworld.com/2009/07/30/the-50th-law/, Internet, accessed 6 November 2009.
7. http://www.youtube.com/watch?v=mBpGlWShkQI, Internet, accessed 6 November 2009.
8. http://www.youtube.com/watch?v=mBpGlWShkQI, Internet, accessed 6 November 2009.
9. http://www.youtube.com/watch?v=mBpGlWShkQI, Internet, accessed 6 November 2009.
10. http://www.youtube.com/watch?v=tlp66y9ML3o, Internet, accessed 6 November 2009.
11. http://www.sohh.com/2009/09/50_cent_breaks_down_50th.html, Internet, accessed 6 November 2009.
12. http://www.sohh.com/2009/09/50_cent_breaks_down_50th.html, Internet, accessed 6 November 2009.
13. Monica R. Miller, "Don't Judge a Book By Its Cover." *Bulletin for the Study of Religion* (Equinox) Special Issue: "What's this 'Religious' in Hip Hop Culture?" 40, no. 3 (September 2011): 26–31.

14. Robert Greene and 50 Cent, *The 50ᵗʰ Law* (New York: G-Unit Books, 2009), vii.
15. Bruce Lincoln, *Authority: Construction and Corrosion* (Chicago: University of Chicago Press, 1994), 10–11.
16. Lincoln, *Authority*, 11.
17. Greene and 50 Cent, *The 50ᵗʰ Law*, ix.
18. Greene and 50 Cent, *The 50ᵗʰ Law*, 14.
19. Jacques Derrida, and Elisabeth Rudinesco, *For What Tomorrow: A Dialogue* (Stanford, CA: Stanford University Press, 2004), 20.
20. Derrida and Rudinesco, *For What Tomorrow*, 21.
21. Greene and 50 Cent, *The 50ᵗʰ Law*, 33.
22. Sudhir Venkatesh, *Off The Books: The Underground Economy of the Urban Poor* (Cambridge: Harvard University, 2006), 7.
23. Venkatesh, *Off The Books*, 18.
24. Venkatesh, *Off The Books*, 93.
25. Venkatesh, *Off The Books*, 170.
26. Howard S. Becker, *Outsiders: Studies in the Sociology of Deviance*, (London: Free Press, 1963), 15.
27. Becker, *Outsiders*, 147.
28. Pierre Bourdieu, "The Forms of Capital," in J. Richardson, ed. *Handbook of Theory and Research for the Sociology of Education* (New York, Greenwood, 1986), 241–258.
29. Pierre Bourdieu, *Language and Symbolic Power* ed. John B. Thompson, trans. Gino Raymond and Matthew Adamson Cambridge: Harvard University Press, 1991), 107.
30. Bourdieu, *Language and Symbolic Power*, 116.
31. Greene and 50 Cent, *The 50ᵗʰ Law*, x.
32. Bourdieu, *Language and Symbolic Power*, 117.
33. Michel Foucault, *The Archeology of Knowledge* trans. A. M. Sheridan Smith (New York: Pantheon, 1972), 50.
34. Russell T. McCutcheon, *Manufacturing Religion* (New York: Oxford University Press, 1997), 117.
35. Greene and 50 Cent, *The 50ᵗʰ Law*, x.
36. Greene and 50 Cent, *The 50ᵗʰ Law*, 3.
37. Greene and 50 Cent, *The 50ᵗʰ Law*, 18.
38. Greene and 50 Cent, *The 50ᵗʰ Law*, 102.
39. Greene and 50 Cent, *The 50ᵗʰ Law*, 19.
40. Greene and 50 Cent, *The 50ᵗʰ Law*, 21.
41. Greene and 50 Cent, *The 50ᵗʰ Law*, 21.
42. Greene and 50 Cent, *The 50ᵗʰ Law*, 22.
43. Greene and 50 Cent, *The 50ᵗʰ Law*, 288.
44. http://www.hiphopdx.com/index/news/id.9241/title.krs-one-delivers-hip-hop-gospel, Internet, accessed 6 November 2009.
45. http://allhiphop.com/stories/news/archive/2009/08/20/21903171.aspx, Internet, accessed 6 November 2009.
46. http://www.guardian.co.uk/music/2009/sep/01/krs-one-gospel-hip-hop, Internet, accessed 6 November 2009.
47. http://www.guardian.co.uk/music/2009/sep/01/krs-one-gospel-hip-hop, Internet, accessed 6 November 2009.
48. http://www.youtube.com/watch?v=Z675H-PkwZ0, Internet, accessed 6 November 2009.
49. http://www.youtube.com/watch?v=oS3ZpqY_u6A&feature=related, Internet, accessed 6 November 2009.
50. KRS One, *The Gospel of Hip Hop*, 6.
51. KRS One, *The Gospel of Hip Hop*, 7.
52. KRS One, *The Gospel of Hip Hop*, 7.

53. KRS One, *The Gospel of Hip Hop*, 8.
54. Talal Asad, *Genealogies of Religion: Discipline and Reasons of Power in Christianity and Islam* (Baltimore, MD: Johns Hopkins University Press, 1993), 29.
55. Asad, *Genealogies of Religion*, 37.
56. Asad, *Genealogies of Religion*, 43.
57. Asad, *Genealogies of Religion*, 45.
58. KRS One, *The Gospel of Hip Hop*, 15.
59. KRS One, *The Gospel of Hip Hop*, 8.
60. KRS One, *The Gospel of Hip Hop*, 10.
61. KRS One, *The Gospel of Hip Hop*, 13.
62. Bourdieu, *Language and Symbolic Power*, 166.
63. KRS One, *The Gospel of Hip Hop*, 14.
64. KRS One, *The Gospel of Hip Hop*, 14.
65. KRS One, *The Gospel of Hip Hop*, 15.
66. KRS One, *The Gospel of Hip Hop*, 26.
67. KRS One, *The Gospel of Hip Hop*, 28.
68. KRS One, *The Gospel of Hip Hop*, 61.
69. KRS One, *The Gospel of Hip Hop*, 62.
70. http://hypebeast.com/2009/09/rza-tao-wu-book/, Internet, accessed 6 November 2009.
71. http://www.youtube.com/watch?v=aCTgQUcqhWk, Internet, accessed 6 November 2009.
72. http://www.youtube.com/watch?v=aCTgQUcqhWk, Internet, accessed 6 November 2010.
73. The RZA and Chris Norris, *The Tao of Wu* (New York: Penguin Group, 2009), vi.
74. RZA and Norris, *The Tao of Wu*.
75. Michel de Certeau, *The Practice of Everyday Life* (Los Angeles: University of California Press, 1984), 30.
76. de Certeau, *The Practice of Everyday Life*, 30.
77. de Certeau, *The Practice of Everyday Life*, 36.
78. de Certeau, *The Practice of Everyday Life*, 36–37.
79. RZA and Norris, *The Tao of Wu*, 4.
80. RZA and Norris, *The Tao of Wu*, 26.
81. RZA and Norris, *The Tao of Wu*, 41.
82. RZA and Norris, *The Tao of Wu*, 47.
83. RZA and Norris, *The Tao of Wu*, 48.
84. RZA and Norris, *The Tao of Wu*, 49.
85. RZA and Norris, *The Tao of Wu*, 58.
86. RZA and Norris, *The Tao of Wu*, 108.
87. RZA and Norris, *The Tao of Wu*, 109.
88. RZA and Norris, *The Tao of Wu*, 113.
89. RZA and Norris, *The Tao of Wu*, 120.
90. RZA and Norris, *The Tao of Wu*, 124.
91. RZA and Norris, *The Tao of Wu*, 124–125.
92. RZA and Norris, *The Tao of Wu*, 139.

NOTES TO CHAPTER 3

1. James A. Beckford, *Social Theory and Religion* (Cambridge: Cambridge University Press, 2003), 15.
2. John L. Jackson, *Racial Paranoia: The Unintended Consequences of Political Correctness* (New York: Basic Civitas, 2008), 147.

3. "Interview With 2Pac," available from http://www.tupacnet.org/life/interview.htm, accessed 2 January 2009.

4. Representative of such notable treatments are the work of Anthony B. Pinn, Cornel West, Michael Eric Dyson, and Anthony B. Pinn and Monica R. Miller.

5. Here, I deploy the phraseology of "im/possibility" in a Derridian sense. Derrida uses the deconstructive terminology of "impossibility" to connate that it is the same conditions that often enable possibility, that likewise constrain such potentiality. This rubric transgresses birfucated and dualistic thinking. Thinking more specifically about the topic at hand, Hip-Hop culture—Hip Hop retains a potentiality of religion (through the play with master signifiers and perceived religious language)—and yet it is the play that enables such possibility that likewise makes space for the "impossible" task—that is, searching for "religion" in a modality that is not inherently or innately religious. The religious studies scholar is searching for religious "meaning" and "essence" in practices that in fact may call the enabling of such quest or search into question in both form and content of the culture itself.

6. Talal Asad, *Genealogies of Religion: Discipline and Reasons of Power in Christianity and Islam* (Baltimore, MD: Johns Hopkins University Press, 1993), 45.

7. Jonathan Z. Smith, *Imagining Religion: From Babylon to Jonestown* (Chicago: University of Chicago Press, 1982), xi.

8. Asad, *Genealogies of Religion*, 44.

9. Malory Nye, "Religion, Post-Religionish, and Religioning: Religious Studies and Contemporary Cultural Debates," *Method & Theory in the Study of Religion* 4, no. 12 (2000), 468–469.

10. Jacques Derrida, "Faith and Knowledge: The Two Sources of 'Religion' Within the Limits of Mere Reason" in *Acts of Religion*, eds. Jacques Derrida and Gianni Vattimo (Stanford, CA: Stanford University Press, 1998), 71.

11. For an extended conversation on Derrida and aporia see: Niall Lucy, *A Derrida Dictionary* (Malden: Blackwell, 2004) and Nicholas Royale, *Critical Thinkers: Jacques Derrida* (London: Routledge, 2003).

12. See Jacques Derrida's: "Structure, Sign, and Play in the Discourse of the Human Sciences" in *Writing and Difference*, trans. Alan Bass (London: Routledge, 1978), 278–294.

13. Jackson, *Racial Paranoia*, 147.

14. Jackson, *Racial Paranoia*, 150.

15. See: Bruce David Forbes and Jeffrey H. Mahan ed. *Religion and Popular Culture in America* (Berkeley: University of California Press, 2005).

16. Omar McRoberts, *Streets of Glory: Church and Community in a Black Urban Neighborhood* (Chicago: University of Chicago Press, 2003), 81–99.

17. See Mary Patillo, *Black Picket Fences: Privilege and Peril Among the Black Middle Class* (Chicago: University of Chicago Press, 1999).

18. Ralph C. Watkins, *The Gospel Remix: Reaching The Hip Hop Generation* (Valley Forge: Judson Press, 2007), ix–x.

19. Watkins, *The Gospel Remix*, 2.

20. For an extended conversation on the workings of *hegemony* see: Antonio Gramsci, *Selections from the Prison Notebooks,* trans. Quintin Hoare and Geoffrey Nowell Smith (London: Lawrence & Wishart, 1971).

21. Watkins, *The Gospel Remix*, 41.

22. Otis Moss III, "Real Big: The Hip Hop Pastor as Postmodern Prophet," in Watkins, *The Gospel Remix*, 111.

23. Efrem Smith and Phil Jackson, *The Hip-Hop Church: Connecting with the Movement Shaping Our Culture* (Downers Grove: InterVarsity Press, 2005), 25.

24. Smith and Jackson, *The Hip Hop Church*, 25.

25. Louis Althusser, "Ideology and Ideological State Apparatuses (Notes towards an Investigation)," in Louis Althusser, *Lenin and Philosophy and Other Essays*, trans. Ben Brewster (New York: Monthly Review Press, 1971).

26. Althusser, *Lenin, Philosophy, and Other Essays*, 138.

27. Althusser, *Lenin, Philosophy, and Other Essays*, 121.

28. Gramsci, *Selections From The Prison Notebooks*, 170.

29. Michael Eric Dyson, *Open Mike: Reflections on Philosophy, Race, Sex, Culture and Religion* (New York: Basic Civitas, 2002), xiii.

30. Dyson, *Between God and Gangsta Rap*.

31. Michael Eric Dyson, *Holler if You Hear Me: Searching for TuPac Shakur* (New York, Basic Civitas, 2006), 204.

32. Dyson, *Holler If You Hear Me*, 204.

33. Dyson, *Holler If You Hear Me*, 209

34. Dyson, *Holler If You Hear Me*, 209.

35. In West African tradition, a griot is known as a storyteller who places emphasis on the oral tradition.

36. Dyson, *Holler If You Hear Me*, 210.

37. Dyson, *Holler If You Hear Me*, 209.

38. Dyson, *Holler If You Hear Me*, 244.

39. Michael Eric Dyson, *Open Mike: Reflections on Philosophy, Race, Sex, Culture and Religion* (New York: Basic Civitas, 2002), 275.

40. Dyson, *Open Mike*, 276.

41. Dyson, *Open Mike*, 276.

42. Cornel West, *The Cornel West Reader* (New York: Basic Civitas, 1999), 482.

43. Cornel West, *Race Matters* (New York: Vintage, 2001), 148.

44. West, *Democracy Matters*, 179.

45. West, *Race Matters*, 148.

46. West, *Democracy Matters*, 179.

47. West, *Race Matters*, 162.

48. Pinn, *Noise and Spirit*, 3.

49. Pinn, *Noise and Spirit*, 21.

50. Pinn, *Noise and Spirit*, 95.

51. Anthony B. Pinn and Monica R. Miller, "Introduction: Intersections of Culture and Religion in African-American Communities" in *Culture and Religion* 10, no. 1 (2009): 3.

52. Pinn and Miller, "Introduction," 3.

53. Pinn and Miller, "Introduction," 3.

54. Paul Tillich, *Dynamics of Faith* (New York: Perrenial, 2001), 1–2.

55. Pinn and Miller, "Introduction," 4.

56. Gordon Lynch,"The Role of Popular Music in the Construction of Spiritual Identities and Ideologies," *Journal for the Scientific Study of Religion* 45 no. 4 (2006): 481–88.

57. Lynch, "The Role of Popular Music," 12.

NOTES TO CHAPTER 4

1. Jacques Derrida, *Speech and Phenomena: And Other Essays on Husserl's Theory of Signs*, trans. David B. Allison (Evanston: Northwestern University Press, 1973), 62–63.

2. Derrida, *Speech and Phenomena*, 104.

3. In his work *Writing and Difference*, Derrida understands the *trace* as an emptying of presence, "not a presence but . . . rather the simulacrum of a presence that dislocates, displaces, and refers beyond itself. The trace has,

properly speaking, no place for effacement belongs to the very structure of the trace. . . . In this was the metaphysical text is understood; it is still readable, and remains read." See Jacques Derrida *Writing and Difference*, trans. Alan Bass (London: Routledge, 1978), 403.

4. Charles H. Long, *Significations: Signs, Symbols, and Images in the Interpretation of Religion* (Philadelphia: Fortress, 1986), 7.
5. Long, *Significations*, 7.
6. Anthony B. Pinn, *Terror and Triumph: The Nature of Black Religion* (Minneapolis: Fortress, 2003), 133–134.
7. Pinn, *Terror and Triumph*, 137.
8. Pinn, *Terror and Triumph*, 137.
9. Pinn, *Terror and Triumph*, 157.
10. Pinn, *Terror and Triumph*, 175.
11. Pinn, *Terror and Triumph*, 158.
12. Pinn, *Terror and Triumph*, 158.
13. Pinn, *Terror and Triumph*, 159.
14. Pinn, *Terror and Triumph*, 159–160.
15. Pinn, *Terror and Triumph*, 177.
16. Pinn, *Terror and Triumph*, 177.
17. Pinn, *Terror and Triumph*, 177.
18. Pinn, *Terror and Triumph*, 178.
19. Pinn, *Terror and Triumph*, 180.
20. Pinn, *Terror and Triumph*, 181.
21. Pinn, *Terror and Triumph*, 182.
22. Pinn, *Terror and Triumph*, 186.
23. McCutcheon, *Critics Not Caretakers*, 11.
24. Long, *Significations*, 16.
25. Long, *Significations*, 33.
26. Russell T. McCutcheon, *Critics Not Caretakers: Redescribing the Public Study of Religion* (Albany: State University of New York Press, 2001), 11.
27. William James, *Varieties of Religious Experience: A Study in Human Nature* (New York: The Modern Library, 1902) 10.
28. James, *Varieties*, 31.
29. James, *Varieties*, 126.
30. James, *Varieties*, 126.
31. James, *Varieties*, 188.
32. James, *Varieties*, 189.
33. James, *Varieties*, 196.
34. James, *Varieties*, 193.
35. Pinn and Miller, "Introduction," 3.
36. Pinn and Miller, "Introduction," 3.
37. Pinn and Miller, "Introduction," 3.
38. Pinn and Miller, "Introduction," 7.
39. McCutcheon, *Critics Not Caretakers*, xi.
40. McCutcheon, *Critics Not Caretakers*, 5.
41. William David Hart, "Review: Terror and Triumph: The Nature of Black Religion," *Journal of the American Academy of Religion* 72, no. 3 (2004): 797.
42. Anton van Harskamp, "Existential Insecurity and New Religiosity: An Essay on Some Religion-Making Characteristics of Modernity," *Social Compass* 55, no. 9 (2008): 9.
43. Jacques Derrida, and Elisabeth Rudinesco, *For What Tomorrow: A Dialogue* (Stanford, CA: Stanford University Press, 2004), 3–4.
44. Jacques Derrida, *Writing and Difference*, trans. Alan Bass (London: Routledge, 1978), 278.

45. Derrida, *Writing and Difference*, 278.
46. Derrida, *Writing and Difference*, 279–280.
47. Derrida, *Writing and Difference*, 292.
48. Pierre Bourdieu, *Outline of a Theory of Practice* trans. Richard Nice (Cambridge: Cambridge University Press, 1977), 72.
49. Bourdieu, *Outline of a Theory of Practice*, 79.
50. Pierre Bourdieu, *Logic of Practice* trans. Richard Nice (Cambridge: Blackwell, 1990), 58.
51. Pierre Bourdieu, *Distinction: A Social Critique of the Judgment of Taste* trans. Richard Nice (Cambridge: Harvard University Press, 1984), 6.
52. Nye, *Religion*, 114.
53. McCutcheon, *Manufacturing Religion*, viii.
54. McCutcheon, *Manufacturing Religion*, 31.
55. James A. Beckford, *Social Theory and Religion* (Cambridge: Cambridge University Press, 2003), 3.
56. Beckford, *Social Theory and Religion*, 15.

NOTES TO CHAPTER 5

1. There are few studies in general that have looked at religious participation among young adults; see the following websites: http://www.youthandreligion.org/news/4–15–2002.html, Internet, accessed 13 January 2010 (the National Study of Youth and Religion out of the University of Notre Dame); http://store.nfcymoffice.net/shop/pc/viewPrd.asp?idcategory=11&idproduct=87#details, Internet, accessed 13 January 2010 (the national study of youth and religion, 2004, specific to Catholic youth); http://www.spiritualdevelopmentcenter.org/Display.asp?Page=FastFacts5, Internet, accessed 13 January 2010 (national study of youth and religion by the center for spiritual development in childhood and adolescence—primarily interested in how societal institutions influence and affect religion and spirituality for youth in contemporary American culture); and http://blackyouthproject.uchicago.edu/primers/reviews/8.shtml, Internet, accessed 13 January 2010 (the national Black Youth Project University of Chicago looks at and considers the role, consequences and importance of religion and its institutions on black youth). While only one of these studies focused solely on urban youth of color, what is common among these studies is looking at the construct of religiosity from an institutional perspective, rather than focusing specifically on the everyday practices outside of (but certainly influenced by) institutions such as churches.
2. David Morgan, ed., *Religion and Material Culture: The Matter of Belief* (New York: Routledge, 2010), 2.
3. Morgan, *Religion and Material Culture*, 7.
4. Gordon Lynch, *After Religion 'Generation X' and the Search for Meaning* (London: Darton, Longman, and Todd, 2002), 3.
5. Richard W. Flory and Donald E. Miller, ed. *GenX Religion* (New York: Routledge, 2000), 2.
6. Flory and Miller, *GenX Religion*, 3.
7. Tupac Shakur, available from http://www.youtube.com/watch?v=KNWQ0SzRdb8, Internet, accessed 04, July 2012.
8. Howard S. Becker, *Outsiders: Studies in the Sociology of Deviance* (London: Free Press, 1963), 8.
9. Christian Smith, Melinda Lundquits Denton, Robert Faris, and Mark D. Regnerus, "Mapping American Adolescent Religious Participation," *Journal for Scientific Study of Religion* 41, no. 4 (2002): 597.

10. Smith et al., "Mapping American Adolescent Religious Participation," 597.
11. Smith et al., "Mapping American Adolescent Religious Participation," 609–610.
12. Smith et al., "Mapping American Adolescent Religious Participation," 600.
13. Smith et al., "Mapping American Adolescent Religious Participation," 598.
14. Christian Smith, Robert Faris, and Melinda Denton, "Mapping American Adolescent Subjective Religiosity and Attitudes of Alienation Toward Religion: A Research Report," *Sociology of Religion* 64. no. 1 (2003): 111.
15. Smith, Faris and Denton, "Mapping American Adolescent Subjective Religiosity and Attitudes of Alienation Toward Religion," 125.
16. Smith, Faris and Denton, "Mapping American Adolescent Subjective Religiosity and Attitudes of Alienation Toward Religion," 127.
17. Smith, Faris and Denton, "Mapping American Adolescent Subjective Religiosity and Attitudes of Alienation Toward Religion," 130.
18. Christian Smith and Lundquist Denton, *Soul Searching: The Religious and Spiritual Lives of American Teenagers* (New York: Oxford University Press, 2009), 5.
19. Smith and Denton, *Soul Searching*, 5.
20. Smith and Denton, *Soul Searching*, 27.
21. Smith and Denton, *Soul Searching*, 27.
22. Smith and Denton, *Soul Searching*, 45.
23. Smith and Denton, *Soul Searching*, 67.
24. Smith and Denton, *Soul Searching*, 162–163.
25. Smith and Denton, *Soul Searching*, 163.
26. Smith and Denton, *Soul Searching*, 164.
27. Smith and Denton, *Soul Searching*, 171.
28. Smith and Denton, *Soul Searching*, 257.
29. Smith and Denton, *Soul Searching*, 257.
30. Smith and Denton, *Soul Searching*, 258.
31. Christian Smith with Patricia Snell, *Souls in Transition: The Religious and Spiritual Lives of Emerging Adults* (New York: Oxford University Press, 2009), 4.
32. Smith and Snell, *Souls in Transition*, 166–68.
33. See Chapter 9 of Smith and Snell *Souls in Transition*, 257–278.
34. Mary Patillo-McCoy, "Church Culture as Strategy of Action in the Black Community," *American Sociological Review* 63, no. 6 (1998): 767.
35. Cathy J. Cohen, "Black Youth Project: Research Summary," University of Chicago Press, http://blackyouthproject.uchicago.edu/writings/research_summary.pdf, accessed 12 January 2010, 24.
36. Smith and Snell, *Souls in Transition*, 265–276.
37. Christian Smith, "Theorizing Religious Effects Among American Adolescents," *Journal for the Scientific Study of Religion* 42, no. 1 (2003): 17–18.
38. Smith, "Theorizing Religious Effects Among American Adolescents," 20.
39. Smith et al. , "Mapping American Adolescent Religious Participation," 609.
40. Byron R. Johnson, "The Role of African-American Churches in Reducing Crime Among Black Youth," Center for Research on Religion and Urban Civil Society, University of Pennsylvania, and Adjunct Fellow, Center for Civic Innovation, Manhattan Institute (2008): 8.
41. Johnson, "The Role of African-American Churches in Reducing Crime Among Black Youth," 3.
42. Nancy T. Ammerman, ed. *Everyday Religion: Observing Modern Religious Lives* (New York: Oxford University Press, 2007), v–vi.
43. Ammerman, *Everyday Religion*, 6.
44. Smith and Denton, *Souls in Transition*, 167–168.
45. Flory and Miller, *Gen X Religion*, 3.
46. Mary Douglas, *Purity and Danger: An Analysis of Concepts of Pollution and Taboo* (New York: Routledge, 1966), 3.

47. Gordon Lynch, "Object Theory: Towards a Mediated, Dynamic and Inter-subjective Theory of Religion," in *Religion and Material Culture: The Matter of Belief*, ed. David Morgan (London: Routledge, 2010), 40.
48. Miller with Dixon-Roman, "Habits of the Heart," 84.
49. Smith et al., "Mapping American Adolescent Religious Participation," 598.
50. Cathy J. Cohen, "The Attitudes and Behaviors of Young Black Americans: Research Summary," available from http://www-news.uchicago.edu/releases/07/pdf/070201.cohen-byp.pdf, Internet, accessed 1 April 2010.
51. Byron R. Johnson, Sung Joo Jang, Spencer De Li and David Larson, "The 'Invisible Institution' and Black Youth Crime: The Church as Agency of Local Social Control," *Journal of Youth and Adolescence* 29, no. 4 (2000): 10.
52. Johnson, "The Role of African-American Churches in Reducing Crime Among Black Youth," 9.
53. Smith and Denton, *Soul Searching*, 107.
54. Smith and Denton, *Soul Searching*, 273–274.
55. Smith and Denton, *Soul Searching*, 106–112 and 272–291.
56. Monica Miller with Ezekiel Dixon-Roman, "Habits of the Heart: Youth Religious Participation as Progress, *Peril* or Change?" *The Annals of the American Academy of Political and Social Science* (Sage), Special Issue: 'Race, Religion, and Late Democracy' 637, no. 1 (September 2011): 78–98.
57. Smith and Snell, *Souls in Transition*, 113.
58. Miller with Dixon-Roman, "Habits of the Heart," 97.

NOTES TO CHAPTER 6

1. Dragon, from the documentary RIZE.
2. "Behind the Scenes of David LaChapelle's Documentary 'RIZE,'" available from http://www.dancespirit.com/articles/1452), Internet, accessed 16 December 2009.
3. Lynch, "Object Theory," 42.
4. Pinn, *Terror and Triumph*, 159.
5. "Behind the Scenes of David LaChapelle's Documentary 'RIZE,'" available from http://www.dancespirit.com/articles/1452), Internet, accessed 6 January 2010.
6. de Certeau, *The Practice of Everyday Life*, 29.
7. Russell T. McCutcheon, "Critical Trends in the Study of Religion in the United States," in Peter Antes, W. Geertz, and Randi R. Warne, eds., *New Approaches to the Study of Religion* (New York: Walter De Gruyter, 2004), 317.
8. McCutcheon, "Critical Trends in the Study of Religion in the United States," 321–322.
9. de Certeau, *The Practice of Everyday Life*, xv.
10. Available from http://www.charlierose.com/view/interview/864, Internet; accessed 6 January 2010.
11. Claude Levi-Strauss, *The Savage Mind* (Chicago: The University of Chicago Press, 1966), 22.
12. McCutcheon, "Critical Trends in the Study of Religion in the Unites States," 322.
13. van Harskam, "Existential Insecurity and New Religiosity."
14. Available from http://www.charlierose.com/view/interview/864, Internet, accessed 1 January 2010.
15. "Behind the Scenes of David LaChapelle's Documentary 'RIZE,'" available from http://www.dancespirit.com/articles/1452), Internet, accessed 6 January 2009.

16. Susan Bordo, *Unbearable Weight* (Berkeley: University of California Press, 1993), 15.
17. Bordo, *Unbearable Weight*, 16.
18. Catherine Bell, *Ritual Theory, Ritual Practice* (New York: Oxford University Press, 1992), 92–93.
19. Available from http://www.charlierose.com/view/interview/864, Internet, accessed 6 January 2010.
20. Gordon Lynch, ed., *Between Sacred and Profane: Researching Religion and Popular Culture* (London: I.B. Tauris, 2007), 137.
21. See Bourdieu, *Distinction*.
22. Available from http://www.charlierose.com/view/interview/864, Internet; accessed 6 January 2010.

NOTES TO THE CONCLUSION

1. "Interview With 2Pac"; Available from http://www.tupacnet.org/life/interview.htm; Internet; accessed 2 January 2009.

Bibliography

"50 Cent Presents 'The 50th Law'—Book with Robert Greene." 50CentMusic Channel. September 07, 2009. YouTube. Online Video Clip. http://www.youtube.com/watch?v=tlp66y9ML3o (accessed 6 November 2009).

"50 Cent Robert Greene Preview 'The 50th Law' new book in 10th September." September 03, 2009. Ghettonumber3 Channel. YouTube. Online Video Clip. http://www.youtube.com/watch?v=mBpGlWShkQI (accessed 6 November 2009).

Althusser, Louis. "Ideology and Ideological State Apparatuses (Notes towards an Investigation)." In *Lenin and Philosophy and Other Essays*, by Louis Althusser, translated by Ben Brewster. New York: Monthly Review Press, 1971.

Ammerman, Nancy T., ed. *Everyday Religion: Observing Modern Religious Lives.* New York: Oxford University Press, 2007.

Asad, Talal. *Genealogies of Religion: Discipline and Reasons of Power in Christianity and Islam.* Baltimore, MD: Johns Hopkins University Press, 1993.

Attack of the Show. "Wu-Tang Clan's RZA Talks About His Book 'The Tao of Wu'." YouTube. Online Video Clip. December 14, 2009. http://www.youtube.com/watch?v=aCTgQUcqhWk (accessed 6 November 2010).

Becker, Howard S. *Outsiders: Studies in the Sociology of Deviance.* London: Free Press, 1963.

Beckford, James A. *Social Theory and Religion.* Cambridge: Cambridge University Press, 2003.

Bell, Catherine. *Ritual Theory, Ritual Practice.* New York: Oxford University Press, 1992.

Berger, Peter. *Sacred Canopy: Elements of a Sociological Theory of Religion.* New York: Anchor, 1990, c1967.

Bordo, Susan. The Flight to Objectivity: Essays on Cartesianism and Culture. Albany, NY: State University of New York Press, 1987.

———. *Unbearable Weight.* Berkeley, CA: University of California Press, 1993.

Bourdieu, Pierre. *Distinction: A Social Critique of the Judgment of Taste.* Translated by Richard Nice. Cambridge, MA: Harvard University Press, 1984.

———. *Language and Symbolic Power.* Edited by John B. Thompson. Translated by Gino Raymond and Matthew Adamson. Cambridge, MA: Harvard University Press, 1991.

———. *Logic of Practice.* Translated by Richard Nice. Stanford, CA: Stanford University Press, 1990.

———. *Outline of a Theory of Practice.* Translated by Richard Nice. Cambridge: Cambridge Univeristy Press, 1977.

———. "The Forms of Capital." In *Handbook of Theory and Research for the Sociology of Education*, edited by J. Richardson. New York: Greenwood, 1986.

Butler, Judith. "Against Proper Objects. Introduction." *A Journal of Feminist Cultural Studies* 6, nos. 2 and 3 (1994).

————. *Bodies that Matter: On the Discursive Limits of Sex.* New York: Routledge, 1993.

————. *Excitable Speech: A Politics of the Performative.* New York: Routledge, 1997.

————. *Gender Trouble.* New York: Routledge, 1990.

————. *Undoing Gender.* New York: Routledge, 2004.

Brydson, Nicole. "Rapper on the Mount: KRS-ONE Delivers The Gospel of Hip Hop." *Brooklyn The Borough,* May 30, 2009. http://brooklyntheborough.com/?p=1003 (accessed 15 November 2009).

Cohen, Cathy J. "The Attitudes and Behaviors of Young Black Americans: Research Summary." http://www-news.uchicago.edu/releases/07/pdf/070201.cohen-byp.pdf (accessed 1 April 2010).

————. *Democracy Remixed: Black Youth and the Future of American Politics.* London: Oxford University Press, 2010.

————. "Black Youth Project: Research Summary." University of Chicago Press. http://blackyouthproject.uchicago.edu/writings/research_summary.pdf (accessed 12 January 2010).

————. *The Boundaries of Blackness: AIDS and the Breakdown of Black Politics.* Chicago: University of Chicago Press, 1999.

————. "Punks, Bulldaggers, and Welfare Queens: The Radical Potential of Queer Politics." In *Black Queer Studies: A Critical Anthology,* edited by E. Patrick Johnson and Mae G. Henderson. Durham, NC: Duke University Press, 2005.

Cohen, Stanley. *Folk Devils and Moral Panics.* 3rd Edition. New York : Routledge, 2002, c1972.

Danz, Dawn and Phalary Long. KRS Plans New Hip-Hop Religion With 'Gospel of Hip Hop' Thursday, August 20, 2009. AllHipHop Website. http://allhiphop.com/stories/news/archive/2009/08/20/21903171.aspx (accessed 6 November 2009).

de Certeau, Michel. *The Practice of Everyday Life.* Los Angeles: University of California Press, 1984.

Derrida, Jacques. "Faith and Knowledge: The Two Sources of 'Religion' Within the Limits of Mere Reason." In *Acts of Religion,* edited by Jacques Derrida and Gianni Vattimo. Stanford, CA: Stanford University Press, 1998.

————. *Speech and Phenomena: And Other Essays on Husserl's Theory of Signs.* Translated by David B. Allison. Evanston, IL: Northwestern University Press, 1973.

————. *Writing and Difference.* Translated by Alan Bass. London: Routledge, 1978.

Derrida, Jacques, and Elisabeth Rudinesco. *For What Tomorrow: A Dialogue.* Stanford, CA: Stanford University Press, 2004.

"Don Imus and Nappy Headed Hos." MSNBC video. YouTube. Online Video Clip. http://www.youtube.com/watch?v=RF9BjB7Bzr0 (accessed 3 February 2010).

Douglas, Mary. *Purity and Danger: An Analysis of Concepts of Pollution and Taboo.* New York: Routledge, 1966.

Dyson, Michael Eric. *Between God and Gangsta Rap.* New York: Oxford University Press, 1996.

————. *Holler If You Hear Me: Searching for TuPac Shakur.* New York: Basic Civitas, 2001.

————. *Is Bill Cosby Right (Or Has the Black Middle Class Lost Its Mind?).* New York: Basic Civitas, 2005.

————. *Open Mike: Reflections on Philosophy, Race, Sex, Culture and Religion.* New York: Basic Civitas, 2002.

Flory, Richard W., and Donald E. Miller. *GenX Religion.* New York: Routledge, 2000.

————. *Finding Faith: The Spiritual Quest of the Post-Boomer Generation.* Piscataway, NJ: Rutgers University Press, 2008.

Forbes, Bruce David, and Jeffrey H. Mahan. *Religion and Popular Culture in America*. Berkeley. CA: University of California Press, 2005.

Foucault, Michel. *The Archeology of Knowledge*. Translated by A.M. Sheridan Smith. New York: Pantheon Books, 1972.

Gramsci, Antonio. *Selections from the Prison Notebooks*. Edited by Quintin Hoare and Geoffrey Nowell Smith. Translated by Quintin Hoare and Geoffrey Nowell Smith. London: Lawrence & Wishart, 1971.

Greene, Robert, and 50 Cent. *The 50th Law*. New York: G-Unit Books, 2009.

Hart, William David. "Review: Terror and Triumph: The Nature of Black Religion." *Journal of the American Academy of Religion*, 72, no. 3 (September 2004): 795–797.

hooks, bell. *Outlaw Culture*. New York: Routledge, 1994.

Hoover, Stewart M. "The Cross at Willow Creek: Seeker Religion and the Contemporary Marketplace." In *Religion and Popular Culture in America*, edited by Bruce David Forbes and Jeffrey H. Mahan. Berkeley, CA: University of California Press, 2000.

"Imus Calls Girls Nappy Headed Hoes & Jiggaboos!?" April 4 edition of MSNBC's Imus in the Morning. Thejakester1 channel. YouTube. Online Video Clip. http://www.youtube.com/watch?v=bmF8iIeOVEo (accessed 3 February 2010).

"Interview With 2Pac." TupacNet.org. http://www.tupacnet.org/life/interview.htm (accessed 2 January 2009).

Jackson, John L. *Racial Paranoia: The Unintended Consequences of Political Correctedness*. New York: Basic Civitas, 2008.

James, William. *Varieties of Religious Experience: A Study in Human Nature*. New York: The Modern Library, 1902.

Johnson, Byron R. *The Role of African-American Churches in Reducing Crime Among Black Youth*. CRRUS Report, University of Pennsylvania, Philadelphia: Center for Research on Religion and Urban Civil Society, 2001.

Johnson, Byron R., Sung Joo Jang, Spencer De Li, and David Larson. "The 'Invisible Institution' and Black Youth Crime: The Church as Agency of Local Social Control." *Journal of Youth and Adolescence* 29, no. 4 (2000): 7.

Johnson, E. Patrick, and Mae G. Henderson. *Black Queer Studies: A Critical Anthology*. Durham, NC: Duke University Press, 2005.

Jones, Jen. "Behind the Scenes of David LaChapelle's Documentary 'Rize'." September 1, 2005. *Dance Spirit* Magazine. http://www.dancespirit.com/articles/1452 (accessed 6 January 2010).

Kanye West. "Bush Doesn't Care About Black People." From "A Concert for Hurricane Relief." NBC. Telethon for Hurricane Katrina, 2005. YouTube. Online Video Clip. http://www.youtube.com/watch?v=zIUzLpO1kxI (accessed 3 February 2010).

KRS One. "First Overstanding: Hip Hop Connects us to our Humanity." From KRS One—GOSPEL OF HIP HOP. powerHouseTVnetwork and I AM HIP HOP. February 18, 2009. YouTube. Online Video Clip. http://www.youtube.com/watch?v=Z675H-PkwZ0 (accessed 6 November 2009).

KRS One. *The Gospel of Hip Hop: The First Instrument*. Brooklyn, NY: I Am Hip Hop, 2009.

Koroma, Salima. "KRS-One Delivers Hip Hop Gospel." June 03, 2009. Hiphopdx.com. http://www.hiphopdx.com/index/news/id.9241/title.krs-one-delivers-hip-hop-gospel *(accessed 6 November 2009).*

Langhorne, Cyrus. 50 cent drops '50th Law' Book, "Create Your Own Five-Year Plan For Success" [video]. September 8, 2009. SOHH.com. 4Control Media, inc. http://www.sohh.com/2009/09/50_cent_breaks_down_50th.html (accessed 6 November 2009).

Levi-Strauss, Claude. *The Savage Mind*. Chicago, IL: University of Chicago Press, 1966.

Lincoln, Bruce. *Authority: Construction and Corrosion*. Chicago: University of Chicago Press, 1994.

Long, Charles H. *Significations: Signs, Symbols, and Images in the Interpretation of Religion*. Philadelphia: Fortress Press, 1986.

Lucy, Niall. *A Derrida Dictionary*. Malden, MA: Blackwell, 2004.

Lupe Fiasco. "Hip Hop Saved My Life featuring Nikki Jean." The Cool. Audio Compact Disc. CD Track 9. Atlantic/ Wea. 2007.

Lynch, Gordon. *After Religion 'Generation X' and the Search for Meaning*. London: Darton, Longman, and Todd, 2002.

———. "Object Theory: Towards a Mediated, dynamic and Intersubjective Theory of religion." In *The Matter of Belief*, edited by David Morgan. London: Routledge, 2010.

———. "The Role of Popular Music in the Construction of Spiritual Identities and Ideologies." *Journal for the Scientific Study of Religion*, 45, no. 4 (2006): 481–488.

———. *Understanding Theology and Popular Culture*. Malden, MA: Blackwell Publishing, 2005.

———. *Between Sacred and Profane: Researching Religion and Popular Culture*. London: I.B. Tauris, 2007.

McCorquodale, Charlotte, Shepp, Victoria, and Leigh Sterten. "National Study of Youth and Religion: Analysis of the Population of Catholic Teenagers and Their Parents." A Research Report Produced for The National Federation for Catholic Youth Ministry and Ministry Training Source. December 2004. http://store.nfcymoffice.net/shop/pc/viewPrd.asp?idcategory=11&idproduct=87#details (accessed 13 January 2010).

McCutcheon, Russell T. "Critical Trends in the Study of Religion in the United States." Vol. 1, in *New Approaches to the Study of Religion*, edited by Peter Antes, Armin W. Geertz and Randi R. Warne. New York: Walter de Gruyter, 2008.

———. *Critics Not Caretakers: Redescribing The Public Study of Religion*. Suny Series, Issues in the Study of Religion. Albany, NY: State University of New York Press, 2001.

———. *Manufacturing Religion*. New York: Oxford University Press, 1997.

McRoberts, Omar. *Streets of Glory: Church and Community in a Black Urban Neighborhood*. Chicago: University of Chicago Press, 2003.

Media Matters. "Imus called women's basketball team 'nappy headed hos'." http://mediamatters.org/items/200704040011 (accessed 10 February 2010).

Michaels, Sean. "KRS-One writes 'gospel of hip-hop' Stand aside Christianity, Islam and Judaism, a new rap religion is set to take over the world and KRS-One is its prophet." 1 September 2009. Guardian News and Media Limited, London. http://www.guardian.co.uk/music/2009/sep/01/krs-one-gospel-hip-hop (accessed 6 November 2009).

Miller, Monica "Don't Judge a Book By Its Cover." *Bulletin for the Study of Religion* Special Issue: "What's this 'Religious' in Hip Hop Culture?", 40, no. 3 (September 2011): 26–31.

———. [with Ezekiel Dixon-Roman]. "Habits of the Heart: Youth Religious Participation as Progress, *Peril* or Change?" *The Annals of the American Academy of Political and Social Science* (Special Issue): "Race, Religion, & Late Democracy", 637, no. 1 (September 2011): 78–98.

Morgan, David, ed. *Religion and Material Culture: The Matter of Belief*. New York: Routledge, 2010.

Moss, III, Otis. "Real Big: The Hip Hop Pastor as Postmodern Prophet." In *The Gospel Remix: Reaching The Hip Hop Generation*, edited by Ralph C. Watkins. Valley Forge: Judson Press, 2007.

Nas (Nasir Jones). "Hip Hop Is Dead." Hip Hop Is Dead. Audio Compact Disc. CD Track 5. Def Jam. 2006.

Nye, Malory. "Religion, Post-Religionism, and Religioning: Religious Studies and Contemporary Cultural Debates." *Method & Theory in the Study of Religion*, 12, no. 1–4 (2000): 447–476.

———. *Religion: The Basics*. 2nd Edition. London: Routledge, 2008.

Patillo, Mary. *Black Picket Fences: Privilege and Peril Among the Black Middle Class*. Chicago: University of Chicago Press, 1999.

Patillo-McCoy, Mary. "Church Culture as Strategy of Action in the Black Community." *American Sociological Review*, 63, no. 6 (1998): 767–784.

Piatt, Christian and Amy Piatt. *MySpace to Sacred Space: God for a New Generation*. St. Louis, MO: Chalice Press, 2007.

Pinn, Anthony B. "On a Mission from God: African American Music and the Nature/Meaning of Conversion in Religious Life." In *Between Sacred and Profane: Researching Religion and Popular Culture*, edited by Gordon Lynch. London: I.B. Tauris, 2007.

———. *Noise and Spirit: The Religious and Spiritual Sensibilities of Rap Music*. New York: New York University Press, 2003.

———. *Terror and Triumph: The Nature of Black Religion*. Minneapolis: Fortress Press, 2003.

Pinn, Anthony B., and Monica R Miller. "Introduction: Intersections of Culture and Religion in African-American Communities." *Culture and Religion*, 10, no. 1 (2009): 1–9.

Pinn, Anthony B. and Paul Easterling. "Followers of Black Jesus on Alert: Thoughts on the Story of Tupac Shakur's Life/Death/Life." *Black Theology: An International Journal*, 7 no. 1 (2009): .31–44.

Puar, Jasbir K. *Terrorist Assemblages: Homonationalism in Queer Times*. Durham, NC: Duke University Press, 2007.

Racialicious Blog, maintained by Carmen Van Kerckhove. "Oprah's Town Hall Meetings on Misogyny and Hip Hop." Nina, Guest Contributor. 20 April 2007. http://www.racialicious.com/2007/04/20/oprahs-town-hall-meetings-on-misogyny-in-hip-hop/ (accessed 20 February 2010).

Reid, Shaheem. "MTV News Exclusive: Nas Previews Hip-Hop Is Dead . . . The N. MC works with Dre, Kanye, Will.I.Am; says he's about to be the 'craziest' [artist] on Def Jam." October 10, 2006. MTV Networks. MTV.com. http://www.mtv.com/news/articles/1542740/20061009/nas.jhtml (accessed 6 November 2009).

Rivera, Racquel Z. *New York Ricans from the Hip Hop Zone*. New York: Palgrave MacMillan, 2003.

Royale, Nicholas. *Critical Thinkers: Jacques Derrida*. London: Routledge, 2003.

Ruano, L. "The RZA: The Tao of Wu Book " September 29, 2009 Hypebeast Website. http://hypebeast.com/2009/09/rza-tao-wu-book/ (accessed 6 November 2009).

Schneider, Laurel C. *Beyond Monotheism: A Theology of Multiplicity*. New York: Routledge, 2008.

Schneider, Laurel C. "What Race Is Your Sex?" In *Disrupting White Supremacy from Within*, edited by Jennifer Harvey , Karin A. Case, Robin Hawley Gorsline. Cleveland, OH: Pilgrim Press, 2008.

Smith, Christian. "Theorizing Religious Effects Among American Adolescents." *Journal for the Scientific Study of Religion*, 42 , no. 1 (2003): 17–30.

Smith, Christian, Melinda Lundquist Denton, and Mark Regnerus. "Religious Affiliation by Race." National Study of Youth and Religion. University of North Carolina at Chapel Hill. 15 April 2002. http://www.youthandreligion.org/news/4-15-2002.html (accessed 13 January 2010).

Smith, Christian, Melinda Lundquist Denton, Robert Faris, and Mark D. Regnerus. "Mapping American Adolescent Religious Participation." *Journal for Scientific Study of Religion*, 41, no. 4 (2002): 597–612.

Smith, Christian, and Melissa Lundquist Denton. *Soul Searching: The Religious and Spiritual Lives of American Teenagers*. New York: Oxford University Press, 2009.

Smith, Christian, and Patricia Snell. *Souls in Transition: The Religious and Spiritual Lives of Emerging Adults*. New York: Oxford University Press, 2009.

Smith, Christian, Robert Faris, and Melinda Denton. "Mapping American Adolescent Subjective Religiosity and Attitudes of Alienation Toward Religion: A Research Report." *Sociology of Religion*, 64, no. 1 (2003): 111–133.

Smith, Efrem, and Phil Jackson. *The Hip-Hop Church: Connecting with the Movement Shaping Our Culture*. Downers Grove: InterVarsity Press, 2005.

Smith, Jonathan Z. *Imagining Religion: From Babylon to Jonestown*. Chicago: University of Chicago Press, 1982.

Spivak, Gayatri Chakravorty. "Can the Subaltern Speak?" In *Marxism and the Interpretation of Culture*, edited by Cary Nelson and Lawrence Grossberg. Urbana, IL: University of Illinois Press, 1988.

Stone, Micha J., Portland Humanist Examiner. "Rap religion: KRS-One to release Hip-Hop Bible." Clarity Digital Group LLC d/b/a Examiner.com. http://www.examiner.com/x-10853-Portland-Humanist-Examiner~y2009m8d25-Rap-religion-KRSOne-to-release-HipHop-Bible (accessed 5 January 2010).

Sylvan, Robin. *Traces of the Spirit: The Religious Dimensions of Popular Music*. New York: New York University Press, 2002.

———. *Trance Formation: The Spiritual Dimensions of Global Rave Culture*. New York: Routledge, 2005.

T. Magic. "The 50th Law. July 30th 2009. TMagicworld website. http://tmagic-world.com/2009/07/30/the-50th-law/ (accessed 6 November 2009).

The Black Youth Project. University of Chicago. http://blackyouthproject.uchicago.edu/primers/reviews/8.shtml (accessed 13 January 2010).

The Charlie Rose Show. Public Broadcasting Service (PBS). A conversation about the documentary "Rize" with Tommy Johnson, Christopher Toler and David LaChapelle. Wednesday, June 22, 2005. http://www.charlierose.com/view/interview/864 (accessed 6 January 2010).

The RZA and Chris Norris. *Tao of Wu* . New York: Penguin Group, 2009.

Tillich, Paul. *Dynamics of Faith*. Reprint. New York: Perrenial, 2001.

TMZ Staff. "Kramer's" Racist Tirade—Caught on Tape." Nov 20th 2006. TMZ.com website. http://www.tmz.com/2006/11/20/kramers-racist-tirade-caught-on-tape/ (accessed 25 February 2010).

"Transcript: Don Imus on Al Sharpton's Radio Show." *New York Times* 9 April 2007, Media and Advertising Section, http://www.nytimes.com/2007/04/09/business/media/09imus_transcript.html (accessed 10 Februrary 2010).

van Harskamp, Anton. "Existential Insecurity and New Religiosity: An Essay on Some Religion-Making Characteristics of Modernity." *Social Compass*, 55, no. 1 (2008): 9–19.

Venkatesh, Sudhir. *Off the Books: The Underground Economy of the Urban Poor*. Cambridge, MA: Harvard University Press, 2006.

Watkins, Ralph C. *The Gospel Remix: Reaching the Hip Hop Generation*. Valley Forge: Judson Press, 2007.

West, Cornel. *The Cornel West Reader*. New York: Basic Civitas, 1990.

———. *Democracy Matters: Winning the Fight Against Imperialism*. Reprint. New York: Penguin Books, 2004.

———. *Race Matters*. New York: Vintage, 2001.

Williams, Corey. "NAACP Buries Symbolically Buries N-Word." *Washington Post* 9 July 2007, http://www.washingtonpost.com/wp-dyn/content/article/2007/07/09/AR2007070900609.html (accessed 10 February 2010).

Young, Iris Marion. *Justice and the Politics of Difference*. Princeton, NJ: Princeton University Press, 1990.

Index